Understanding Family Process

For permission to reprint copyrighted material the author and publisher gratefully acknowledge the following:

UNDERSTANDING
Family
Process

BASICS
OF FAMILY
SYSTEMS
THEORY

Carlfred B. Broderick

SAGE Publications
International Educational and Professional Publisher
Newbury Park   London   New Delhi

For information address:

SAGE Publications, Inc.
2455 Teller Road
Newbury Park, California 91320

SAGE Publications Ltd.
6 Bonhill Street
London EC2A 4PU
United Kingdom

SAGE Publications India Pvt. Ltd.
M-32 Market
Greater Kailash I
New Delhi 110 048 India

Printed in the United States of America

Library of Congress Cataloging-in-Publication Data

Broderick, Carlfred B.
   Understanding family process : basics of family systems theory /
Carlfred B. Broderick.
         p.   cm.
   Includes bibliographical references (p.   ) and index.
   ISBN 0-8039-3777-6 (cloth).   —ISBN 0-8039-3778-4 (pbk.)
   1. Family.   2. System theory.   3. Communication in the family.
I. Title.
HQ728.B745   1993
306.85—dc20   92-40083

93   94   95   96   10   9   8   7   6   5   4   3   2   1

Sage Production Editor: Judith L. Hunter

Contents

Preface

To some degree, this book affords me the opportunity to pull together the disparate strands of my professional career. The pursuit of knowledge about the inner workings of the family has always been at the center of my scholarship, but the outer boundaries have pulsed and changed shape like an amoeba sending pseudopodia now in this direction, now in that. This shifting profile may result partly from my affinity for marginality. The view from the top of the interdisciplinary fence is the one I cherish. In another part, I suppose, the profile results from an inbred distaste of wearing anyone's label but my own. Early in my life, I discovered the potency of multiple alliances as a strategy for avoiding domination or definition by any. But partly such a profile must grow out of my academic history. Without much master planning on my part, every academic setting I have ever studied or taught in has been devoutly and uniquely ecumenical.

This "policy" began during my undergraduate years at Harvard, where I discovered that it was not possible to major in sociology, as I had intended. Instead offered was social relations, which was a potpourri of sociology, social psychology, clinical psychology, and social anthropology.[1] It continued in graduate school. The doctoral program in child development and family relations at Cornell was more narrowly focused, but the faculty members were equally scattered among the disciplines (besides which I took minors in both sociology and psychology). The pattern persisted in my postgraduate career. My first two academic appointments at the University of Georgia for 4 years and then at The Pennsylvania State University for 11 years were in colleges of home economics. In these settings, one interacted regularly with colleagues whose pragmatic perspective on family functioning was quite foreign to that of the behavioral sciences.

During my stay at Penn State, I took a sabbatical year at the University of Minnesota to take training in marriage and family therapy. This helped to prepare me for my current, mix-and-match academic placement at the University of Southern California, where, for the past 21 years, I have headed a doctoral program in marriage and family therapy that is uniquely situated in a Department of Sociology.

If I have learned anything from this 40-year immersion in multiple perspectives it is that no one discipline has a corner on scholarly interest in or insight into how families function. Each has a great deal to learn from the others, but the free exchange of information is inhibited by the dense special vocabularies and conceptual models that each develops and by the fact that we mostly do not read one another's parochial journals. I have been encouraged, however, over the past two or three decades to see an integrative movement emerge under the title of family process or family systems theory. At the forefront of the movement have been some of the more creative family therapists, but scholars from a wide variety of backgrounds also have cross-borrowed and contributed to the growing body of understanding. The cross-disciplinary dialogue still stumbles, but it is occurring.

This volume is an attempt to contribute to that process of communication and integration, trusting that my heterodox background might be an asset. The strategy of the book is to develop an economical but reasonably comprehensive model of family process theory and then to tie into it as wide a range of pertinent family scholarship as possible without doing violence to the logic of either the model or the original work. Ideally, the result would move family process theory a step or two forward. I also have desired to reduce the technical jargon to the minimum consistent with rigor and to make the book as lively and readable as possible given its purposes.

These were the goals at the beginning. As I review the effort at its completion, I am painfully aware that they were only partially and imperfectly realized. Yet I hope this volume may be useful to a wide range of family scholars if only as a temptation to improve upon it.

Carlfred B. Broderick

Note

1. The Harvard Department of Social Relations was a wonderful place in the early 1950s. Talcott Parsons and George Homans taught the basic sociology courses, Gordon Alport taught the introductory course in social psychology, Clyde Kluckholm social anthropology, Robert Sears child development, and Carle C. Zimmerman the family. Introductory statistics was taught by Samuel Stouffer and advanced statistics by Frederick Mosteller. My clinical courses were taught by the author of the TAT and the head of the famous Judge Baker Clinic for Child Psychiatry. To be instructed exclusively by independent-minded creative scholars, by men of ideas, was a heady experience, and although at the time I lacked the perspective to fully understand how rare a collection of mentors this was, even then I knew that I was being fed intellectual haute cuisine.

Acknowledgments

This project has bumped along for several years. It is therefore no small matter that my editor, Mitch Allen, has been unfailingly encouraging and, when necessary, gracefully patient. I am particularly grateful to my distinguished colleagues who critiqued several of the early chapters. I cannot imagine an author being better served by his peers. Their extraordinary collective scholarship was exceeded only by their extraordinary collective generosity. They called my attention to pertinent references—indeed, to whole areas of pertinent research that I had overlooked; tactfully took exception to several of my unwarranted conclusions and unacknowledged biases; made constructive suggestions as to how I might smooth out the style of presentation, and did their best to protect me from my penchant for overly vivid writing.

It is also no small matter to have a supportive spouse during so extended a project. I am grateful for this and for much else to Kathleen, my wife of 40 years.

PART I

The Systemic Approach to Families

CHAPTER 1

The Foundations of Family Process Theory

Introduction

Family process theory emerged at a particular point in the history of the social sciences to satisfy an unmet intellectual need, just as has every other system of social explanation. In this case, the need was created by a whole new set of observations of human interaction that came from the emerging family therapy movement.

As these pioneering clinicians met daily with whole families and attempted to help them address the problems they confronted, they could find no ready-made body of theory to guide their efforts. So, being men and women of revolutionary boldness and ingenuity, they set about constructing theory to meet their needs. Because they were independent-minded folk from a variety of backgrounds, they did not all approach the task from the same perspective and did not all come to the same conclusions. Even when they did agree, it was not always immediately apparent: Each had invented his or her own vocabulary. Although they tended to be strong-willed individualists, they also saw themselves as constituting a community of clinical innovators. As a community, they consulted and compared and critiqued one another's views and debated the issues; from all of this has emerged a new, reasonably coherent set of constructs for the analysis of what sociologist Gerald Handel (1967) called "the psychosocial interior of the family."

The new conceptual framework was most often called *family process theory* (Jackson, 1965; Kantor & Lehr, 1975), and, almost as frequently, *family systems theory* (Kantor & Lehr, 1975; Broderick & Smith, 1979). This book will use the terms interchangeably. Although the theory began as a unifying framework of the family therapy movement, over the years it has emerged as a major paradigm for family analysis among other, non-clinical disciplines such as sociology, psychology, home economics, social work, and human communications.

As intellectual fashions go, family process theory must be considered one of the more recent additions to the collection of major conceptual frameworks available to students of the family. Only a little more than 30 years ago, Hill and Hansen (1960) meticulously surveyed the field of family theory and failed to include either family systems or family process theory among the conceptual frameworks that informed the family scholarship of that day. On the other hand, many observers are already willing to write the theory off as having come and gone in the intervening decades. They declare it passé. Obviously, I would not have written this book if I were of that opinion. In my view, Mark Twain's famous remark—that the reports of his death had been greatly exaggerated—apply equally to family process theory. One of the purposes of this volume is to present compelling evidence not only of this conceptual framework's current good health, but also of its hardy future prospects.

No social or intellectual movement can be said to have come into being at a particular moment, but in the case of the family process movement, a good place to begin tracking its development is with the founding of the journal *Family Process* in 1961, just one year after the Hill and Hansen survey. The journal was established as the "house organ" of the new family therapy movement. The majority of the great, inventive minds that sparked that revolution in the treatment of dys-function were on its board. Among the most lucid and articulate of that group was Don Jackson, the founder of the Mental Health Institute in Palo Alto, California, and cofounder of *Family Process*. By 1965, he was able to publish an exposition of the basic tenets of the new theory as the lead article in Volume 4 of the new journal (Jackson, 1965).

Mainline (i.e., nonclinical) family scholars did not take note of these new conceptualizations for some time. For example, Nye and Berardo's

1966 book-length update and expansion of the Hill and Hanson survey failed to mention this new theoretical approach, as did the 1968 review of developments in family theory by Klein, Calvert, Garland, and Polomo. The theory was not taken note of by the nonclinical establishment until 1971, a full decade after the establishment of *Family Process*. That year, a review of developments in the field of family theory during the 1960s offered the first acknowledgement of the new systems approach's growing importance (Broderick, 1971).

One might argue that the approach was not fully established as a serious contender for a place among the other major family conceptual frameworks until the 1975 publication of Kantor and Lehr's *Inside the Family: Toward a Theory of Family Process*. So far as we know, this was the first book-length effort to describe, analyze, and explain how families operate in real time (i.e., in seconds, minutes, hours, and days). Certainly, by the end of the 1970s the theory was recognized as a framework to be reckoned with. This recognition was evidenced by the theory's inclusion in the massive and authoritative, two-volume compendium *Contemporary Theories about the Family* (1979a), which was edited by Wesley Burr, Reuben Hill, Ivan Nye, and Ira Reiss.

Three of the 29 chapters reviewed various aspects of the new approach (Raush, Greif, & Nugent, 1979; Broderick & Pulliam-Krager, 1979; and Broderick & Smith, 1979). Today, I believe that any fair-minded evaluation would have to conclude that the theory ranks as one of the most influential and generative of all of the family conceptual frameworks.

As noted, one purpose of this book is to document that conclusion. In the chapters that follow, I have attempted to spell out some of the major contributions of process-oriented research and scholarship. As we will see, there are many generally unacknowledged points of intersection between the work of process-oriented scholars and the contributions of other students of the family. In attempting to call attention to these points of convergence, I hope to stimulate further dialogue among scholars of different conceptual persuasions for the benefit of all. On the other hand, this volume is intended to be a critique of the theory as well as an exposition. Where I have encountered blind spots, or unwarranted assumptions, I have challenged them. In a few cases, I have made more or less ambitious attempts to modify or extend the theory. More often, I have merely identified critical tasks that await the next generation of family process scholars.

Family Process Theory and the Social Sciences

To understand the history of the family process movement, we will review its interweavings with four other major conceptual currents—structural functionalism, inductive empiricism, general systems theory, and the eclectic academic field known as family relations—that shaped its early development, each in a different way.

The notion of viewing the family as a social system did not begin with family process theory. It was at the core of *structural functional theory*, one of the most influential paradigms in social anthropology and sociology for 30 years. Conceivably, family systems theory could have developed directly from this conceptual framework, building on its strengths and correcting its weaknesses, but, for reasons that will become evident, it did not.

One of those reasons—and one of the main weaknesses of structural functionalism as practiced by sociologists—was its failure to root itself in systematic, empirical observations of the social systems it attempted to explain. Partly in reaction against this type of armchair theorizing, the majority of American sociologists gradually turned to far more modest, ad-hoc theories based on empirically based generalizations. Especially among family scholars, the decade of the 1970s was noted far less as the period in which family process theory emerged than as the time of the intensive quest for a comprehensive, integrated system of empirically based propositions about how families operated. This major effort culminated in the publication of the previously mentioned, two-volume *Contemporary Theories About the Family* (Burr et al., 1979). Except for the three chapters dealing with various aspects of the new process theory, however, the entire volume was based on the premise that social causes and effects were connected to one another in a strictly linear fashion that excluded consideration of any of the concepts that were distinctive to the systems approach.

By contrast, during the same period, a new paradigm for the analysis of complex systems was gaining adherents across a broad spectrum of disciplines. The earliest architect of *general systems theory* was biologist Ludwig von Bertalanffy. In an intersecting development, Norbert Wiener, an engineer, and his associates developed the science of self-correcting systems, which they called *cybernetics*. Early in their development, these two conceptual systems merged and fed directly into the family process movement through the active participation of key scholars such as Gregory Bateson in both movements.

Finally, in interaction with all of these, and acting in some degree as the conduit between the community of family therapists and the community of nonclinical sociologists and psychologists were a group of interstitial *family relations specialists*. These academics often had some clinical training, and many of them later became involved in training family therapists at their institutions. Their main roots, however, were typically in academic departments with names such as Human Development and Family Relations and Family Science.

Earliest Uses of the Systems Approach:
The Structural Functionalists

From the earliest tribal spinners of tales to the latest professorial expounders of theories, humans have found it necessary, or at least satisfying, to put forth explanations of how the world ought to be conceived. Every people of every age have borrowed or created their own versions of the laws of nature and their own understandings of the nature of laws. No one can say when the concept of *systems* first emerged as an element in those explanations.

Certainly by the time of Aristotle and his famous dictum, "The whole is greater than the sum of its parts," the idea was a familiar part of the intellectual fabric of the Western world. When Paul, the great Christian missionary of the first century, wanted to impress the concept of harmonious relationships on the contentious members of the congregation at Corinth, systemic imagery came readily to hand. "For just as the body is one and has many members, and all the members of the body, though many, are one body, so it is with [the Church of] Christ," he wrote. "If the whole body were an eye, where would be the hearing? If the whole body were an ear where would be the sense of smell? . . . The eye cannot say to the hand 'I have no need of you,' nor again the head to the feet, 'I have no need of you.'. . . If one member suffers, all suffer together; if one member is honored, all rejoice together" (Paul's First Letter to the Corinthians, chapter 12).

In our own era, the concept of system has been a core element in the theoretical work of many branches of the social sciences, but few theorists have given it as central a position in their construction of social reality as have the social anthropologists and sociologists who developed the theory that has come to be called *structural functionalism*. Anthropologists such as Radcliff-Brown (1922, 1952) and Malinowski (1922) searched out semi-isolated, tribal societies that were sufficiently small and sufficiently self-contained to be studied as wholes. After months of careful observations and interviews, they concluded that, without exception, the customs, practices, and beliefs of such societies, although outlandish to European eyes, were functional for their particular societies. Moreover, in each society, the whole system of folk-ways fit together in such a way that each part needed to maintain its shape so that the rest of the system could maintain *its* shape. A corollary was that, because changes in any part of the system had consequences for every other part and for the whole, all systems functioned to resist change and maintain an ongoing equilibrium. Harvard sociologist Talcott Parsons later called this "the law of inertia of social process" and noted that "this concept is similar to that of homeostasis in physiol-ogy" (1951, p. 482).

As this systems paradigm was applied to an increasing number of societies, a further corollary was derived: Societies might vary in their particular social features, but underlying all were irreducible, univer-sal requirements that every society must meet in some way if it were to survive as a system (Parsons, 1951, pp. 26ff.). These observers put forth various lists of these universal societal requirements, (which they called *functional requisites*). For example, they argued that every social system must come up with some means of meeting its members' minimal nutritional and biological needs.

The *social mechanisms* or *structures* for accomplishing this function might vary from society to society or over time in the same society. The group's members might hunt and gather, or grow their own crops, or manufacture something suitable to trade for food, or raid and plunder their neighbors, or combine some of these approaches, but if they did not find some successful means of performing this necessary function, they would not survive. Other frequently listed functional requisites were replenishing membership; maintaining internal order; defending the system and its boundaries against external predators; providing a sense of group loyalty, identity, and morale; and providing a set of palatable explanations for the uncontrollable natural forces that im-pinged upon them.

In this paradigm, the family was accorded a place of particular impor-tance. In every society, some arrangement of biologically related per-sons took the main responsibility for performing one of the universally necessary functions, the recruiting of new members through reproduc-tion and socialization. The particular form the family might take in any given society, of course, depended on the structural constraints within that particular social system. With the compilation of ethnographies into central repositories such as the Human Area Files at Yale, system-atic comparisons among hundreds of societies became possible. Using this resource, anthropologists such as Murdock (1949) were able to look for cross-cultural correlations between the way family relations were structured and other key societal characteristics. Murdock found a rich set of patterns that linked family forms to other features in the social system, supporting to that degree the doctrine of systemic interrelationships within the structure of societies. But his research also led him to conclude that the conceptualizations of the social system put forth by Radcliff-Brown and Malinowski were overly deterministic and static. In one of the earliest critiques of that brand of social systems theory, Murdock wrote the following:

> Although the functional anthropologists have contributed to our understanding of the interrelatedness of the elements of social organization, they have done little to illuminate the dynamics of cultural change. Indeed, so strongly have they emphasized the internal integration of social systems that they have almost made no theoretical provision for change. If nearly perfect integration is a universal characteristic of social structure, only additive change is possible. (1949, pp. 196-197)

We have already cited Talcott Parsons. Among sociologists, he is undoubtedly the theorist most centrally identified with structural functionalism. In his 1951 book *The Social System*, he offered an interesting explanation for his own almost exclusive focus on system stability rather than on system change. Having devoted the body of his book to developing a general model of the social system, its major structural components, and the motivational processes that were required to keep it operational, Parsons finally turned, in the next to the last chapter, to the question of changes in the structure of the system itself. The essence of his long, discursive argument is distilled in the following extracts from that chapter:

> [I]t is necessary to distinguish clearly between the processes *within* the system and the processes of change *of* the system. (p. 481)
>
> [W]e are dealing [here] with the boundary-maintaining type of system. The definition of a system as boundary-maintaining is a way of saying that, *relative to its environment*, that is to fluctuations in the factors in its environment, it maintains certain constancies of pattern, whether this constancy be static or moving. . . . Theory, relative to such systems, is directed to the analysis of the conditions under which such a given constant system pattern will be maintained and conversely, the conditions under which it will be altered in determinate ways. (p. 482)
>
> The impetus to a process of change may perfectly well originate in the development of a cultural configuration, such as a development of science, or of religious ideas. It may also perfectly well originate in a change in the genetic constitution of the population, or in a shift in the physical environment such as the exhaustion of a strategic resource. . . . Another very important

possibility lies in the progressive increase of strains in one strategic area of the social structure which are finally resolved by a structural reorganization of the system. . . . [Such a] structured strain may well be the point at which the balance between forces tending towards reequilibration of the previous structure and toward transition to a new structure may be most evident. (p. 493)

The essential point is that for there to be a theory of *change* of pattern, under these methodological assumptions, there must be an initial and a terminal pattern to be used as points of reference. (p. 483)

It is a necessary inference from the above considerations that *a general theory of the process of change of social systems is not possible in the present state of knowledge.* The reason is very simply that such a theory would imply complete knowledge of the laws of process of the system and this knowledge we do not possess. (p. 486) (Parsons, 1951, emphases in the original)

Fortunately, this dictum did not prevent other sociologists from using a systems perspective to explain both social stability and social change. One of Parsons's students, Robert Merton (1949), provided a useful conceptual tool for this purpose when he proposed that, in addition to the intended and acknowledged functions ascribed to any given social mechanism, there was always another set of unintended and unacknowledged (although equally consequential) functions. He called the intended set the *manifest functions* of the mechanism and the unintended set its *latent functions.* Many aspects of family-related behavior became clarified through this type of analysis. For example, the turn-of-the-century movement toward coeducation at the college level can be seen not only as a major step toward the extension of equal opportunities for education to both sexes (its manifest function), but also as a new and improved mechanism for promoting interaction and romance among those of equal social and intellectual rank (its equally consequential latent function).

In a widely reprinted article, sociologist Kingsley Davis was able to use a similar type of functional analysis to explain the perverse stability of that universally disdained institution, prostitution. Its manifest function—to provide illicit sex to its male clientele—can be shown to be reinforced by other real or perceived latent functions such as providing employment to otherwise unemployable young women, as well as protecting the daughters of the genteel from the rude pressures of oversexed single men and their mothers from the importunities of their oversexed husbands (Davis, 1937).

My own estimate of the validity of this analysis shifted in the positive direction in response to a series of events that took place while I was on the faculty of the University of Georgia in the late 1950s. After much pressure from local church groups, the sheriff finally closed down the two houses of prostitution in the county that had been the moral nemeses of so many young college men over the years. To the surprise of many citizens, within weeks the houses had to be reopened because of protests from an unexpected quarter (at least unexpected to those who had not read Davis's analysis). The *mothers* of the university's coeds demanded that the houses be opened again so that their virginal daughters could once more walk the streets of Athens unmolested by their sexually unrequited male counterparts!

As suggested earlier, functional analyses were used to good effect in the analysis of social change as well as in the analysis of social stability. William F. Ogburn and Meyer F. Nimkoff's 1955 book, *Technology and the Changing Family*, was dedicated to tracing the unintended effects of various technological innovations on the Western family. The prime example was the dramatic shift in American courtship practices that resulted from the mass production of automobiles in the early 1920s. Invented as a means for moving people from point A to point B in a minimum time and with minimum discomfort, the automobile blossomed overnight into a combination roller-coaster type of joyride and parlor-away-from-home for the courting young. It established a new criterion for heterosexual desirability (car ownership) and jump started the sexual revolution.

Parsons himself continued to develop his systems model in collaboration with colleagues. In the 1953 *Working Papers* (with Bales and Shils), he developed a simplified, four-fold typology of universal functional requisites. In retrospect, the binary logic that led him to the construction of his rectangular model of social system functioning seems remarkably naive and simplistic. Yet its impact on the field was enormous at the time, and no fledgling American sociologist could have passed his qualifying examinations in that era without being able to describe and explain the A-G-I-L model, as it came to be known (see Figure 1.1).

The upper left-hand (A) quadrant contained the generic systems task that Parsons called *adaptive instrumental*. It involved dealing directly with the job of survival. If the social system under scrutiny were a society, then the subsystem most centrally involved in the processes of this quadrant was the *economy*.

In the upper right-hand (G) quadrant was the generic systems task that Parsons labeled *goal gratification*. It had to do with selecting goals and mobilizing the system toward fulfilling them. In a society, the subsystem most centrally involved in the performance of this task was the *government*.

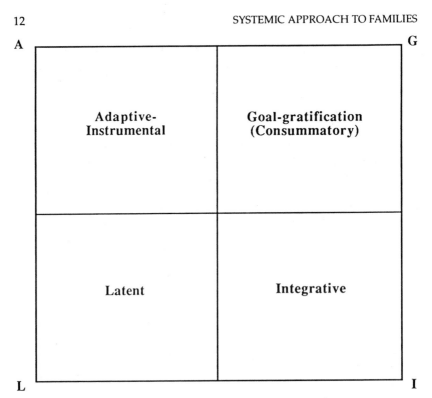

Figure 1.1. The A-G-I-L Model: Phase Patterns of Task-Performance
Adapted from Parsons and Bales, 1955, Fig. 1, p. 39

In the lower right-hand (I) quadrant was the generic systems task that Parsons called *integrative*. It had to do with the maintenance of morale and cooperation and the containment of hostility and competition. In a society, the subsystem most centrally involved in the performance of this task was the *family* through its mechanisms of socialization and social control.

Finally, in the lower left-hand (L) quadrant was the generic systems task that Parsons originally labeled *pattern maintenance*. (Unhappily, when he joined forces with Robert F. Bales, he felt it necessary to relabel it *latent* to make it correspond to the fourth phase, the period between group meetings, in Bales's four-step group process model. The term made perfect sense in Bales's model, but none in Parsons's. To understand the unseemly eagerness to superimpose these two quite dissimilar rectangular models on each other, one must understand that these men considered themselves hot on the trail of a universal, four-celled reality.) The systems task assigned to this quadrant had to do with maintaining the continuity of social patterns over time. In a society, the subsystem most centrally involved in the performance of this task was the *institution of religion*.

Like other systems theorists before and after him, Parsons conceived of human society as consisting of a hierarchy of nested social systems. He considered his four-fold model as equally applicable at each level. At the top of the systems hierarchy was the world system. At that level, the four quadrants of the model were occupied by various national societies, assigned according to the major value system around which they were organized. For example, the United States of America was assigned to the A cell, because it was determined that the nation's most developed interest was in getting the work of the world done and its most developed institution was its economy. The Soviet Union was assigned to the G cell. In their avid pursuit of the goal of world communism, the Soviets' central institution was their governmental apparatus. As the example of an I-cell nation, Parsons chose the classical, Confucian Chinese society with its emphases on interpersonal harmony and the extended family as its core institution. In the fourth cell, Parsons placed the highly stratified traditional society of classical India with its religiously rooted caste system (Parsons, 1951b).

One step down from the world society was the national society. As we have already indicated, at this level the four major institutions—the economy, the government, the family, and institutionalized religion— were allocated to the four cells of the model. One step down from the national society, at the third level of the social systems hierarchy, were these very same institutional subsystems, although this time considered as four-celled systems in their own right. Thus, like all other systems, if the family were to survive, it had to develop within itself mechanisms to meet the requirements of all four quadrants.

It was Parsons's ill-fated conclusion that the standard solution to this dilemma was the nuclear family's gender-by-generation structure and its four (of course!) basic roles: father, mother, son, and daughter. Without a backward glance, he declared a matchup between the father role and the adaptive instrumental function (which also corresponded exactly to Bales's *instrumental* group leader). The role of mother, Parsons felt, fit seamlessly with the goal gratification function and corresponded with Bales's *expressive* group leader. Then, in a further demonstration of the Olympics-class conceptual gymnastics that came easily to these folks, the integrative task was assigned to the daughter role and the pattern-maintenance (or latent) task to the son role.

In 1955, Parsons and Bales elaborated on this system in a series of essays published under the title *Family, Socialization and Interaction*

Process. This volume brought the model one step farther down the nested-systems stepladder, using the four-celled family system as the template for an introjected four-celled protopersonality. (Through cell division, the personality eventually developed into a 16-celled entity.) It is a social commentary on the times that for more than a decade this was a well-received theoretical formulation. As may be imagined, it did not survive the more sophisticated and politically sensitive scrutiny of the following decades. Indeed, few sociological constructions have ever come under more scathing fire than did Parsons's model of the generic family with its instrumental father and its expressive mother. It was identified, with some reason, as the very incarnation of a rigidly sexist model of society.

Despite its limitations, however, the systems theory of the structural functionalists incorporated many of the features of more contemporary systems approaches:

1. The focus of the model was on the interdependence of the parts and on the emergent qualities of the system as a system; that is, "the whole was greater than the sum of its parts."
2. Social systems were perceived as boundary-maintaining and equilibrium-maintaining in the face of a wide range of internal and external perturbations. Only when internal or external disruptive forces exceed these limits was the basic structure of the system placed under sufficient pressure to transform itself into a different structure.
3. Social systems were seen as having intrinsic requirements for survival, including: (a) an economic function that stimulates and regulates internal productivity as well as both initiating and regulating exchanges with the external environment; (b) an executive or political function that maintains order and provides both the goals and priorities for the system and the motivation to achieve those goals and priorities; (c) a morale- and loyalty-maintaining function; and (d) a stabilizing, homeostatic function. Each function requires social mechanisms or social structuring to achieve its goals.
4. Social systems may be thought of as hierarchically arranged or "nested"; that is, systems may be component parts of more inclusive systems, and their own subunits may also be systems in their own right.

Structural-functional approaches to the family also exhibited certain limitations that, in my view, doomed them to become conceptual blind alleys:

1. They were incurably static and abstract. All of the rules that were held to govern families were societal rules that were frozen in time and external to the family itself. Real families operate in real time with evolving rules,

many of which are idiosyncratic to themselves, and they invariably adapt societal norms to their individual circumstances. Real families also vary widely in their goals, styles of interaction, and structural anatomies.

2. Although the original anthropologists based their functional theory on observations of actual families, the social systems theories of the Parsonian era lacked an empirical data base. Some armchair theorists did not hesitate to cite confirming data if they were available, but their basic tools were their own talents for logical analysis and persuasive exposition. Even a few hours spent observing a representative array of real families in real-time interaction would have forced a reconsideration of most of their global assertions. As we shall see, contemporary family systems theory grew out of just such a set of observations.

Empirical Systems of Variables:
Partitioning Variance in Linear Models of Social Reality

About the same time that Parsons and his associates were attempting to generate an all-inclusive theory of social action that would explain social (including familial) patterns of behavior, Samuel Stouffer, a Harvard sociologist with an office just a few doors down from Parsons, was engaged in a scholarly enterprise that would leave an even greater imprint on the history of social explanation. By 1950, systematic empirical investigation of families and other social groups already had a long history, one that dated from Le Play's analysis of the spending habits of 36 French working-class families almost a hundred years earlier (1885/1935). However, the dominant approach to social explanation over that century was the type of grand theorizing that Parsons's work exemplified. Theorists of this stamp did not rely on carefully designed studies to test their conclusions. They wrote in the ancient and honorable tradition of Aristotle and the generations of social philosophers who followed him.

Samuel Stouffer and his small army of collaborators were cut from a very different cloth. During World War II, they were employed by the Research Branch of the U.S. Army to study the adjustment of enlisted men to army life. In the charge of bureaucratic hacks, such an assignment might easily have produced nothing but a large volume of in-house boiler plate. But in the hands of Stouffer and his remarkable company of scholars, the final product was a four-volume document, *The American Soldier* (1949-1950), that redefined the aspirations of the discipline and launched a new era in the social sciences. Stouffer listed 130 collaborators on the project. Among them were many whose later contributions were notable, including John A. Clausen, Leonard S. Cottrell, Jr., John Dollard,

Paul Glick, Louis Guttman, G. Frederick Kuder, Paul F. Lazarsfield, Rensis Likert, Robert K. Merton, Frederick Mosteller, Arnold M. Rose, Paul Wallin, Robin M. Williams, Kimball Young, and Eugene J. Zander, just to name a few whose subsequent work I have particularly admired. Together with their colleagues, over a 5-year period these researchers developed more than 100 attitude scales and other instruments and administered one or more of them to more than half a million respondents. Their consuming goal was to explain the variance in a set of "dependent" or "outcome" variables of interest to the army (such as troop morale).

Like all conscientious craftsmen, these researchers understood that to do a good job at the ultimate task required the use of quality tools. Perhaps more than any group of social scientists before them, they gave detailed attention to the issues of measurement, of validity and reliability, and to whether their results could be replicated in a different sample.

Their guiding conceptual framework was the classic scientific model that had led to the discovery of the laws of physics centuries earlier. Surely, buried under all of the confounding complexity, must be equally fundamental laws of social interaction, and these searchers meant to participate in the task of identifying them. They made every effort to model their research procedures on those that had been so productive in the physical sciences. Where possible, they set up controlled experiments, a procedure more feasible in a military setting than in most other sectors of society. When this was not feasible, they developed the best approximations permitted by the circumstances.

Like all social scientists, their ultimate goal was to produce social explanation—that is, to generate theory. But they had little patience with philosophical principles or abstract deductive reasoning. The theory they hoped to construct was to be inductive, grounded in empirical data, and subject to confirmation or disconfirmation by well-designed research.

As Stouffer put it in the forward to the final volume,

[T]he future of social psychology and sociology calls for three developments:
1. Formulation of theories, at least of some limited generality, which can be operationally stated such that verification is possible, and from which predictions can be made successfully to new specific instances.

2. Such theories demand that the objects of study be isolated and adequately described, preferably by measurement.

3. Once the variables are identified, the test of the adequacy of the theory, in comparison to alternative theories, must be rigorous, preferably evidenced by controlled experiment, and preferably replicated.

> By its contributions to measurement and prediction this volume seeks to accelerate the advance of the social sciences. (Stouffer et al., Vol. 4, 1950, p. vi)

A new brand of theorists emerged in sociology who based their work on this inductive premise. It is safe to assert that this has remained the prevailing paradigm in American sociology to this very day.

In the early 1970s, a consortium of family scholars under the leadership of Wesley Burr, Reuben Hill, Ivan Nye, and Ira Reiss agreed to attempt to develop a more systematic, integrated, and comprehensive corpus of midrange theories about the family. The hope was that a foundation might be laid for an eventual master theory of the family. The strategy, following the lead of the new breed of sociological theorists (such as Merton, 1945, 1949; and Zetterberg, 1963) was to be twofold. First, existing minitheories pertaining to particular family issues were to be analyzed, the variables cleaned up and specified, overlapping sets of propositions consolidated, and finally the entire domain reduced to systems of empirically testable propositions. Second, the research literature was to be surveyed, critiqued, and integrated so that the existing degree of support for the various theoretically derived propositions might be assessed and critical gaps identified (see Chapter 1 in Burr et al., 1979b, Vol. 1). Although this strategy included both deductive and inductive components, from the beginning it clearly rested on the same philosophical foundation spelled out by Stouffer and his colleagues. The ultimate product was to be a series of empirically supported propositions that attempted to predict variation in certain socially significant dependent family variables by identifying the system of independent variables that influenced them. The model was *positivistic* (i.e., all conclusions were rooted in research evidence), *linear* (i.e., the causes all ran in one direction, from the independent to the dependent variables), *static* (i.e., the relationships among variables were all frozen in time), and *deterministic* (i.e., it was assumed that if it were possible to measure all of the pertinent independent variables without measurement or sampling error, then it would be possible to account for all of the variance in the dependent variable).

The final product of the seven-year project was the aforementioned two-volume report *Contemporary Theories about the Family* (Burr et al., 1979a). The first volume consisted of the reports of 22 authors (or teams of authors), each of whom had taken some aspect of family relationships and attempted to integrate the pertinent theory and research in the manner agreed upon. (See Box A for an example of one of the more successful efforts).

BOX A

Figure 1.2 is taken from Reiss and Miller (1979). It attempted to represent graphically the system of determinants of heterosexual permissiveness that were identified by the authors as a result of following the prescribed procedures. In the system of notation used here (and in most of the other chapters), the boxes represent variables. The arrowed lines that connect boxes represent causal relationships (with the causal influence running in the direction of the arrows). In a refinement to the basic causal diagram, Reiss and Miller have incorporated *contingency variables* into their model. These are represented by boxes with arrowed lines that end in another line rather than in a box. They are intended to indicate that the causal relationship represented by the targeted line (which itself connects two variables) is modified by the contingency variable. Whether the relationship is strengthened or weakened by an increase in the value of the contingency variable is indicated by a circled S with an *arrow up* if strengthened and an *arrow down* if weakened. One also can indicate when an increase in the contingency variable may actually cause the relationship between independent and dependent variable to reverse in sign. One instance of this is indicated in Figure 1.2 by a circled (Lo = −, Hi = +). ▲

As a contributing author, I stood only on the periphery of this ambitious process and was not involved in the interpersonal struggles, the volumes of correspondence, and the hours of debate and drudgery that the editors and their close associates endured. My impression is that those involved came to revise their estimates of how soon the family field might generate a unifying set of interlinked midrange theories. I thought I sensed a certain retreat, not just from the daunting magnitude of the task, but also from the definition of the task. At the beginning, I believe many of us shared the hope that after each of the 22 teams had done its work, certain patterns of variables would be discovered in many of the models. These recurring patterns would provide the unifying links between the formerly discrete minitheories. At the very least, we collectively hoped that this exercise in consolidation might be a productive first step and point the way toward some

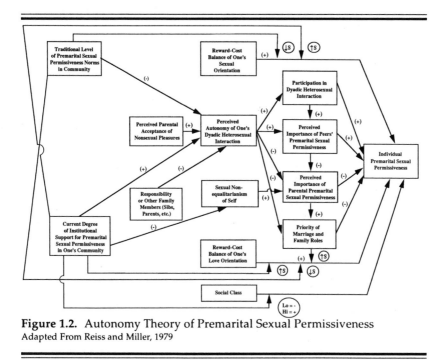

Figure 1.2. Autonomy Theory of Premarital Sexual Permissiveness
Adapted From Reiss and Miller, 1979

future achievement of the ultimate goal—an overarching, articulated macromodel of family relationships.

Alas, no such network of overlapping patterns emerged. The explanatory variables in each model seemed to be related in unique patterns that proliferated endlessly. Beyond this, some of the authors, including myself, found that the theory and empirical research in their topical areas did not lend themselves to presentation in the format set up by the editors. My own topic was family process and child outcomes. The presentation attempted to summarize and integrate work based on the family process theory of that period. These systems-oriented theorists and researchers did not share the foundational assumptions of the scholarly tradition upon which the whole family theories project was based. Although my coauthor and I were willing to compromise to the extent of making the model linear (i.e., omitting feedback), we needed to adopt a format that permitted multiple, qualitatively distinct outcomes rather than fluctuations in a single, continuous outcome variable. With some difficulty, I got the editors to let me substitute the conventions of computer flow charts. These could be under-

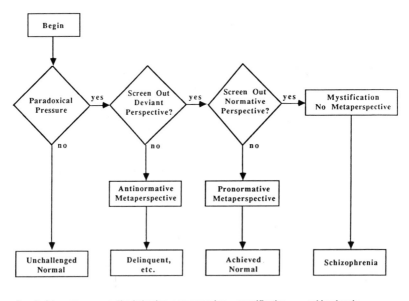

Paradoxial pressure × nondiscriminating over screening × mystification = schizophrenia.
Paradoxial pressure × nondiscriminating under screening × metaperspective = delinquency.
Paradoxial pressure × discriminating screening × metaperspective = achieved normal.
No paradoxial pressure ------------------------------------ = unchallenged normal.
                        (no metaperspective)

Figure 1.3. Family Process and Child Outcomes
From Broderick and Pulliam-Krager, 1979, Fig. 23.1

stood by most readers without much special instruction and were much better suited to represent the flow of social processes with choice points along the way. (See Figure 1.3.) My impression was that they thought me a poor sport not to follow the guidelines they set up, but this was not a matter of willful lack of cooperation, simply a basic conceptual incompatibility between the two scientific paradigms.

Volume 2 of *Contemporary Theories About the Family* consisted of five general essays on the more prominent competing theoretical approaches to social relationships from which theories about the family were derived. James Smith and I were invited to write the chapter on general systems theory. A brief history of that movement is the subject of the next section of this chapter. More pertinent to the present topic is our attempt in that 1979 chapter to analyze the exact nature of the incompatibilities between the notational systems required for presenting process models and those used to represent linear causal pathways such as those prescribed by Burr and his associates. Quite apart from the inclusion of choice points and feedback, we argued that basic systems notation is literally the inverse of the notation used in the linear causal model. As explained in Box B and illustrated in Figure 1.4 (both are extracted directly from the 1979 Broderick and Smith chapter), the boxes in one become the arrowed lines in the other and vice versa.

BOX B   CONVERTING CAUSAL MODELS INTO SYSTEMS NOTATION

In causal models such as social scientists are used to seeing the variables are in the boxes and the nature of the relationship between them is represented by connecting arrows. In a linear equation this relationship or *rule of transformation* is represented by a slope that expresses the degree of influence of one variable upon the other. In systems notation the variables are seen as inputs or outputs and are represented by arrows, while the rule of transformation is in the box. The reversal is not trivial. Systems theory focuses on the rules of relationships among units rather than on variation in the inputs and outputs.

The three examples in Figure [1.4] illustrate the difference in notation, first for a simple two-variable causal model, second for a slightly more complex path model involving five variables, and finally for a nonlinear model where one variable is a contingency variable, that is, it modifies the relationship between the other two variables. ▲

The Emergence of General Systems Theory

Many minds contributed to the intellectual construction of what has come to be known as general systems theory, but two stand out as having had critical influence: biologist Ludwig von Bertalanffy and mathematician and engineer Norbert Wiener.

As early as 1928, Bertalanffy wrote:

Since the fundamental character of the living thing is its organization, the customary investigation of the single parts and processes cannot provide a complete explanation of the vital phenomena. This investigation gives us no information about the coordination of parts and processes. (Bertalanffy, 1934)

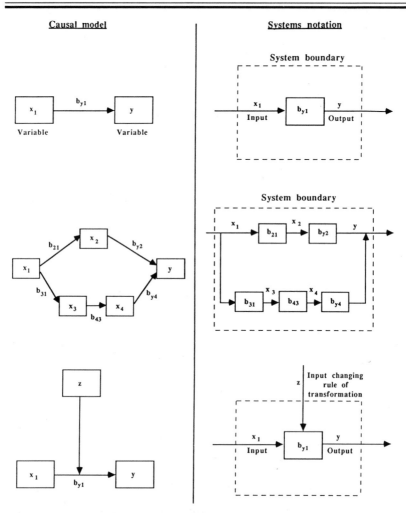

Figure 1.4. Illustrations of System Notation
Reprinted from Broderick and Smith, 1979, Fig. 3.9.

Having identified the problem, Bertalanffy began working on solutions, incorporating his evolving ideas into his lectures and seminars. However, not until the 1950s were his claims for the broad utility of his new approach presented in print in English (1951, 1952, 1955). By that time he was writing in a more assertive vein:

We postulate a new discipline called *General Systems Theory*. General systems theory is a logico-mathematical field whose task is the formulation and derivation of those general principles that are applicable to "systems" in general. In this way, exact formulations of terms such as wholeness and sum, differentiation, progressive mechanization, centralization, hierarchical order, finality and equifinality, etc., become possible, terms which occur in all sciences dealing with "systems" and imply their logical homology. (Original German 1947; cited in Bertalanffy, 1972, p. 26)

From the beginning, Bertalanffy viewed psychological and social systems as lying well within the scope of his theory. They belonged to the third and highest tier of his hierarchical model of system types. At the lowest levels were *inanimate systems*, at the intermediate level were *living systems*, and at the highest level were *symbolic systems*, which dealt with meanings (Bertalanffy, 1959). (This point has been provocatively elaborated by social anthropologist Roy D'Andrade, whose views are summarized in Box C. What Bertalanffy called "symbolic systems," D'Andrade called *semiotic systems*.)

BOX C D'ANDRADE'S THREE-TIERED MODEL OF SCIENTIFIC PARADIGMS

In a classic article, social anthropologist Roy D'Andrade (1986) has argued that each of the three levels of systems has a distinctive and appropriate type of scientific inquiry and explanation, one that cannot be applied to the other two without producing serious errors.

The classic scientific paradigm was designed to investigate the laws of the *physical sciences* and assumes "an almost completely homogenous universe where all generalizations apply equally through all time. There are only a few basic objects and a few forces, and their interrelations can be stated in quantitative mathematical form" (D'Andrade, 1986, pp. 20-21). This permits the formulation of "laws" or quantitative statements that use few terms and require minimal specifications of restrictions or boundary conditions.

D'Andrade calls the second level the domain of the *natural sciences*, and he includes complex ecological and meteorological systems as well as biological systems. Because of the complexity and the particularity of each instance of such a system, he argues that the task of scientific investigation is to discover the order underlying the complexity. This involves describing how each system is constituted and how it works (that is, how each part relates to and affects the other parts, and what higher-level systemic features are emergent from this interaction). To the extent possible, systems that operate in parallel ways are grouped together, and more general principles of organization pertaining to that class of systems may be adduced. However, generalizations based on such investigations are necessarily restricted to particular systems or classes of systems that exist for only a particular limited time under particular circumstances. These generalizations can only be adequately stated in long, complex, natural-language statements. Because modern systems theory grew out of attempts to analyze and describe this type of system, most of the systems literature (including much of the family systems literature) is pitched at this level.

D'Andrade calls the third level the domain of the *semiotic sciences* (from the Greek, *sema*, meaning sign or symbol). At this level, scientific inquiry probes the nature of systems in which the order is imposed, not by the nature of the component parts nor even by the emergent features growing out of their interaction, but by the *meanings* of each of these to sentient participants in the system. Such systems are intrinsically more complex than natural systems because they involve individual decision making and the interpersonal construction of shared meanings. Clearly this is the appropriate level of analysis for family systems. ▲

In 1954, the Society for the Advancement of General Systems Theory (later renamed the Society for General Systems Research) was established as a broad cross-disciplinary forum for the discussion of Bertalanffy's ideas. Much of the development of the theory since that time has been stimulated by the discussions and publications of the participants in those meetings.

Meanwhile, quite independent of these developments, Norbert Wiener and a group of colleagues spent World War II developing control systems for antiaircraft batteries that were trying to compensate for enemy aircrafts' advances in speed and maneuverability. In the process, they worked very closely with Vannevar Bush and the new computing machines he had pioneered. Their work led them to develop a new science of feedback systems and communication technology that they eventually named *cybernetics*, after the Greek word for a "steersman." Like Bertalanffy, Wiener and his associates perceived early on the more general applications of their model. To them, for example, the principles of feedback, self-regulating systems, and information processing clearly applied to both the human brain and the electronic control system. As soon as the end of the war left them free to pursue the matter, they sought financial support from the Josiah Macy Foundation to bring together a select group of scholars from a variety of disciplines to discuss these broader implications. The 20 members would present papers to one another for discussion and critique in a series of two-day seminars at six-month intervals. Included in the distinguished company were psychologist Kurt Lewin and anthropologists Gregory Bateson and Margaret Mead (Wiener, 1948).

Lewin began to incorporate the concept of feedback into his explanations of human behavior as early as 1947. He was a social psychologist in the Gestalt tradition, and his writings offered a bold alternative to the prevailing view that humans were basically driven by instinct. Rather, he conceived of them as goal-seeking beings whose strategy of life involved successive approximations and course corrections based on feedback (not at all unlike Wiener's target-seeking missiles). Instead of looking inward to biological drives or even to learned responses, Lewin looked outward to the way individuals perceived and interacted with their immediate "life space" (1951). In this context, life space looked very much like both Wiener's "environment" and Bertalanffy's "external system."

Anthropologist Gregory Bateson went on to become one of the most influential founders of the family process movement—even though he was never a family therapist. Like many of the intellectuals of the day, he maintained an active correspondence that cut across disciplinary lines. Among those with whom he exchanged ideas regularly were Kurt Lewin, psychiatrist Harry Stack Sullivan, and Bertalanffy. Their influence is evident in the book Bateson wrote with psychiatrist Jurgen Ruesch, *Communication: The Social Matrix of Society* (Ruesch & Bateson, 1951). It outlined the principles of communication theory as they might be applied to the field of psychiatry. In a later section of the chapter, we shall review the circumstances that led to the incorporation of Bateson's ideas in the intellectual and conceptual foundation of the family process movement.

Bateson was not the only early student of systems who reaped benefits from integrating the ideas of Wiener and Bertalanffy. Although cyberneticists and general systems theorists at first attempted to maintain distinct identities (they refrained from citing each other's works and so forth), ultimately all but the most devout purists were promiscuously intermixing the contributions of the two approaches without regard for their origins. In this book, I intend, for the most part, to follow this libertine practice myself.

Transactions With the Other Family Discipline

As noted earlier, family process theory has not remained the exclusive province of family therapists. A broad array of other academic disciplines has found its perspective and constructs useful. In medicine, the theory sparked the development of the new subdiscipline of family medicine; in psychology, it gave birth to a new specialty, family psychology (now one of the fastest-growing sections of the American Psychological Association); in social work, it contributed to the emergence of ecological systems as a major theoretical framework for contemporary practice; and in home economics, it gave rise to a new, systemic approach to family resource management. This book will not track the intellectual contagion wrought by this theory, but it is germane to our purpose to review some of the transactions between the emerging family process theory and the preexisting body of family scholarship known variously as family relationships, family studies, and family science. Not only is this the nonclinical discipline within which family process theory fits most obviously, but also it is my own discipline, one that I have closely observed and in which I have actively participated.

The field of family relations had its earliest roots in sociology if only because this was the discipline that most concerned itself with the contemporary family. So far as we can determine, the first course at an American university that focused exclusively on the family was offered in 1893 by Charles R. Henderson, a sociologist at the University of Chicago (Mudd, 1951, p. 6). By 1908, according to a survey by Bernard, approximately 20 such courses were being offered across the country (Bernard, 1908). But the subject matter of these courses was not everyday interactions among family members nor ordinary transactions between family members and non-family members in the larger society. Rather, it was a more abstract, cross-cultural consideration of the family as a social institution.

When Ernest W. Burgess decided to teach a class on the contemporary American family at the University of Chicago in the mid-1920s, he was appalled to find that "among all the volumes upon the family, ethological, historical, psychological, ethical, social, economic, statistical, radically realist or radically idealist, there was to be found not a single work that even pretended to study the modern family as behavior or as social phenomenon" (Burgess, 1926, p. 3). If his students were to be exposed to a more dynamic view of families, then he would have to provide it himself.

Elsewhere I have written:

To say that the modern field of family relations was inaugurated by Ernest W. Burgess's remarkable essay "The Family as a Unit of Interacting Personalities" (1926) is probably only a modest overstatement.... [In it] he proceeded to outline some of the conceptual elements that he considered essential to any analysis of the family "as a living being rather than a dead form." (Broderick, 1988, p. 570)

In one remarkable conceptual leap, Burgess seems almost to have anticipated the family systems perspective. He wrote:

By a unity of interacting personalities is meant a living, changing, growing thing. I was about to call it a super personality. At any rate the actual unity of family life has its existence not in any legal conception, nor in any formal contract, but in the interaction of its members. For the family does not depend for its survival upon the harmonious relations of its members, nor does it necessarily disintegrate as a result of conflicts among its members. The family lives as long as interaction is taking place. (Burgess, 1926, p. 3)

At about the same time, on the East Coast, another sociology professor was also responding to student demands for a more pragmatic and helpful approach to the relational issues they faced. It is probably not irrelevant to note that Ernest R. Groves was a minister before he became a sociologist. In any case, in 1922 he was the head of the Department of Sociology at the University of New Hampshire, and when the students pressed the school to offer a down-to-earth, noncredit Preparation for Marriage course, the dean appointed him to head the team of academics and medical practitioners whose assignment was to develop and present such a course. One by one, the other members of the team dropped out, concerned about the possible negative reflection on their own reputations that might result from participation in such a radical enterprise. Groves found it necessary to develop and offer the course himself, bringing in professionals from related fields such as law, medicine, and sexual hygiene to lecture in areas where his own expertise was insufficient. When he moved to the University of North Carolina in 1927 (perhaps encouraged by Burgess's paper, which he had almost certainly heard given at the Family Section of the American Sociological Society meetings in New York the previous year), Groves introduced into the sociology department's regular curriculum—for the first time anywhere—a family course that was "functional" rather than academic in its focus. Because it was intended to be helpful to students in their real-life challenges, it included a great deal of non-sociological, pragmatically useful material and excluded a great deal of standard sociological analysis (for example, cross-cultural surveys of family forms). Groves not only had to produce his own text for the course (1931), but also founded the Groves Conference on the Conservation of Marriage and the Family in 1934 to foster this approach among other professional educators (Green, 1985).

Not surprisingly, this new breed of family life educators often became involved in counseling with their students and eventually with others. It was a natural extension of their core commitment to improve family relationships as well as to study them. Long before the family therapy movement was initiated, Groves taught the first university-level course on marriage counseling at Duke in 1937 (Green, 1985). In the mid-1940s, he was the chief force behind the organization of the American Association of Marriage Counselors (forerunner of the current American Association for Marriage and Family Therapy, or AAMFT).

One other reflection of the clinical involvement of family scholars in this early period might be noted. When the National Council on Family Relations was founded in 1937 as the professional organization for the new family discipline, one of its early organizational elaborations was to include a therapy section along with its research and education sections. Even today, the connection between the academic study of family relations and the clinical treatment of families is strong. It is not uncommon to find that the university location of the graduate program in marriage and family therapy is in a Department of Family Sciences (by whatever name).

As we shall see in a later section, the roots of the family therapy movement were not in the discipline of family relations, but in social psychiatry and general systems theory. However, if the architects of family process theory managed their achievement with relatively little comment from traditional family scholars, there was a substantial influence in the opposite direction. As might be supposed, the first impact was in the clinical area. As practiced in the Groves tradition, *marriage counseling* was the part-time, often unremunerated, auxiliary activity of certain family life educators (not to mention certain gynecologists, lawyers, and pastors). The practice was widely acknowledged as lacking a unifying, undergirding theory. For an academic practitioner in this tradition, encountering the theory-rich rhetoric of the emerging family therapy movement was a heady experience. The first impression was of confusion. Each of the dynamic founders of the new movement had invented a unique vocabulary and argued passionately on behalf of his or her own model of family reality against all others. But the ultimate seduction for the theory-deprived outsider was the perception that through the obscuring smoke of sectarian debate an earnest seeker might discern a flickering, unifying image.

Recall that this was a period in which a concerted effort was made within the community of mainline family scholars to construct a unifying framework of family theory. Those who became aware of the family process movement found it hard not to hope that when the ego fires had burned out, a splendid, integrative template for family analysis might shine forth from the ashes. Of course, nothing quite that satisfying emerged. But, as this book shall attempt to show, what has emerged is sufficiently substantial and provocative to make it worthy of the attention of any family scholar of whatever theoretical persuasion.

In the foregoing discussion, I have averred that the bridge between the two family disciplines was pretty much a one-way thoroughfare. Indeed, for the most part it was, especially in the early years. An exception of some significance, however, was the role of Reuben Hill. During the 1960s and 1970s when the family process movement was in its most productive and creative period, Hill was widely regarded as the dean of traditional family scholars. He had been one of the chief authors of the family development conceptual framework and of the ABC-X model of family crisis. Hill was the unanimous choice to become the first recipient of the Burgess Award for career contribution to the field of family scholarship, the most prestigious recognition of the National Council on Family Relations. He was the first, and so far the only, family specialist to be elected president of the International Sociological Association. But more to the point, he was also one of the first scholars within his discipline to see the potential of a systems approach to family phenomena. Because of this and his general prominence as senior statesman among the mainline family scholars of that period, the founders of the *Family Process* journal invited him to become a member of their editorial board. In those days, the editorial board constituted the living core of the family process movement, and Hill's membership on it, together with his unparalleled command of the general literature in family theory and research, permitted him to act as a consultant and, in some degree perhaps, as a mentor to the core architects of the emerging theory.

When he accepted an honorary degree at the University of Leuven, Belgium, in December 1970, Hill delivered an address, "Modern Systems Theory and the Family: A Confrontation" (Hill, 1971). It was one of the very first critiques of the new approach from the perspective of the older discipline. Unhappily, it was published in a European journal that was not readily accessible to American scholars, although Hill was generous in his distribution of reprints among his state-side colleagues.

A quite different set of circumstances led to my own involvement as an interpreter of family process theory to my disciplinary colleagues. About the same time that Hill was working with the board of *Family Process*, I had become the new editor of the *Journal of Marriage and the Family*, which served somewhat the same role for the mainline family discipline as *Family Process* did for the family therapy establishment. Impressed with the remarkable richness and variety of family research and theory produced during the 1960s, I determined to dedicate a couple of issues to integrate and critique this widely dispersed material for our equally widely dispersed readership. The result was the first of the *JMF Decade Reviews*, which began a tradition that, happily, has been carried on by subsequent editors. I assigned myself the article that reviewed developments in family theory over the decade. Being one of those family scholars who was also involved in clinical work (in the Groves tradition), I had read a good deal of the published material from the new family therapy group and was a subscriber to *Family Process*. As a result, I included a section on general systems theory in my review, briefly tracing its influence on the family process movement and optimistically suggesting that it might provide a conceptual umbrella for the integration of the various competing family theories (Broderick, 1971). So far as I am aware, this paper and Hill's were the first to call attention to the new approaches in a nonclinical scholarly journal.

As noted previously, when a consortium of major family scholars dedicated themselves in 1972 to a seven-year theory-construction project, I was able to prevail upon them to include chapters based on a systems approach even though that approach did not conform to the overarching positivist model they had set up for authors to use (Broderick & Pulliam-Krager, 1979; Broderick & Smith, 1979). Subsequently, I have continued to publish material on family process theory in the family relations literature. One recent example is a chapter in Sprey's *Fashioning Family Theory* (Broderick, 1990), that attempted to summarize the current status of the theory in terms that would communicate to an uninitiated student of the family. The present volume represents a still more ambitious effort in that direction.

At least one other bridging scholar must be mentioned: David Olson of the University of Minnesota. His background is in family relations (in fact, although I was not at all involved in any of his later contributions to the field, I cannot resist noting that he was one of my doctoral students in the Department of Human Development and Family Relations at The Pennsylvania State University in the 1960s), and he also has received clinical training. His circumplex model of marital and family systems, together with a variety of associated measurement instruments—FACES I, II, III, and IV; PAIR, PREPARE, and ENRICH (Olson, Sprenkle, & Russell, 1979; Olson, McCubbin, Barnes, Larsen, Muxen, & Wilson, 1983; Olson, Russell, & Sprenkle, 1989)—has received more attention and generated more research (and more controversy) here and abroad than any other model of family behavior. Outside the tight circle of original founders, Olson is one of the most frequently cited writers in the family therapy literature. He would doubtless also rank among the top dozen or so in the nonclinical family literature and also is widely referred to in the literatures of a broad range of other disciplines. We will have occasion to refer to his ideas at several points in the body of this book.

Development of the Family Therapy Movement and Emergence of Family Process Theory

Family therapy emerged as a rebellion against the limiting doctrines of traditional, one-on-one psychotherapy. At one point, Freud had actually been persuaded to attempt the concurrent analysis of a husband and wife (James and Alex Strachey, who later became his English translators) (Stone, 1971). This disconcerting experience led him to write, "When it comes to the treatment of relationships I must confess myself utterly at a loss and I have altogether little faith in any individual therapy of them" (Freud, 1912). Three years later, he took an even more adamant position: "When the husband's resistance is added to that of the wife, efforts are made fruitless and therapy is prematurely broken off. . . . We had undertaken something which under existing conditions was impossible to carry out" (Freud, 1915).

As a result of his own unsuccessful experience, Freud made it a doctrine among analysts that seeing more than one member of a family at a time was anathema. As with all such rules, it was only a matter of time before independent-minded therapists challenged it (although none went public with their experiments until after Freud had died).

In some degree, the path of rebellion and innovation was prepared by the development of social psychiatry in the United States after the close of World War II. Hitler's anti-Semitic policies had led many of the most creative European psychiatrists to flee to the United States during the late 1930s. Here, freed from the orthodoxy of the analytic establishment, they explored a wide variety of new ideas, including

those of sociologists Charles H. Cooley (1909) (who described the importance of the perceptions of others in the construction of the "looking
glass self") and George Herbert Mead (1934) (whose similar view was
that personality developed as a function of the introjection of the
"generalized other"). As a result of these and other influences, innovators such as Eric Fromm (1941, 1947) and Harry Stack Sullivan (1947,
1953) began to describe personality and personality disorders as the
product of social processes rather than as the product of internal psycho-
dynamic processes.

From that perception, it was not an unimaginable step to consider
the possibility that personality disorders, especially among children,
might best be dealt with by intervening in the ongoing social processes
that created them. The majority of those who broke the rules and
started seeing whole families were frustrated child psychiatrists. In the
typical case, a therapist would find himself stuck in the treatment of
some recalcitrant young patient, often perceiving that the patient's
family was colluding in the sabotage of the therapeutic enterprise.
Finally, in exasperation, he would call in the whole group in an effort
to mobilize support for what he was trying to accomplish. The results
were often gratifying and sometimes almost miraculous. Small wonder that a therapist with two or three such experiences might consider
setting aside Freudian prohibitions and experimenting with a whole-
family approach.

Nathan Ackerman and Murray Bowen are good examples of psychiatrists who found themselves led in this fashion, step by step, into the
unexplored territory of family therapy. By coincidence, each had his
first experience meeting with family members (as an auxiliary to child
therapy) while working on the staff of the Menninger Clinic in Topeka,
Kansas, early in his career. Each, quite independent of the other,
proceeded to experiment with switching his therapeutic approaches
increasingly to whole-family interventions. Each eventually founded
a major center for training family therapists, Ackerman in New York
and Bowen in Washington, D.C.

For certain of the pioneers, their discovery of the family systems
approach to treating an individual's symptoms did not derive entirely from their clinical experience. For example, Lyman Wynne, like
Ackerman and Bowen, began his career as a psychiatrist working with
children with serious psychiatric problems. In his case, he was part of
a team headed by Erich Lindemann at the Massachusetts General Hospital that was investigating the causes of severe psychophysical disorders in young people. As in the other cases, he and the other members
of the team became aware of the impact of family events on the manifes-

tations of their patients' symptoms. But, unlike the others, Wynne's insights into the properties of family systems were fed from an additional source. In the midst of his work with the Lindemann group, he managed to find time and energy to complete a four-year Ph.D. in social relations at Harvard. The chair of his doctoral committee was none other than Talcott Parsons, the reigning sage of systems.

Among the founding fathers and mothers of the family therapy movement, perhaps none was more explicit in incorporating the concepts of modern systems theory than Don Jackson. Like Wynne, he had assistance in articulating his thoughts from both clinical and nonclinical mentors. He began with an advantage, having been trained in psychiatry under the tutelage of that great innovator, Harry Stack Sullivan. He began his career working as a psychiatric resident at Sullivan's Chestnut Lodge, a treatment center for young schizophrenics in Rockville, Maryland. Meanwhile, 3,000 miles away at the Veterans Hospital in Palo Alto, Sullivan's old friend and correspondent, Gregory Bateson, found himself about to undertake a research project with schizophrenics and needed a psychiatric consultant. Sullivan suggested Jackson.

Bateson, of course, was an anthropologist who had been very involved in the development of general systems theory, cybernetics, and communication theory. In truth, he had no special interest in schizophrenia per se, but he was intrigued by a particular type of paradoxical communication. He had already spent two years sponsored by a Rockefeller Grant, pursuing other manifestations of this communication pattern. His team in that project had included Jay Haley and John Weakland. Haley had been brought onto the research team because of his earlier work with films that included interaction between cartoon characters and live actors (an example of the type of paradoxical discourse that interested Bateson). His assignment on the grant had involved traveling to Arizona to study the work of the remarkable hypnotherapist Milton Ericson, whose trademark was the therapeutic use of paradox. Weakland's interest was in Chinese culture and films and especially in humor based on paradox.

By 1956, the Bateson team had used up its first grant and was casting about for a "sexy" aspect of the topic that might attract further funding. The members hit upon a project that focused on Bateson's notion that schizophrenia was the result of having been caught in a paradoxical bind with one's mother while growing up. The grant application (to the Macy Foundation) described the schizophrenigenic mother as being "driven not only to punish the child's demand for love, but also to punish any indication which the child may give that he knows he is not loved" (Haley, 1976a, p. 67). Because no team member had any credentials or experience with schizophrenics, such a project clearly would require adding a specialist in the subject. The first major expenditure of the new grant was to bring Jackson to Palo Alto.

Out of that project came perhaps the most discussed paper in modern psychiatry, "Toward a Theory of Schizophrenia" (Bateson, Jackson, Haley, & Weakland, 1956), which enlarged and documented Bateson's theory with clinical examples. Schizophrenia in young people was attributed to an ongoing pattern of maternal "double binding." This involved the mother's repeated demands for something at one level of discourse (for example, verbal complaints that she never got enough affection from her son) while simultaneously contradicting this demand on another level (for example, manifesting strong aversion through her body language to demonstrations of affection). Because two different levels of discourse were involved, the contradiction was not easy to confront, and part of the pattern was to prohibit any effort to do so. The final element in this toxic pattern was an emotionally loaded injunction never to abandon the "crazy-making" situation.

The new theory proposed that any child thus bound had only one recourse—madness. Effective treatment thus must focus less on the youthful victim and more on the double-binding pattern of mother-child interaction. Freed of this paradoxical straightjacket, the young person was enabled to reestablish rational behavior. The arguments and observational data set forth in this article were compelling. For a generation, the double-bind theory was the most influential explanation of mental illness among both progressive professionals and the general public. As we shall see in subsequent chapters, time and further research has not been kind to the theory. Nevertheless, this paper by the Palo Alto group became a foundational document for the family process movement.

While working on Bateson's research project, Jackson founded his own clinically oriented organization, the Mental Research Institute, or MRI as it is more commonly known. In the next few years, the staff was joined by such talents as Paul Watzlawick and Virginia Satir. It was in the crucible of debates among these impressive intellects that Bateson's insights into social systems, cybernetics, and communication theory were blended with Ericson's paradoxical therapeutic strategies (Jay Haley being the chief advocate) and Jackson's theoretical and clinical lucidity into one of the major schools of family therapy. Also in that crucible was laid the foundation of family process theory.

In 1961, Don Jackson in Palo Alto and Nathan Ackerman of the Family Institute in New York joined forces in establishing a new journal, *Family Process*. The first editor was Jay Haley. As we have noted earlier, most of the early pioneers were invited to be on the editorial board (along with a few outsiders such as Reuben Hill), and the meetings of that board provided the forum for the debates that generated much of the superstructure of the theory as it developed. (For a more detailed history of the founding of the family therapy field, see Broderick and Schrader, 1991.)

The End of the Beginning

From these roots and beginnings, family process (or systems) theory has developed along many lines. I have no ambition either to attempt a comprehensive review of the entire process literature or to comment on all of the debates, issues, and permutations that intrigue its many practitioners. The task is too daunting, and even were it possible to accomplish, the resulting tome would make dull reading. Instead, my effort will be to present what I perceive to be the enduring core features of the theory in as lucid a manner as possible. If it could be achieved, I would love to make it a lively as well as a lucid presentation, but, given the constraints of responsible scholarship, perhaps all that can be expected are occasional lively interludes. The next chapter is an overview of the gross structure of the theory. In the chapters that follow, I hope to explore some of the substructures more critically and in more depth. In the process, I should like to participate in the ongoing cross-fertilization between the family process movement and the nonclinical scholarly establishment by identifying areas in each literature that, in my view, have exciting implications for the other.

CHAPTER 2

The Family as a System: An Overview

This chapter provides an overview of family process theory, a birds-eye view, as it were, of the whole terrain. In the following chapters, as we explore some of the more engaging byways and neighborhoods in more detail, the reader will better understand how each particular topic fits into the larger schema.

We might begin with the most basic definition of a system. As Hall and Fagan (1956) put it, a system is "a set of objects together with relationships between the objects and between their attributes." Virtually any assemblage of distinct parts would meet these modest criteria (a chair, for example). To define the essential features of a living system such as a cell or an individual organism requires a more complex set of descriptors. Bertalanffy's contribution was to establish the critical features that differentiate open, living systems, which exchange energy and information with their environments, from closed, mechanical systems (1950, 1959). In his 1967 book *Sociology and Modern Systems Theory*, Buckley in turn focused his attention on the qualities that differentiate social from biological systems. Still other theorists, such as Jackson (1965) and Kantor and Lehr (1975), began to specify the distinctive qualities of that unique social system, the family. More recently, variations among families have received considerable scholarly attention. For example, Ahrons and Rogers (1987) contrast the standard nuclear family organization with the binuclear families that result from divorce; McGoldrick and her associates offered a book of readings on ethnic variations in family processes (McGoldrick, Pearce, & Giordano, 1982); and still others have called our attention to the impact of members with particular needs or incapacities on family functioning.

All of this together has led to the general conclusion that the family is an example of an open, ongoing, goal-seeking, self-regulating, social system, and that it shares the features of all such systems. In addition, certain features—such as its unique structuring of gender and generation—set it apart from other social systems. Beyond this, each individual family system is shaped by its own particular structural features (size, complexity, composition, life stage), the psychobiological characteristics of its individual members (age, gender, fertility, health, temperament, and so on), and its sociocultural and historic position in its larger environment.

Our strategy in this overview of family process theory, will be to look first at the characteristics held in common by all *open, ongoing systems*, and then examine those characteristics shared by that subset of such systems that are also *goal-seeking and self-regulating*. We then review those additional features peculiar to *social systems* and the features unique to that subset of social systems designated as *families*. Finally, we will consider the effects of *variations* in the structural features of the family, in the psychobiological characteristics of its members, and in the sociocultural and historical context of its operations.

Characteristics of Open, Ongoing Systems

To describe a system as "open" is not to suggest that it has no boundaries between itself and its environment; we say only that energy, matter, and information flow back and forth across that barrier. That which is received from the environment is called *input*; that which is given back to the environment is called *output*. By logical necessity, with both inputs and outputs, the system is involved in changes not only internal to itself (in order to incorporate inputs and generate outputs), but also in relation to its environment.

To describe a system as "ongoing" as well as "open" is merely to call attention to the fact that change can occur only in relationship to time.

That which changes has a past, a present, and a future; it is ongoing. The following principles, then, can be seen as flowing directly from the definitions of open, ongoing systems:

1. By definition, *open, ongoing systems* are not static and may not be fully described in static or structural terms. Rather, the parts are dynamically related to one another and to the environment. The student of open, ongoing systems therefore focuses on processes and on the patterning of those processes over time. Walter Buckley put it well when he wrote, "Process, then, focuses on the actions and interactions of the components of the ongoing system, such that varying degrees of structuring arise, persist, dissolve, or change" (1967, p. 18). Admittedly, theorists within the movement discuss such systemic structural features as boundaries, hierarchies, and coalitions at some length. However, the purists among them insist that while processes may be observed directly, structures may only be inferred. They would claim that the use of such static constructs is likely to seduce the theorist into thinking of these structures as concrete realities rather than as the ephemeral, ever-shifting patterns of interaction that Buckley described above. One strategy for avoiding static thinking is to use verb forms rather than nouns when discussing the characteristics of systems. Thus, the purist speaks of structuring rather than of structures, of bounding rather than of boundaries, and of ordering or ranking rather than of hierarchies. In this book I have not always chosen to follow this convention where it has seemed awkward to do so, but the focus remains on process, whatever the language.

2. It follows that the qualities of an open, ongoing system are *emergent* out of the interaction of its parts; that is, as Aristotle and many others since have noted, the whole is greater than the sum of its parts and has qualities that cannot be deduced from the combined characteristics of each part.

   In an early application of this principle to family systems, Jackson wrote, "Even if the object of study is ostensibly the family unit, any examination of the characteristics of the various individual family members remains in the domain of individual theory. . . . It is only when we attend to the transactions between individuals as primary data that a qualitative shift in conceptual framework can be achieved. . . . We need measures which do not simply sum up individuals into a family unit; we need to measure the characteristics of the supra-individual family unit" (1965, p. 5).

3. The quality that defines a set of ongoing processes as a system is their organization into recurring, repetitive patterns that may be observed over time. From these observed regularities, we can deduce the *rules* that govern the system. Again we may turn to Jackson's 1965 article for a lucid application of this generic systems principle to the family:

   Briefly stated, the major assertion of the theory . . . is that the family is a rule-governed system: that its members behave among themselves in an organized, repetitive manner and that this patterning of behaviors can be abstracted as a governing principle of family life (p. 6). . . . Just as a relatively few rules permit games as complex as chess or bridge, so a few family rules can cover the major aspects of ongoing interpersonal relationships. (p. 11)

4. The rules governing systems complex enough to be open and ongoing are hierarchically structured. It seems to be inherent in the organization of complex sets of rules that they be hierarchically structured; that is, all rules are not equal in their breadth of application. Some are narrowly applicable to immediate inputs such as "open the door when someone knocks." Others are more comprehensive, perhaps governing who should answer the door when several family members are present or what circumstances might lead to deciding not to open the door when a knock is heard. In systems parlance, these are called *metarules* (from the Greek *meta*, meaning "beyond, over, transcending"). Logically, beyond metarules are infinite series of *meta-meta*, *meta-meta-meta*, and so on rules at increasing levels of abstraction and breadth of application. For purposes of this discussion, distinguishing only three levels above the concrete, particular, first-level rules seems sufficient. We may refer, as above, to metarules that specify the conditions under which various first-level rules are brought into operation. Beyond this, *midlevel policies* incorporate broad sectors of family concern, such as the style of child discipline considered appropriate at particular ages or whether changes in the family's situation warrants changes in the permeability of the family's boundaries. Finally, we will have occasion to discuss top-of-the-pyramid *family paradigms* that represent the core philosophy of the family enterprise and therefore shape the evolution of its policies. These integrative paradigms themselves may evolve over time, but they constitute family members' most enduring and most centrally held values and commitments.

Certain sets of rules (hierarchically arranged, as we have seen) seem to be intrinsic in systems that, although they are open to inputs from the environment, maintain continuity and identity over substantial periods of time. One such set of rules regulates the relational distances among family members (this is the subject of Chapter 4, Distance Regulation Within the Family System). These rules govern the moving balance between the forces working to *bond* the members together into a coherent unit and the counterforces working to *buffer* the members and thus preserve a measure of independent personal identity and limit the degree of enmeshment. Other rules regulate traffic across family boundaries. These govern the balance between the energies expended in *bridging* to the outside world and the opposing energies dedicated to *maintaining a boundary* between the family and the outside world (this is the subject matter of Chapter 5, The Regulation of Transactions Across Family Boundaries).

These points may be summarized in the following systems principles:

5. If they are to survive as such, all ongoing systems must regulate relationships among members to ensure that they are bonded enough to maintain the system's integrity and yet sufficiently buffered to maintain each member's integrity.

6. If they are to remain open and ongoing, all such systems must regulate traffic across their borders so that they are able to access necessary resources from the environment while protecting themselves from threatening or unwelcome incursions from that same environment. Because, by definition, all living systems are open, it is regrettable that so many family process theorists have followed the lead of Kantor and Lehr in describing families as ranging from "open to closed." We would more accurately acknowledge that *all* viable families occupy a relatively narrow band toward the open end of the open-to-closed spectrum. They vary only from "more open" to "less open."

In summary, we have noted six characteristics shared by *all* open, ongoing systems—by ferns, finches, and federations as much as by families. An open and ongoing system has the following characteristics:

1. It may be conceptualized as a set of *patterned, interactive processes*.
2. These processes have qualities that are *emergent* rather than merely summative.
3. These processes have regularities that permit *rules* to be inferred.
4. These rules are *hierarchically structured*.
5. These rules include well-developed sets of guidelines for maintaining and regulating relationships *among their component elements*.
6. These rules also include well-developed sets of guidelines for maintaining and regulating relationships *between the system and its environment*.

Characteristics of Goal-Seeking, Self-Regulating Systems

One foundational concern of systems theory pioneers was to illuminate the features of systems that had the capacity to pursue a goal. In the case of Norbert Wiener, the originator of cybernetics, the initial object was to design mechanical systems that had this capacity, such as antiaircraft batteries that could track moving objects, factor in changes in wind velocity and so on, and effectively bring down enemy planes

(1948). In the decades since World War II, the development of electronic guidance systems has resulted in remarkably effective goal-seeking machines. At a minimum, any such system must include at least four features: (1) a means of identifying the goal, (2) a means of calculating and pursuing a path toward that goal, (3) a means of perceiving deviations from that planned trajectory in real time, and (4) a mechanism for correcting course so that the objective is realized. Today's sophisticated military hardware may also incorporate secondary agendas in their design that are derivative from the prime directive. For example, they may have built-in defensive capability, enabling them to avoid detection, identify and evade or destroy interceptors, circumvent obstacles, and even self-destruct under certain circumstances.

Some social systems would appear to have prime directives nearly as sharply focused as these electronic-guidance systems. Businesses are geared toward the pursuit of profit; unions struggle against the odds to improve the wages, benefits, and working conditions of their members; schools exist to educate their students; and hospitals have the clear purpose of caring for the ill and injured. Like their more sophisticated electronic counterparts, all such social systems incorporate derivative goals and subsystems for achieving them. To succeed, businesses must also maintain at least a minimal level of employee morale; unions must profitably manage investment of their retirement funds; schools must attend to the health needs of their students; and hospitals must maintain ongoing training programs for their staffs.

The Family as a Goal-Seeking System

To my knowledge, no one has ever challenged the assertion that families, like the other social systems cited above, are goal-seeking. We can fairly summarize the general view as follows:

1. Like every cybernetic system, families pursue goals.
2. To pursue goals, a logical prior task is to select goals and mobilize support for them among family members.
3. To pursue goals, the means to these ends, the tactics best calculated to achieve them, their intermediate destinations, and so on must be identified. This requires the operation of an executive function.
4. To pursue goals to a successful conclusion, progress must be monitored and corrections made for perceived deviations from the planned trajectory.

Although virtually all family systems theorists take these truths to be self-evident, I think that it is not at all obvious that real families operate in this way. For starters, identifying the prime directives of a family system is not easy. At some points in the life cycle, the focal activity of the family might be having and raising children; at other points, it might be launching these same children out of the family. For a certain span of years, much else might be sacrificed in pursuit of career success for certain family members; at a later period, career may be sacrificed to care for an aging parent. Families' prime directives seem to be far more complex, diffuse, and shifting than those of most other organizations and thus more difficult to bring into sharp focus.

Another problem with fitting families neatly into the cybernetic mold has to do with the range of degrees of goal orientation that can be observed among them. While certain families invest a great deal of very focused attention on the achievement of certain goals, others seem to lack any such commitment, drifting along passively in the currents of their life course. Also, as discussed more fully in Chapter 7 (Family Meanings and Shared Realities), some families seem to be unified in their identification of key goals and in their efforts to pursue them, while others seem instead to be collections of individuals who live together but have quite disparate agendas for their lives.

If families can be said to have goals, then clearly these are far more complex matters than they are for those more focused systems from which the model was derived. My own attempt to resolve this issue is the subject matter of Chapter 3, From Cybernetic to Transcybernetic.

However family goals may be conceptualized, there can be no doubt that they are complexly organized. According to the systems principle noted earlier, they, like family rules, must be hierarchically structured. Short-term, immediate goals are at the bottom of the pyramid, and overarching life objectives (such as health, wealth, happiness, and, perhaps, eternal life) are at the top.

In his analysis of multilevel systems, Mesarovic (1970) observes that higher level subsystems have a natural slower rate of change than do lower level subsystems and that they relate to system issues that involve longer time periods. We have noted that family priorities may shift as their circumstances shift over the life cycle. Based on Mesarovic's principle, we should expect to find that, for the most part, the changes occur most readily at the bottom of the pyramid and more slowly at the top. We are reminded of the findings during the revolutionary 1960s and 1970s that the most radical students turned out to be the children of liberal activists. Although the parents were alarmed at their offsprings' extreme behaviors, in truth these children had only adopted radical new strategies to pursue their parents' most basic social and political values.

The following principle, then, may safely be added to the list of those accepted without dissent by systems theorists across the spectrum:

5. Family goals are organized into hierarchies. Higher level goals define the priorities among lower level goals and are intrinsically less likely to be revised or abandoned.

Of course, having hierarchically organized goals is only one requirement of a cybernetic system. To be self-regulating, such a system also must stipulate some means of self-surveillance and some capacity for course correction.

The Family as a Self-Regulating System

Figure 2.1 summarizes the core requirements of any cybernetic system. Of course, each tidy box in this figure must be assumed to represent a complex subsystem in its own right. The value of this simplistic representation is that it focuses our attention away from those complications and on the basic processes inherent in all self-regulating systems. Whether the variations and complexities of real families can be somehow stuffed into such a framework without doing violence either to themselves or to the model is a key question. Again, the careful consideration of that issue is deferred to the next chapter.

In Figure 2.1, the executive function or decision-making process is activated by information from three sources. As Walter Buckley wrote (1967):

> For effective "self-direction" a . . . system must continue to receive a full flow of three kinds of information: (1) information of the world outside; (2) information from the past with a wide range of recall and recombination; and (3) information about itself and its own parts. (p. 56)

In the model, we have designated these three sources of information, respectively as (1) the *family context monitoring function,* (2) the *family archival function,* and (3) the *family status monitoring function.* The interactions among the units in the model are actually continuous and circular, but each cycle is more easily thought of as beginning with a comparison between the family's goals (stored with much else in the collective memory represented by the archival function box) and its current status with respect to those goals (this estimate is provided by various mechanisms of self-surveillance and assessment as shown in the status monitoring box). The assumption is that if the executive

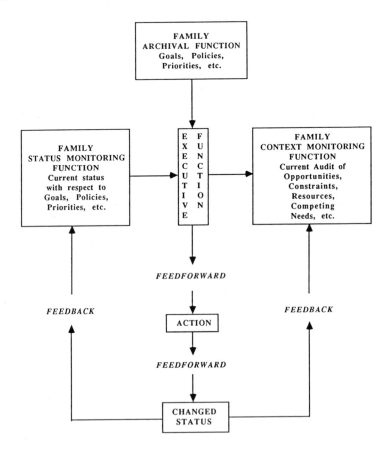

Figure 2.1. Schema of the Family Self-Regulation Function

subsystem perceives few discrepancies between the two—that is, if it discovers the family to be performing in a manner consistent with its goals—then it will continue its present course without correction.

If, on the other hand, the executive subsystem finds significant discrepancies between its goals and its current status—or, better yet, between its goals and its current *trajectory* toward those goals—then it will be motivated to act to change its course. Before acting on that impulse, however, it will need to consider its current situation with respect to its environment. In particular, it must assess the current status of its opportunities, obligations, resources, constraints, competing needs, and so on via the mechanisms represented in the context monitoring box. This further evaluation will finally result in the choice of a particular course of action.

This action will in turn have some impact on the family's status (not necessarily the anticipated one), which results in a changed status. In systems parlance, the transformation of a decision into an action and then into a consequence is often called *feedforward* (Meetham, 1969; Ford, 1987). This changed status necessitates a reevaluation of the family's newly achieved current situation by both the status monitoring function and the context monitoring function in a process known as *feedback*. This sets up the whole system for another round of comparison and action.

If the family is to be considered a goal-seeking, self-correcting, cybernetic system, then it must be observed to lurch toward its goals in endless iterations of some such cycle.

Perhaps we might well comment briefly on the penchant of early family process theorists to focus on the energy and ingenuity that families expend in pursuit of *homeostasis* (that is, resisting change) rather than on their ongoing pursuit of as-yet-unrealized goals (see, for example, Jackson, 1959). Because virtually all of these pioneering theorists were also pioneering family therapists, it should surprise no one that their daily encounter with resistance should lead them to a preoccupation with this particular manifestation of family self-regulation. In similar circumstances, Freud, the founding father of individual psychotherapy, found himself in daily confrontations with his patients' resistance. Out of that ongoing encounter developed a psychology based on the analysis of individual defense mechanisms. In both cases, attempts to understand and overcome resistance led to new levels of insight into how humans operate. In both cases, such analysis also led to a focus on rigidity and dysfunction rather than on adaptive functioning. As we shall see in Chapter 3, contemporary models of self-regulation give at least as much attention to the mechanisms of adaptive change as to the mechanisms of stability. Both are seen as essential elements in family process.

The Principle of Requisite Variety and the Default Response

One element in any self-regulating system is the limitation imposed by the principle of *requisite variety*, which states that a system (or its executive subsystem) must have in its repertoire of responses sufficient variety to match the variety of inputs it encounters. Lacking sufficient variety, the system has only three choices: (1) It can close down operations, refusing to respond at all; (2) it can fall back on a standard default response; or (3) if it is a sufficiently complex system, it may generate a new, previously untried response. This generation of an entirely new response is called *morphogenesis* (literally, the creation of a new form or structure). Of course, the family's external structure has not been reshaped in such a case, but its internal catalog of rules and responses has. In Chapter 6, we will expand upon this principle and illustrate the various options.

Characteristics of a Social System

Communication

Social systems have certain qualities that set them apart. True, they share the common attributes of all living systems; that is, they are open, ongoing, goal-seeking, and self-regulating. But unlike any other type of system, their component parts are self-aware, self-directed, independent entities. For these freestanding beings to form themselves into a system, each must share with the others a common set of meanings. The most significant connectors among them are symbolic, not tangible, and the structure of the relationships among them can be understood only through an analysis of these shared meanings.

Many in the "semiotic sciences" (to recall D'Andrade's term from the last chapter) have studied the communicative interactions of social beings, and have discovered that the messages exchanged are multi-layered, subtly shaded, and complex. They are likely to involve a bewildering array of simultaneous signals on a variety of channels. Posture, expression, tone, vocabulary, immediate context, and shared history all contribute to the meaning imputed to a message. Not only is information (and often deliberate misinformation) exchanged, but also signals of relative social position, such as "We are equals," "I am to be deferred to and obeyed," "I love you," and "I defy you." Bateson and his colleagues (Ruesch & Bateson, 1951; Watzlawick, Beavin, & Jackson, 1967) were the first to introduce the notion that messages between social beings always contain both an informational component, called the *message*, and a relationship-defining component, called the *metamessage*. They further asserted that when two social beings were aware of each other, communicating was impossible to avoid. As Bateson et al. have put it, "you cannot not communicate." Even two strangers attempting to ignore each other communicate both a message and a metamessage. In words, their double-decker messages to each other would be: "Do not approach me. I regard you to be a stranger whom it is appropriate to ignore."

According to these authors, the analysis of the communication process in a social system requires separate evaluation of its three aspects of *syntactics, semantics,* and *pragmatic* (Watzlawick et al., 1967, pp. 21ff). It is of passing interest that different sets of family therapists have attached different importance to these three aspects of communication in devising their own "brand name" strategies of intervention with dysfunctional families. *Syntactics* is concerned with how accurately a message (and its attendant metamessage) is conveyed from one party to another. It considers such issues as how the messages are coded and decoded, what channels are used, how much redundancy is in the message, and the like. These topics have been of central concern to engineers in the communications industry, who have a major stake in achieving "clear channel" communication and in diagnosing and eliminating distortions and interference—"noise")—in the system. Applications of their noise-reduction models to the family date back to the work of Swedish sociologist Georg Karlsson (1951). Certain family therapists have also incorporated this type of model as part of their programs for enhancing communication between family members (e.g., Bach & Wyden, 1969; Miller, Nunnally, & Wackman, 1975; Guerney, 1977; Thomas, 1977; Jacobson & Margolin, 1979, chap. 7; Broderick, 1988, chap. 5).

Semantics is concerned with meaning. The question addressed is what was really meant by the message (irrespective of how it might have been encoded, which channels were used, and so on). By extension, semantics also includes the issues of understanding and accurate empathy. Within social psychology, a long tradition of research and theory is concerned with the construction of meanings and shared meanings and the consequences of misperceptions and unshared meanings. From its beginning, the concept has also played an important part in family process theory. Kantor and Lehr (1975, pp. 50-55) list *pursuit of meaning* as one of the three generic goals that individuals hope to achieve through family interaction (the other two are *power* and *affect*). Other family scholars have written about *family themes* (Hess & Handel, 1959), *family myths and legends* (Wynne, Rychoff, Day, & Hirsch, 1958; Ferreira, 1966; Byng-Hall, 1988), and *family stories* (Stone, 1988) as mechanisms for creating and sustaining shared meanings (this is the subject matter of this volume's Chapter 7). In addition, a variety of therapists use this dimension in their treatment of families, choosing to alter the family patterns through *reframing* particular types of interaction (that is, by redefining their meaning).

Pragmatics concerns itself with the impact of communication on behavior. Put differently, it is the power of one communicative action or sequence to evoke another. This aspect of the subject has been most fully elaborated in Watzlawick et al.'s *Pragmatics of Human Communication* (1967) and by Jay Haley (1976a, 1976b), a close associate in the Palo Alto group. Those researchers who are most committed to the importance of this aspect of communication are likely to reflect this belief in their approaches to therapy. Insight and understanding, the core elements of traditional therapy, are of little interest to them. They are likely to point out that, as research shows, most of the patterns of interaction in families are not evident to the participants. So long as the therapist can see the patterns clearly enough to induce beneficial changes in them, family understanding does not seem necessary.

Psychopolitical Negotiation

Joint decisions by members with individual needs and independent wills require a far more elaborate executive mechanism than is found in other types of systems. Social systems cannot function without some process for interweaving individual members' perceptions, evaluations, and influences into a single fabric. Differences in emotional as well as pragmatic agendas must be addressed and a conjoint action negotiated. The student of biological systems confronts nothing quite so complicated. Nor is it clear that those who study social systems have mastered these considerations. By having acknowledged such complexities, however, they have at least taken some preliminary steps toward developing models that take them into account. Various aspects of the psychopolitical process will be discussed in Chapters 3 and 6.

Attribution at the Social Systems Level

One common error made by those who study social systems is to describe them in ways that only apply—only *can* apply—to their individual members. For example, people frequently refer to marriages as either happy or unhappy, although a marriage itself lacks the capacity to feel anything. It is a mere social system, without the mechanisms required to experience emotions. In fact, as Jesse Bernard long ago reminded us, in every case there are two marriages: his and hers. Although research has shown a positive correlation between the scores of husbands and wives filling out marital adjustment inventories, it is only about 0.5. This certainly allows a difference in experience: His marital experience may be wonderful at the same time that hers is miserable, or vice versa (Bernard, 1972). Despite this, some unsophisticated researchers trouble themselves with measuring the happiness of each partner, only to then *average* the two scores to get a "more accurate estimate" of "the actual level" of marital morale. Their assumptions seem to be (1) that an actual level of satisfaction is attributable to the dyad as an entity; (2) that the partners' scores are both estimates of that true value; and (3) that any differences between their scores thus are manifestations of errors of measurement. Such an "estimate," of course, is meaningless. The average of two discrepant marital satisfaction scores represents an opinion of the relationship that is held by neither participant and which is attributed to a social system that—like all social systems—is intrinsically incapable of any opinion at all. In a similar fashion, families with deviant members are often characterized as deviant, families in which a member is experiencing a crisis are often referred to as families *in* crisis, and so forth. To make any sense at all, qualities attributed to social systems must pertain to the system as systems. That is, such descriptors must pertain not to the qualities of the system's component parts, but to those qualities that are emergent through their interaction. Thus, systems may be appropriately described in terms of their size or internal structure or external articulation with superordinate systems. They may be characterized as having more rigid or less rigid rules or more or less permeable boundaries, or even as having more or less congruence among their members, but *not* as more happy or less happy. We shall have occasion to return to this topic in several subsequent chapters.

Social Distance Regulation

In a previous section, we noted the importance of distance regulation, of finding that shifting balance in every ongoing system between connection and partition. In biological systems, the various component parts of the system are related to one another in three-dimensional space. The boundaries of the system enclose a measurable volume, and the connections between the parts are tangible. Of course, social systems also operate in three-dimensional space. But the dimensions of social geography are symbolic, not spatial. Members may (and regularly do) move in and out of spatial proximity without changing their relational coordinates at all. Although it is convenient to use a spatial metaphor when discussing social relationships—speaking of them being *close* or *distant*—we must never forget that the usage is only metaphorical. The geography of social space lies entirely in the mind.

Or perhaps we might more precisely say that it exists entirely in the shared perceptions of social beings.

The founders of family process theory shared a pervasive concern with the balance between the bonding forces that connect family members and the buffering forces that insulate them from one another. Clinical experience led these men and women to be particularly wary of overly tight family bonds and overly tight family boundaries, which they identified as among the chief roots of family dysfunction. Each made the point in his or her own vocabulary. Bowen (1960, 1974) warned about the dangers of the *undifferentiated family ego-mass*, Minuchin (1974) of *enmeshment*, and Wynne and associates (Wynne et al., 1958; Wynne & Singer, 1963) of *pseudo-mutuality* and *rubber-fences*. They all believed, however, that overconnection was dangerous and that one of therapy's main goals was *differentiation* (to use Bowen's term).

One historical curiosity of the field is that major studies of large, nonclinical populations (Olson et al.,1983, p. 184; Green, Harris, Forte, & Robinson, 1991) have found that, far from being dysfunctional, cohesive families (with tight bonds and tight boundaries) are the most functional and the most valued by their members. The reasons for the disparity between the clinical and nonclinical findings very much remain a matter of debate. All of these subjects are discussed in greater length in Chapter 4, Distance Regulation Within the Family System, and Chapter 5, The Regulation of Transactions Across Family Boundaries.

Vertical Distance Regulation

The metaphorical space of social systems also has a vertical dimension. Intrinsic to every social relationship is the question of precedence and influence. The subject has long intrigued social scientists of every kind. Among family scholars, differential power in the marital relationship and between the generations has been the subject of literally hundreds of essays and investigations. Within the early family process literature, the topic was most often discussed in the context of dysfunctional family organization. For example, Lidz and his colleagues (1957) were certain that the most important factors for children's mental illness were distortions in the power structure of the marital unit. They noted two varieties: *schism* and *skew*. For Watzlawick and his colleagues (1967), the key issue was whether the exchanged metamessages defined the marital relationship as *symmetrical* (i.e., each having equal status) or *complementary* (i.e., having unequal status). For both Minuchin (1974) and Haley (1976a, 1976b), his long-time associate, the main structural concern was with maintaining the appropriate vertical distance between the generations. Haley's conviction is that "an individual is more disturbed in direct proportion to the number of malfunctioning hierarchies in which he is embedded" (1976b, p. 117).

More recently, feminist scholars (e.g., Hare-Mussen, 1978; Libow, Raskin, & Caust, 1982) have introduced a different perspective on the subject. Their chief concern is that the patriarchal ordering of power and privilege embedded in our social and political system affects families in ways that are dysfunctional for all members.

The processes by which families achieve and maintain their vertical position in the larger social system—their *social class placement* (in sociological terms)—have received less attention from family process scholars. One exception was the early work of Auerswald and Minuchin and their associates. They teamed up to study the families of poor Puerto Ricans in New York City in the early 1960s and discovered that the physical and emotional health problems they observed were more a product of the social displacement of the immigrant families than of any individual pathologies. When these families were helped to find a secure place within the community structure, their members' symptoms disappeared (Minuchin, Auerswald, King, & Rabkin, 1964; Minuchin, Martalvo, Guerney, Rosman, & Schumer, 1967). Auerswald later elaborated on this principle in his own work on community psychiatry (Auerswald, 1968, 1971), but, for the most part, one must look beyond the community of family process scholars to find the most important research and theory in this area.

Sociologists, particularly those who study social networks, have carried most of the load. For example, Granovetter (1983) has studied the intense transactions between family members and their close relatives and friends and the far more casual transactions with acquaintances, co-workers, and neighbors. He calls the former *strong ties* and the latter *weak ties* and finds that previous analyses have grossly underestimated the significance of the weak tie network in establishing and maintaining a family's place in the social hierarchy of the community. Although such scholars have no direct ties to the family process movement, their work fits remarkably well into the overall framework. Chapters 5 and 6 consider these issues in further detail.

Characteristics of Family Systems

Families are a special subset of social systems and are structured by a unique set of intergender and intergenerational relationships. Everyone knows what a family is, yet no one seems to be able to find a definition that is acceptable to everyone. Should the definition include only those people related by blood, marriage, or adoption living under one roof (a frequently offered textbook definition)? Or should a definition also include a daughter away at college, the mother's current live-in lover, the noncustodial husband and his wife, with whom the children spend every other weekend, the grandparent who lives next door but spends most of every day tending the children while the mother works, or, for that matter, the live-in nanny who is no kin at all but who virtually raises the children? Should it include only those who are in daily interaction with one another or also include those absent for extended periods such as the father who is on military duty or in prison or the difficult child who has been sent to live with his grandparents for an indefinite period?

Beyond the strictly logical problems of establishing an unambiguous delineation of what is and is not family, the issue has a political dimension. A wide variety of groups (for example, gay and lesbian couples and certain communes) have a stake in not being excluded. No small wonder then that after days of debate the delegates to the 1980 White House Conference on the Family were unable to agree on how *family* should be defined and that no such conference was even convened in 1990. Fortunately, the task of differentiating the family from other social systems does not require us to establish a universally acceptable rule for determining who should be counted in or out. Establishing particular criteria suitable to our particular analytic purposes is enough here. For the present purpose, we would most usefully adopt the classic definition of a *family* as used by generations of census takers: that is, two or more persons, sharing a common residence, and related by blood, adoption, or marriage.

We also must recognize that there are and have always been many varieties of *family-like systems* that mimic but do not replicate family relationships in a coresidential setting. Thus, live-in lovers (of whatever sexual preference) and adults and children living together in kinlike relationships constitute family-like systems, not families. Households that include both family and family-like relationships are *mixed household systems*, not families. Relatives by blood, adoption, or marriage who do not share a common residence, constitute a *kin network*, but do not meet the criteria we have established for family systems. Much of what family process theorists and researchers have discovered about how family systems operate may apply to family-like systems and to mixed household systems and to kin networks, but at this point, we have an insufficient basis for understanding what can be generalized and what cannot. The focus of this book, then, is on family systems as narrowly defined. At various points, we may comment on related systems, but, lacking an adequate data base, we do not plan any systematic consideration of them.

So far, we have differentiated families from other social systems solely by their criteria for membership. Implicit in that membership, however, are two additional differentiating characteristics. The first is structural. Families are unique in the way they structure genders and generations. Not all families have a heterosexual couple at their core, and some nonfamilies may have one, but only in families is such a couple culturally expected to be sexually and reproductively active. Not all families include more than one generation, and many nonfamilies may include members from across the generational spectrum, but only in families are the younger generation the actual (or, in the case of adoption, the fictive) biological issue of the older generation.

The second differentiating characteristic deriving from the family's membership criteria is the unique quality of family relationships. The sociological literature traditionally categorizes social relationships along various dimensions, with the family anchoring one end of the continuum, and business relationships the other end. Tonnies, Weber, Durkheim, and others put forth their own versions of this relational spectrum, but no one developed as comprehensive a schema as did Talcott Parsons (1951). His model created a four-dimensional social space within which he asserted he could locate, describe, and differentiate every variety of social interaction. He called his four dimensions *pattern variables*.

The first pattern variable discriminates between social interactions that are structured to be very *situation-specific* (as in the relationship between a customer and a sales person, which often does not transcend the transaction between them) or to be very *diffuse* and thus span a great number of situations (as in the relationships between family members).

The second pattern variable discriminates between social interactions governed by either universalistic or particularistic rules. *Universalistic* rules apply equally to every one; for instance, as in the expectation that any judge will dispense justice impartially to any and all who come before his or her bar. *Particularistic* rules vary according to the particular relationship between the parties, as, for example, when husbands are expected to treat their own wives differently from the way they treat other men's wives and their own children differently from the way they respond to children in general.

The third pattern variable discriminates between social interactions that are expected to be either affect-neutral or affective. In an *affect-neutral* interaction, the expression of any but the blandest personal feelings is considered inappropriate (as, for example, in a bureaucratic environment). In an *affective* relationship, the expression of a wide range of personal feelings is considered appropriate (for example, among close friends or family members).

Finally, the fourth pattern variable differentiates between social interactions in either achieved or ascribed relationships. An *achieved* relationship results from some set of voluntary actions on the part of the participants, such as a friendship or a business partnership. In an *ascribed* relationship, status exists independently of any voluntary action on one's own part, such as when it is defined by gender, ethnicity, or kinship.

Literally, only one type of social relationship can be defined as diffuse, *and* particularistic, *and* affective, *and* ascribed: the family relationship. Some of the unique patterns of expectation and interaction that are associated with familial dyads such as husband-wife, parent-child, and sibling-sibling, are explored more fully in Chapter 4, Distance Regulation Within the Family System.

Because of its particular importance, the matter of intergenerational transmission will be treated separately in Chapter 8 (The Socialization Process). Recent years have seen an increased awareness that the child is an active participant in a reciprocating, spiraling, and interactive process rather than the passive recipient of the parents' training. The challenges of Chapter 8 are (1) to develop an integrative summary of the extensive literature based on the linear, noninteractive approach and (2) to incorporate the unique contributions of the interactive, systemic, process-oriented approach.

Variations and Constraints in Family Systems

We have noted some of the essential properties of open, ongoing, goal-oriented, and self-regulating social systems that also meet the criteria of being families. Before concluding this overview of the main elements of family process theory, we must consider certain built-in *constraints* on the family as an ongoing system. A general principle of systems theory holds that the processes of every system are necessarily shaped by (1) the attributes of the particular subsystems from which it is composed, (2) the nature of its own size and structural composition, and (3) the nature of its placement in the larger suprasystem or "ecosystem" of which it is a constituent element. In the case of the family, this requires us to attend to the influence of the family members' particular characteristics (gender, age, physical condition, genetic pre-dispositions, and so forth), the family's structural characteristics (size, composition, and so on), and the family's placement in the larger societal system (its social class, ethnicity, locality, housing, social artic-ulation or isolation, and so forth). These matters have often been ignored by influential writers in the field. Belief in the sovereign sufficiency of generic, family systems-level explanations has often been a matter of loyalty, commitment, and faith, especially among the pioneers. Con-temporary family process scholars are more likely to acknowledge the importance of a more complex, contextual approach.

Variations in the Attributes of Members

Because the family process movement began in part as a protest against the limitations of individual trait psychology, not surprisingly many of its adherents have had a tendency to undervalue the impor-tance of individual attributes. The genius of the new approach was its focus on the family as a system in its own right. The individual and his or her biological and psychological attributes were considered residual and outside the main framework of the process model. Many of the unique contributions of this theoretical perspective undeniably came as a result of this concentration on the family system-level of analysis. Yet from the beginning, some researchers also accorded a place in their models to the attributes of individual family members.

Bowen (1973) was one who kept the importance of individual char-acteristics in focus (such as the internal differentiation of the compo-nents of the self), as did Boszormenyi-Nagy and others of the object relations school of family therapy. In effect, they resisted the wholesale shift away from traditional psychiatric perspectives and embraced the new paradigm cautiously and selectively. But if some theorists were restrained, most of the founders of the movement were not. From the beginning, it was an article of faith within the movement that the genesis of schizophrenia was a young person's effort to adapt to the paradoxical, "crazy-making" demands of his or her family. It was the result of enmeshment in a system of relationships that were double-binding (Bateson et al., 1956; Jackson, 1959; Haley, 1963 and 1971), un-differentiated (Bowen 1960, 1965a, and 1965b), or skewed (Lidz et al., 1957). This view prevailed, virtually unchallenged, for 25 years.

Not until the early 1980s were voices from within the movement heard to caution that a large and persuasive body of evidence showed that the disease has a strong genetic component (Terkelsen, 1983, 1984). Be-fore this point, most members of the family therapy establishment seemed to view this concept in much the same way that creationists viewed the evidence of evolution. The results were sometimes tragic, because these clinicians authoritatively placed the full responsibility for both the origin and cure of a child's mental illness on the shoulders of the hapless parents. Nothing is taken away from the accomplishments of family process theory by acknowledging that children's behavior and personality are the joint products of a variety of influences that include but are not limited to the patterns of interactions that prevailed in their homes as they grew up. Evidence is accumulating that not only schizophrenia, but also mood disorders (such as depression and manic episodes) and anxiety disorders (such as phobias and panic attacks), together with some substance abuse patterns and even life-style choices involved with sexual preference, all have a significant biological component. Recent work on the influence of precise hormone levels on the sexual activity of young men and women (Udry, 1988) and continuing research on the premenstrual syndrome in women give further cause to consider how family process models of socialization might be revised to reflect explicitly the importance of biological factors. One way to do this would be to consider all such attributes of individual members as constraints on the operation of the family system that shape the patterns of interaction and partly define their parameters. The main focus of family process theory must necessarily remain on the patterns of relationships among members, but the impact of the attributes of particular members on those patterns may be entered into the equation.

Variations in Family Size and Structural Composition

By far the most impressive effort to incorporate the dimension of family size and structural composition into the theory has been the systematic elaboration of the family's development on its patterns of interactions and transactions.

The childless couple clearly constitutes a different interactional matrix from that same couple with a newborn baby. Families with preschoolers have quite different patterns of interaction and transaction from those with teenagers. Reuben Hill, one of the originators of the family development conceptual framework, was invited to become a contributing member of the editorial board of the journal *Family Process* almost from its inception (Hill & Rogers, 1964). Partly as a result of his influence, developmental constructs have played an important part in the work of many key figures in the field, including Haley (1973, 1980), Solomon (1973), and Wynne (1984). By all odds, the most influential single contribution to raising the level of collective awareness among family systems scholars was the 1980 collection of papers, *The Changing Family Life Cycle: A Framework for Family Therapy*, which was edited by McGoldrick and Carter. The widely read second edition (1989) has continued to advocate this point of view effectively. The adoption of a family development perspective introduces certain constraints that have to do with the age and generational composition of particular family systems, but it also leaves many other important structural issues unaddressed. Perhaps the most obvious need is for a more developed model for special cases such as single parenthood, binuclear structure, or three-generation households.

More subtle issues, such as the gender and age composition of the sibling subunit, have received still less attention. Even the gross size of the family unit is rarely considered in developing propositions about the interactional network. Yet a family of two and a family of 12 obviously have very different systems properties. The future viability of the family process movement very probably depends on its successful address of these issues.

Variations in Families' Social Placement

At the most general level, a family's interactions and transactions are constrained by what has been called the *opportunity structure* of its immediate environment. In the most straightforward case, family members cannot interact with a person, organization, or object that is not available to them, and they cannot avoid dealing with those that share or force their way into the same space.

But differential opportunities have been shown to influence individual and family actions in far more subtle ways and often with great consequence. For example, the influence of opportunity structure on friend and mate selection has been well documented (see Broderick, 1988, pp. 85-86, 127-130, 305), as has its shaping of such diverse phenomena as the timing and incidence of delinquency (Felson, 1986) and extramarital affairs (Edwards & Booth, 1976) and the timing and target destination of a family's change of residence. None of the above work was done by scholars from within the process framework, but all of it logically articulates with that framework. This subject is considered further in Chapter 3.

On another level of analysis, family process scholars have become increasingly aware that a family's construal of reality and its rules of operation are likely to vary by social status and ethnic background. (Various aspects of this matter are treated in Chapters 5, 6, and 8.)

Nevertheless, we must acknowledge that the task of developing a culturally contextual version of family process theory remains largely before us.

With this brief discussion of the three levels of constraints upon the operations of the family system, we conclude our summary of the main elements of the family process approach.

CHAPTER 3 ▼

From Cybernetic to Transcybernetic

Fitting the Family to the Cybernetic Model

Finding a model for explaining what happens in the common every-day life of families is the ultimate goal of any theory about family processes. More precisely, the object is to find some economical set of interrelated assumptions and principles that can account for both the patterned behavior of family members and the variations in these patterns across and within families over time. Family process theorists have argued that we might profitably look to general systems theory for such a set of constructs. It is the genius of general systems theory that it finds significant parallels in the organizational patterning of very diverse types of systems. This finding allows us profitably to use constructs derived from the analysis of simpler systems (such as, for example, electronic-guidance systems) in attempting to understand the workings of far more complex systems (such as families).

On the other hand, I fear that those of us who write about family systems tend to compare them all too glibly to thermostats or guided missiles or ants or even to human beings. This is a serious error if done so uncritically. The responsible scholar must make a careful judgment as to whether the construct derived in one setting serves usefully in the other. Families may indeed share certain features with electronic and biological systems, but the differences are a good deal more obvious and are often ignored, or at least not carefully considered.

Chapter 2 noted that every self-regulating (that is, cybernetic) system has, at a minimum, the following component elements:

- a set of *system goals* that are (1) hierarchically ordered in a readily available archive, (2) embedded in the decision-making loops of the system, and (3) efficacious (that is, they have significant effects on system decisions);
- an *executive capacity* that can (1) receive and evaluate inputs from several sources, (2) reach decisions on behalf of the system, and (3) act (or cause the system to act) on those decisions;
- an *environment-monitoring capacity* that is embedded in the system's decision-making loop; and
- a *system status-monitoring capacity* that is embedded in the system's decision-making loop.

Our difficulties in fitting family systems to this model begins with the root question: Can families be characterized as having goals in the same sense that self-regulating, cybernetic systems have goals? Certainly, systems theorists write as if this were a settled question, routinely describing families as belonging to that class of systems that are "goal-seeking."

Undoubtedly, an intercontinental ballistic missile meets all of the criteria for a cybernetic system, among them a readily identifiable hierarchy of goals that are programmed into its guidance system. An ant also qualifies: Its behavior is governed by a set of hierarchically ordered imperatives that are embedded in its genetic makeup. Even a human being would appear to meet all of the requirements. According to Maslow's model of personality (1970), we all share a universal, need-based hierarchy of goals, with nonnegotiable survival needs (physiological requirements and personal safety) at the bottom of the pyramid, love and belonging next, and self-actualization at the top. Whatever one may think of this particular schema, such a hierarchy might credibly be encoded in a human brain.

But does the family qualify? For that matter, can any social system logically qualify? In a system composed of independent sentient beings, where is the seat of corporate consciousness in which a goal might be stored? I believe that only two responsible answers to this crucial question are possible. Either they are stored in the collective, congruent commitments of its individual members or, conceivably, they are not stored at all but exist only as emergent directionalities that result from the interaction of individual members but which transcend their individual purposes.

Actually the two processes are not mutually exclusive, and both can be observed in the operations of social systems that are unambiguously goal-oriented, such as work groups, athletic teams, and military units. In these groups, members' personal agendas are expected to be subordinated to the common purpose. This unity of purpose might be achieved through *coercion* (individuals submitting to group direction under threat of punishment), *negotiation* (individuals bartering loyalty to group goals in return for other valuable considerations such as money, security, belonging, approval, and status), or *induction* (individuals incorporating the group's values through socialization or conversion adopting the group's goals as their own). However achieved, this unity of purpose is *summatory* rather than emergent because it consists of the sum of individual commitments to the common goal.

Emergent consensus can also be observed in these settings. In response to certain challenges, a "group spirit" (an "esprit de corps") may emerge that transcends the commitments of individual members and unites them in a single force. This appears to be an example of genuine systemic emergence in which the whole is indeed greater than the sum of its parts.

The problem is that families do not seem by nature to be organized around goal achievement in the same way as are work groups, athletic teams, or military units. Granted, one can find families that for some period of time may be united around the pursuit of some particular goal (such as finding new living quarters, becoming pregnant, getting a breadwinner through school and into employment, making the family business profitable, or seeing that the children get good grades). In these situations, an appropriate argument is that families also might reach consensus through coercion, negotiation, or induction. Furthermore, under certain challenging conditions, they also might experience an emergent unity that transcends their individual purposes. But the reality is that such a focus on joint goal attainment is not a requirement for being a family. Many families seem to have little penchant for focus or commitment, and they drift along passively in the currents of their life course. These are collections of related individuals who live together, but who have quite disparate agendas for their lives. Thus, on the face of it, one major impediment to categorizing families as cybernetic systems is the lack of an obvious goal-driven operation at the core of the family enterprise.

Another consideration may also be seen as problematic. We have adopted the common practice of using the term *goal* to mean a "consciously held objective that a system intentionally pursues." But many studies of families have shown that the course a family says it is pursuing may not correspond well with the path it is observed to follow. If the term *goal* must be restricted to consciously held and intentionally pursued objectives, then what shall we do with observed, recurrent, emergent directionalities that family members do not perceive and that may actually be at cross-purposes to their intentions?

These difficulties in finding a close, natural fit between the nature of families and the nature of the standard cybernetic model suggest the need to reexamine and perhaps modify the model to accommodate the realities of family structure and process. In pursuit of that task, we might profitably review a variety of alternative models that have been designed to account for families' patterned behavior. A wide-ranging survey turned up five interesting cases, each of which offered its own solutions to the issues that separated family systems from the cybernetic model. We might reasonably hope that a critical review of these alternative solutions might suggest a strategy for remodeling the cybernetic paradigm to better fit the realities of family patterns.

Explaining Patterned Behavior in Family Systems

We will label the five approaches as follows: (1) the normative model, (2) the developmental task model, (3) the psychopolitical model, (4) the reflexive spirals model, and (5) the opportunity matrix model. Each offers a unique solution to the problems inherent in characterizing families as goal-seeking, self-regulating systems. Each has certain attractive features and certain limitations. After reviewing the strengths and weaknesses of each of these attempted solutions, we will be in a better position to evaluate the prospect of developing a unified theory of patterned family action that might be termed *transcybernetic*.

The Normative Model

The normative model starts with a premise that has long been accepted as true by virtually all social scientists: Self-regulation is an inherent quality of all social systems. From our discussion of Talcott Parsons in Chapter 1, we will remember that this premise was taken for granted in the structural-functional approach to social systems. But it also has been an unexamined assumption of most other sociologists. According to this approach, the mechanism of self-regulation is the *social norm*, and it can be shown to operate on three levels. First, through the processes of *socialization* or *induction*, the norms of the society are inculcated into each individual, who is assigned the responsibility for monitoring his or her own conformity to these internalized norms. Assuming that this process of internalizing the norms is successful, individual deviations result in painful pangs of *personal guilt*. On the second level, each individual's conformity is monitored informally by his or her family, peers, and associates. Deviations from the norms result in the imposition of *informal social sanctions* that range from mild disapproval to severe punishment. The exposed individual thus experiences *shame*. And finally at the third level, societies reserve to themselves the right to threaten coercive measures and to carry out *formal penalties* for deviant behavior up to and including capital punishment. Awareness of potential punishments further motivates the individual toward conformity by inspiring *fear*. As a last resort, social agents may attempt to enforce their values through *coercion*.

Entire libraries have been written on each of these four levels of social control. Those who take the normative approach to family self-regulation thus draw upon a wealth of research and theory on the dynamics of this process.

Although this model did not originate with systems theory, it can be argued that a norm-driven family meets all of the cybernetic model's requirements. Both the system goals and system rules are incorporated in the concept of social norms; through the process of socialization they are archived in the shared consciousness of all family (and community) members and are also reflected in the society's recorded laws. Performance and system status are monitored by the individual, other socialized family members, and members of the larger community. Deviant behavior (and even the tendencies to consider behaving in a deviant manner) are corrected through a multilevel system response that may evoke various mixes of guilt, shame, fear, and submission to coercion.

The normative approach also has one other feature that makes it attractive to systems theorists who attempt to fit social systems such as the family into the cybernetic mold: a principle of systems theory that rules and goals are hierarchically organized. Although this concept is not native to the sociological version of normative theory, it does no violence to sociological sensibilities. As a result, a fair number of family systems theorists have adopted a hierarchical-normative solution to the problem of fitting families into the cybernetic model. In other words, they see family processes as governed by a multilevel arrangement of normative family rules and goals. In addition to recognizing the level of primary normative rules and goal orientations, they posit at least one and sometimes several levels of more general metarules and metagoals. For example, in my own analysis of normative family rule structure in Chapter 6, I find it useful to adopt a four-level model. At the bottom of the pyramid are *concrete rules* and *immediate goals*; at the next level are *metarules* and *goals* that specify the conditions under which particular first-level rules and goals are implemented; above them are still more general *midrange policies* that govern family activities in whole sectors of their life together; and at the top is the most general, overarching *family paradigm*, that central organizing principle that shapes all of the family's shared assumptions, expectations and commitments (Reiss, 1981, p. 2).

We have reviewed the normative approach, and thus to prepare for comparing it to alternative solutions, we might usefully summarize its obvious strengths and preview some of its most evident limitations.

Strengths of the Normative Model

The normative model has the following four strengths.

1. It provides a set of credible (summative) mechanisms for deriving and archiving family goals and rules and for monitoring and regulating family performance.
2. It ties family self-regulation processes into a substantial matrix of existing theory and research.
3. It explicitly specifies the mechanisms that connect the family system's rules and goals to those of the larger societal system of which they are a part.
4. Although not explicit in the model, the normative approach readily accommodates the important systemic principle that family goals and rules are hierarchically ordered.

Limitations and Weaknesses of the Normative Model

The normative model also has its failings, including the five that follow.

1. All versions of normative theory deal well with shared values and perceptions. Unshared values and perceptions, however, are dealt with poorly and are treated as deviations from the established norm. Both research and clinical data show that much of the ordinary interaction within families (not to mention transactions between families) are driven by the perception that individual family members do *not* share identical agendas or perspectives. In fact, one might claim that a central concern of family sys-

tems theory is the patterned interplay generated by these differences, differences to which normative theory is blind.

2. Normative theory deals only awkwardly with systematic changes in family goals over its life cycle or across historic periods.

3. Normative theory is inherently conservative and structured to support the status quo. It sets up established norms as the sole criterion against which family members' behaviors are measured. The theory thus is problematic for feminists and others who believe that traditional norms ought to be challenged.

4. The normative model is blind to all systems rules that result in counternormative outcomes. This serious limitation results from the model's confusion of two quite separate constructs, *system rules* and *normative rules*. The construct of a normative rule is derived from sociological theory. It may be defined as a conscious, shared, perception of what *ought* to be and not necessarily what *is*. By contrast, systems theory defines a system rule as any observable, patterned regularity of interaction that provides evidence of order and organization within the system. The observed pattern is not required to be consistent with either the society's norms or any member's personal values. As we shall see in a later section, one very important class of systems rules is explicitly counternormative and thus excluded from consideration by the normative model.

5. The normative model makes no allowance for situational constraints on family behavior, although considerable evidence suggests that these factors are important elements in the patterning of family processes.

In summary, the normative theory provides a model of family self-corrective processes that is compatible with the requirements of a cybernetic system and also ties in with a significant body of established sociological theory. The model suffers, however, in its inflexibility in dealing with changes over time, unshared individual values, competing ideologies, counternormative system rules, and situational constraints.

The Developmental Task Model

The developmental task model attempts to correct at least some of the limitations of the normative model. It is more inclusive in the factors it accounts for and is particularly sensitive to systematic shifts in the family's situation over its life cycle. This model defines family goals as growing out of the family's adjustments to the interaction of three forces: (1) evolving *individual developmental needs* of family members, (2) shifting normative prescriptions as families progress from one life-cycle stage to another, and (3) changing challenges imposed by changing family structure and situation. In this model, family goal orientations (or family *tasks*) are seen as emerging from the interaction of these three sets of imperatives rather than as merely summative. Although many developmentalists would probably object to the comparison, the model parallels Freud's famous imagery of the ego as a troika charioteer, struggling constantly to impose coordinate direction on his three spirited steeds: the id, the superego, and reality.

The operational construct in developmental theory is the *family developmental task*, a concept adapted from Robert Havighurst's work (1948) on individual developmental tasks. Havighurst's notion was that at each stage of human development a certain set of tasks is imposed on the individual by his maturing mind and body and by society's age-graded expectations. These tasks are developmentally stacked such that successful achievement of a particular task at one level (for example, achieving standing balance as a young child) is a prerequisite for achieving related goals at later stages of development (for example, participating successfully in children's games such as hopscotch).

Reuben Hill and his associates (Duvall & Hill, 1948; Duvall, 1957; Hill & Rogers, 1964; Mattessich & Hill, 1987) adapted this set of ideas to the family case and then introduced the situational element into their model by citing Glick's (1947) observation, based on an analysis of U.S. census data, that most families go through certain predictable stages of development, just like most individuals. Members are added through birth and eventually subtracted through launching or death at intervals that could be estimated actuarially. As individual members proceed through their predictable developmental challenges, they trigger the family's shift from one predictable circumstance to another. It followed that it should be possible to identify those tasks that the circumstances of each stage imposed upon all families that experienced them.

For example, we may assumed that no married couple bringing a new baby into the family can avoid confronting the task of recalibrating their sexual and affectional life together under these changed circumstances. Following Havighurst's reasoning, the success a couple achieves in this effort should be predicated on their prior success at the related task of their sexual adjustment as a newly married couple. Empirical evidence seemed to support this notion of stacked family developmental tasks. For example, several studies confirmed that, as the theory predicted, couples with better sexual adjustment in early marriage did deal better with the task of maintaining a satisfying sexual relationship through the challenges of pregnancy and early child rearing.

Despite these and many similar confirmatory findings, the developmental task approach to identifying family goals attracted a great deal of criticism, much of it warranted. Contemporary experience has refuted the core assumption of the model, namely, that families are destined to move through a set of developmental stages in an orderly manner, just as individual children sequence through set developmental stages. Millions of children born to single mothers, millions of children being raised in binuclear families, millions of couples who have never had children—all of these bear eloquent witness that no single yellow brick road exists on which all families travel. The assumption of universal, predictable regularities in the life course has proved to be untenable.

Despite this, decades of work done by scholars in this tradition have taught us a great deal about the processes that generate family goal orientations. Independent of the question of universal sequence, we might reasonably retain the premise that families confronting similar challenges are likely to focus on tasks immediately related to coping with these shared dilemmas. It also seems appropriate to retain the notion that successful achievement of tasks at one point in a family's experience is at least partly contingent on its having succeeded at earlier, related tasks. It is only a short step from the developmental concept of patterned family tasks to the systems concept of patterned family goal orientations.

Strengths of the Family Developmental Task Model

Although seriously flawed in certain well-documented respects, the family developmental task approach retains the following four impressive features as a model of family directionality.

1. Like the normative model, the family developmental task model provides a set of credible mechanisms for the generation of family goals, and it connects with a substantial body of research and theory that is relevant to the process of family self-regulation.
2. The model introduces three important additional elements to the normative template: individual needs, situational constraints, and temporal sequencing.
3. Consistent with family process theory, the model sees family tasks as emergent rather than as simply provided by the larger culture through the mechanisms of socialization and so on. This emergence takes place in *developmental time* (which is measured in months and years) rather than in *real time* (that is, time measured in seconds, minutes, and hours). Family tasks and goals are generated by the interplay between the developmental needs of the family's individual members and the changing

external societal and environmental systems through which the family moves in its life course. (Note that this is quite different from such tasks and goals being generated by the interactions of members in real time as in the next three models.)

4. Even though family goals are seen as emergent, they are developmentally patterned and, to that extent, predictable.

Limitations and Weaknesses of the Family Developmental Task Model

Still, the model has the following four failings:

1. It does not explicitly address the cybernetic issue of how family systems achieve self-regulation. However, we may assume that because the model includes social norms as one of its key elements, it implicitly incorporates the mechanisms based on guilt, shame, fear, and coercion that are spelled out in normative theory.

2. The model assumes a simpler and more universal sequence of family life-cycle stages than reality permits. Whether the model can contribute to contemporary family theory depends upon its adoption of a much more complex conceptualization of the family life cycle.

3. It largely ignores individual needs (other than those driven by developmental imperatives), personal agendas, struggles for dominance, and, in short, members' individual purposes and intentions. Unintended or counternormative outcomes also lie outside its scope. In this it is similar to the normative model, most of whose premises it incorporates.

4. Although it gives a prominent place to the role of shifting macrosituational factors in developmental time, the model does not deal with ever-changing microsituational factors in real time.

In summary, the family developmental task model conceives of the family's corporate goals as emerging from the ongoing struggle to meet the ever-shifting demands imposed by individual developmental needs, changing and situation-specific norms, and circumstantial constraints. In many ways, the model is broadly comprehensive, yet it does not deal well with psychopolitical issues, and it ignores entirely those often observed, recurring spirals of reactive behavior that appear to be independent of any member's intentions. Finally, although it is sensitive to the impact of shifting circumstances over developmental time periods, it is not calibrated to consider the minute-by-minute shifts in circumstance that may be presumed to influence minute-by-minute family processes that have traditionally been one of the main foci of concern in family systems theory.

The psychopolitical model has an entirely different set of strengths and weaknesses.

The Psychopolitical Model

The psychopolitical model shares with the normative model the assumption that the archive in which family systems goals are stored is in the shared commitments of the members. The two models differ, however, in the assumptions they make about the processes by which such consensus is achieved. The psychopolitical model assumes that family members have quite independent needs, opinions, and agendas. Consensus on any matter (including family goals) can never be taken for granted and may be achieved only through conscious, purposeful negotiation among members. Individual agendas, priorities, strategies, judgments, and political resources are the central factors involved in determining the outcome. The norms of the larger society as well as the constraints imposed by the family's present situation enter the process only as they might be reflected in the individual members' priorities.

As with the previously discussed models, the psychopolitical model is rooted in a rich theoretical and empirical literature. Scholars from many disciplines have investigated the processes involved in family decision making and negotiation. A central element in most models of that process is the relative *power* of various family members to influence the outcome of contested issues. A detailed discussion of this complex subject is deferred to Chapter 6, which addresses the broader issues of inequalities among family members. For the purposes of this chapter, the simpler model developed by Kantor and Lehr in their 1975 volume, *Inside Families,* will suffice.

Based on their careful study of 19 families observed under "natural" conditions over an extended period, Kantor and Lehr suggest that the process has four basic player parts.

> We contend that members of a family (indeed, members in any social system) have four basic parts to play: *mover, follower, opposer,* and *bystander.* Our premise is that any social action initiated by one member of a family stimulates a reaction from the other members. The initiator of such an action is the mover of the action. The respondents are co-movers. They may exercise one of three logical options: following—agreeing with the action taken by the mover; opposing—challenging the action of the mover; or bystanding—witnessing the mover's action but acknowledging neither agreement nor disagreement with it. . . . Even when there are only two persons present, there are four

parts ready to be played, and if the relationship is to continue, all four parts most certainly will be played. (Kantor & Lehr, 1975, p. 181)

For the purposes of this discussion, the key point is that in the psychopolitical model, family decisions are made and family goals are chosen and implemented through the interaction of the members as they adopt these various player parts in conscious, intentional pursuit of individual goals.

Strengths of the Psychopolitical Model

Like the other approaches, the psychopolitical approach has the following four significant strengths as a general model of family goal seeking and self-regulation:

1. It provides a credible mechanism for the generation and implementation of family rules, policies, and goals as well as for the processes of self-regulation.
2. It ties family self-regulation process into a substantial matrix of theory and research that elaborates on every aspect of the decision-making process.
3. It explicitly acknowledges the independence of individual family members' needs, purposes, and goals and conceptualizes family goals as emergent properties of the system (consistent with the basic premises of systems theory), rather than as prefabricated social norms imported from the larger society.
4. It assumes that no suprapersonal subsystems of the family are responsible for executive decision making or system monitoring; rather, these are seen as emergent phenomena that grow out of the ordinary, real-time interaction of family members.

Limitations and Weaknesses of the Psychopolitical Model

The psychopolitical model also has two basic drawbacks:

1. The model does not preclude the possibility that system rules and even normative rules might emerge from the interaction of separate family members. However, by focusing so narrowly on the independence of members' needs, purposes, and goals, the model takes little account of the patterned, homogenizing influences of socialization and normative constraints or of shared circumstances and interlocking developmental histories.
2. In focusing on the intentionality and conscious purposefulness of family negotiation, the model ignores (but does not preclude) regularly patterned family processes that result in unintended and unwanted outcomes.

In summary, like the previously discussed approaches, the psychopolitical model offers a description of the family self-corrective process that is compatible with the requirements of a cybernetic system and also ties in with a significant body of research and theory—in this case, decision theory rather than normative or developmental theory. Among the model's chief weaknesses are its insensitivity to the influences of patterned pressures from both inside and outside the system. Like the other models, it is blind to the processes involved in unintended emergent outcomes. The next model was designed to shed light on that particular and recurring blind spot.

Reflexive Spirals: The Rapoport Model

The Rapoport model features the unmediated, reflexive, reactivity of family members to one another's inputs. Both clinical observation (e.g., Broderick, 1979; Broderick & Smith, 1979) and research evidence (e.g., Gottman, Notarius, Markman, Yoppi, & Rubin, 1976; Gottman, Markman, & Notarius, 1977; Gottman, 1989; Ting-Toomy, 1983) attest to the fact that families commonly and repetitively engage in patterns of interaction that lead toward outcomes that bear no obvious relationship to the values or goals of any family members; indeed, these outcomes may frequently seem opposed to the family's values or goals. Clearly, no comprehensive discussion of family self-regulation can afford to ignore such a phenomenon; yet, because the term *goal* implies purposeful intentionality, perhaps it would be less confusing to adopt another term such as *vector* for the directional thrust of such spirals.

One difficult feature of the Rapoport model is that it is counterintuitive or at least requires an unattractive degree of cynicism to accept readily. Its main premise is that people's behavior may often be less affected by their personal goals and values than by their interpersonal reflexes. An advantage of this model is that it lends itself to mathematical expression. The benefit of this may not be self-evident, especially to those who do not find differential equations to be user-friendly. However, the interlocking pair of equations that is involved is not difficult to understand if adequately explained. Moreover, understanding them is worth the effort, because useful conclusions can be drawn that are not readily apparent without the benefit of mathematical logic.

As we noted in the beginning of this chapter, systems theory is predicated on the premise that a wide variety of systems have significant similarities in the ways they operate. Beginning with Wiener, cyberneticists have sought to find systems of mathematical equations that are isomorphic with various aspects of biological and social systems' functioning. Anatol Rapoport (1960, 1972) developed the following pair of differential equations in order to predict the conditions under which a social system will either remain in equilibrium, conforming to its members' goals for it, or career off into escalating deviations from those goals. Bernard (1964) and Broderick and Smith (1979) have used the equations to predict the conditions for runaway spirals of hostility among married couples (and also aging parents and caretaking children; see Broderick, in press). They are appropriate representations of any type of unmediated, reflexive interaction between family members, including both vicious and beneficent cycles, as I shall attempt to show.

These are the Rapoport equations:

$$dx/dt = ay - mx + g$$
$$dy/dt = bx - ny + h$$

Suppose we wish to use these equations to predict the conditions under which a runaway escalation of hostility occurs in a marriage. In that case, we will let x equal the level of hostility the husband feels toward his wife at any given moment; y will equal the level of hostility his wife feels toward him at that moment. As we have explained elsewhere:

The expressions dx/dt and dy/dt compare changes in the level of hostility (dx or dy) with changes in the time dimension (dt). Put differently, dx/dt represents the *rate of change* in the husband's hostile feelings toward his wife, while dy/dt represents the concomitant *rate of change* in his wife's feelings toward him. On a graph these rates of change would be indicated by the steepness of the curves representing x and y. The terms a and b stand for the degree to which each partner's level of hostility is dependent upon his or her spouse's level of hostility. These might be called the *coefficients of reactivity*. If they are low, the two might be described as emotionally independent of each other, if high, emotionally interdependent. The terms m and n represent the *cost* to each of his or her own hostile feelings. Social pressure, guilt, and fear of anticipated consequences might determine whether these are high or low. Finally, g and h represent unresolved (or at least unforgotten) former *grievances*. If g and h are positively signed ($+g$), ($+h$), they indicate a history of hostile experiences; if negatively signed ($-g$), ($-h$), they indicate a history of rewarding experiences.

Thus a translation of the first equation into plain English would state that "the rate of change in the husband's level of hostility (dx/dt) depends upon three factors: (1) an escalation factor (ay), consisting of his wife's current level of hostility toward him (y) multiplied by his own level of reactivity toward her (a); (2) as modified by a dampening factor (mx), consisting of his own present level of hostility toward her (x) multiplied by the cost to him of his own level of hostility (m); plus (3) a contingency factor (g) that takes into account the effects of historic grievances ($+g$) or positive experiences ($-g$)." The second equation expresses exactly the same variables from the wife's perspective. The two equations constitute a system because any change in the values of one influences the values of the other (that is, changes in x depend partly on changes in y and vice versa). Through mathematical manipulation of these equations it is possible to demonstrate that four outcomes are possible depending upon the values of the different variables:

1. If the product of the dampening forces (mn) is *greater* than the product of the escalator forces (ab), even though there may be a history of underlying grievances (g and h are positive), there will be stability in the relationship. An expression of hostility on either part will fail to ignite a spiral of escalating hostility between them.

2. If, as in 1, above, the dampening forces (mn) are *greater* than the escalating forces (ab), and if, in addition there is a history of mutual support and forgiveness (g and h are negative), even a negative expression from one or the other will not keep the couple from accumulating more positive experiences together.

3. If the dampening forces (mn) are *less* than the escalating forces (ab) and there is a prior history of underlying grievances (g and h are positive) any hostile act by either party will trigger a runaway escalation of hostility between them that can only be brought under control if at some point the destructiveness of the exchange frightens one or the other into reevaluating the cost of further escalation. Each such episode adds to the reservoir of grievances and eventually, the capacity of the system to survive will be challenged.

4. If the dampening forces (mn) are *less* than the escalating forces (ab) as in 3 above, but the history of the relationship consists largely of mutual support rather than grievance (g and h are negative), the outcome will depend upon the level of the initial input of hostility. If it is above a certain critical threshold, there will be an escalating hostility as in 3 above; if below that threshold, the hostility will decrease as in 2 above. For example, in a particular family physical blows might trigger an escalation of hostility while a verbal attack might be weathered in the generally positive atmosphere. (Adapted from Broderick & Smith, 1979, p. 118)

Figure 3.1 graphically summarizes the four possible outcomes. As mentioned earlier, any two-person vicious (or benign) spiral shares these same dynamics and can be represented by these equations. For example, in the stereotypical cycle involving the increasingly demanding wife and the increasingly resistant husband, x represents his level of resistance and y her level of effort to motivate him.

Cycles involving three or more persons (such as the child-scapegoating spirals described in later chapters) require more complex sets of equations to model, but the basic elements of escalators, dampeners, and contingency factors still are determinative. Individual goals, motivations, and intentions remain irrelevant. Part of the definition of an unmediated response cycle is that it lies outside the scrutiny of the executive function. However, common observation informs us that these "runaway spirals" in fact operate only within certain tolerated limits. If that were not so, every cycle would escalate out of control until one or more of members were killed or at least until the family bond had been sundered. That the great majority of spirals stop short of extreme outcomes suggests that family members (and others) do exercise a sort of metasurveillance. When certain limits of tolerance are exceeded, one or more of the normative constraints (that is, guilt, shame, fear of the consequences, or actual externally imposed restraints) kicks in to abort the escalation.

Strengths of the Rapoport Model

The Rapoport model has the following three strengths:

1. This model accounts for an important class of rule-governed, directional family interaction patterns that each of the other models exclude from consideration.
2. In this model, the directionality of the process is emergent in real time, just as in the psychopolitical model, but it differs from that model in that it does not assume that family members are self-aware or purposeful.
3. This is the only model that explicitly incorporates an archival function (in the g and h terms).

Limitations and Weaknesses of the Rapoport Model

The model also has the following major drawback: a basic incompatibility between its own assumptions and those of the cybernetic model. As we have defined it here, a vector is not a goal. Cybernetic models assume both intentionality and an executive function. This model, while it does include built-in dampeners and contingency factors that function to regulate the system, includes no executive subsystem. The only decision-making function in the loop is the assumption, external to the set of equations themselves, that out-of-control vicious cycles will ultimately trigger some latent normative dampener when certain extreme limits of tolerance are exceeded.

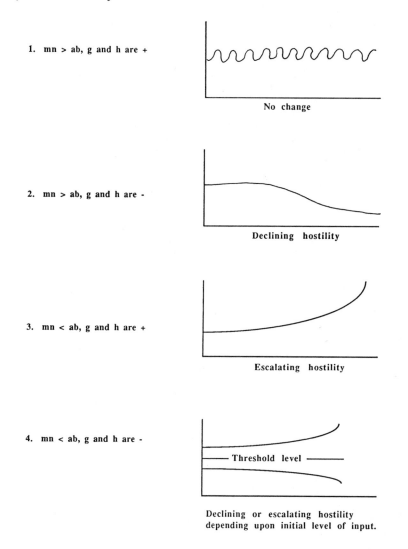

Figure 3.1. Rate of Change in System Level of Hostility in Four Conditions
SOURCE: Broderick & Smith, 1979.

In summary, this model includes an important class of family phenomena—namely, unmediated, reactive spirals of response—that is ignored by the other approaches but ought not to be left out of any comprehensive model of patterned family behavior.

The Opportunity Matrix Model

The final alternative model to be considered was chosen because it also addressed a blind spot in the other approaches. With the exception of the developmental task model, none of the others accounted for the well-established importance of structured environmental or situational factors in patterning family behavior. And, as we have noted, the developmental approach is calibrated to take account only of major shifts in family circumstances over developmental time. The opportunity matrix model, however, grew out of the observation that family actions are substantially shaped by the configuration of the immediate spatial, temporal, material, and social environment (Altman, 1975; Altman & Gauvain, 1981; Werner, Altman, & Oxley, 1985; Werner, Altman, Oxley, & Haggard, 1987; Werner, Altman, & Brown, 1992).

To state the principle that underlies this model in its most universal form, all human action may be thought of as occurring at the intersection of an intention and an opportunity. Cybernetic models tend to focus on the intentions, and, indeed, the intention sometimes seems to be the controlling factor in family behavior as when a family pulls together and "moves heaven and earth" to achieve an elusive goal. At other times, however, the opportunity itself seems to be the more important element, as when a family responds to the unexpected visit of relatives. But in every situation, both are essential elements. No matter how focused and determined the intention, a family cannot interact with a member who cannot be located; no matter how intrusive the opportunity, families will resist acting contrary to their most central commitments. This latter point was illustrated in the Los Angeles riots in May 1992 when, even in the face of the extraordinarily tempting opportunities to join hundreds of their neighbors in looting nearby stores, families with strong commitments to traditional values kept their members at home. The class of exceptions to this point—that is, the circumstances in which families may become involved in escalating exchanges that end by violating their values and intentions—was discussed in the previous section.

As we have seen, human intentions are multileveled and complex. We do not intend to review that part of the equation here, but to understand this model, we must examine the nature of opportunity in some detail.

For many years, ecological psychologists such as Barker and Wright (1951, 1955), Bronfenbrenner (1979, 1986), and Altman and Werner, together with their associates (Altman, 1975; Altman & Gauvain, 1981; Werner et al., 1985, 1987, 1992), have demonstrated the importance of behavioral settings as major determinants of the behavior of individuals. Among sociologists, Stouffer (1940) was the first to introduce the concept of *opportunity structures* as he attempted to account for the pattern of transfers and moves that families make over their lifetimes. Festinger, Schachter, and Back (1950) studied the interfamily visiting patterns of married graduate students at the Massachusetts Institute of Technology and discovered that the prime determinant was whether members of one family had to pass by another family's door in their normal daily routines. Adams (1964, 1968) found that sheer geographical distance was a major factor in accounting for visiting patterns among kin. Homans (1950) developed a theory of human relatedness that posited that individuals whose daily routines brought them into frequent contact would be likely to develop sentiments of liking and increase their interaction beyond the level required by that routine (for example, gossiping with one another or going out to lunch together).

Felson and his colleagues (Cohen & Felson, 1979; Felson, 1987) have developed a comprehensive theory of certain classes of criminal behavior that is based on the mapping of the routine activities of potential criminals, potential victims, and potential guardians. Perhaps the most comprehensive development of this theme among contemporary social psychologists is the recent Ross and Nisbett volume, *The Person and the Situation* (1991).

Based on an analysis of these and similar treatments of the subject, we may conclude that an individual's opportunity structure is the product of four interacting components: (1) *spatial configuration*, or the characteristics of the accessible physical environment; (2) *temporal patterning*, which involves the imposition of routines, schedules, calendars, and so on; (3) the *material milieu*, which concerns the availability of various material objects and utilities (food, furniture, fixtures, vehicles, weapons, tools, toys, and so forth); and (4) the *social milieu*, which is perhaps the most important and concerns the presence or accessibility of particular social categories of individuals (such as parents, pastors, police officers, and prostitutes). Together with the *meanings* attached to each configuration, these components interact to create the routine activity patterns and the opportunity structure for each individual family member.

Our real interest, however, is the dynamic interaction of these individual opportunity structures with one another in what we might call the *family opportunity matrix*. For example, how does the husband's everyday experience of space, time, the material world, and the social world interface with his wife's everyday experiences? Derivative questions might be whether, in that intersection, shared time and space was sufficient to allow marital privacy, planning, and the maintenance of the marital bond and the accomplishment of marital goals? Was community of meaning sufficient for successful communication and coordination? Like individual opportunity structures, family opportunity matrices are the product of the configurations of family space, temporal patterning, and material and social milieu. We may usefully expand on these four components.

Family Spatial Configurations and Their Meanings

The family systems literature deals at some length with two complementary aspects of space utilization within the family domain. The first involves differentiating between family space and non-family space and "patrolling" the perimeter (to use Kantor and Lehr's terminology). Anthropologists, social psychologists, and family scholars have done research on how families maintain their boundaries and the factors that lead some to be more relaxed and others more vigilant in this activity. This set of boundary-maintaining activities is the single subject of Chapter 5.

The second aspect of family spatial patterning involves the allocation of priorities and privileges over family territories and pathways to the various members. It also includes the regulation of personal distances among family members and the maintenance of personal privacy. Other scholars from a variety of disciplines have addressed the subject of interpersonal space in non-family settings. Such investigators have used a wide variety of terms in referring to these phenomena, including *proxemics, personal space, personal distance, territoriality, privacy,* and *body buffer zones* (see L'Abate, 1985, pp. 1222-1225, for a review of this literature). In these discussions, actual physical space is often confounded with relational or metaphorical space. To be "close" or "distant" can refer to physical proximity or relational intimacy. In Chapter 4, we will explore the regulation of relational or metaphorical space in families, but here we refer specifically to the configuration of actual family and personal territories.

People behave differently in cramped space than in open space, in private space than in public space, in secure space than in endangered space, in space that they have personalized than in sterile, impersonal space. Various spaces have particular meanings attached to them that shape the behavior of those in them. People behave differently in kitchens, bedrooms, and bathrooms; in theaters, bars, gyms, churches, factories, stores, schools, airplanes, and jails.

As in all systemic analyses, we will do well to remind ourselves that the influence works both ways. Families and family members not only participate in the choice of their daily pathways through their physical environment, but also routinely make efforts to place their individual stamps on the more important sites for personal and family activities. Werner and her associates (1992) call this *place making*. It can range from carving one's initials in a favorite tree to painting the family name on the mailbox; from putting up a few posters on the college dormitory wall next to your bed to completely redecorating a house or office. In each case, the point is to establish it as personal territory.

Family Temporal Configurations and Their Meanings

All action and interaction can be positioned not only in space, but also in time, and just as all families structure and are structured by their spatial configurations, so a mutual shaping occurs between a family and its temporal patterning. As Kantor and Lehr (1975) concluded from their intensive study of family activities:

> The movements of family members can be traced across two different kinds of time structures: clock time and calendar time. The day and the week are probably the two most important time cycles to examine in order to gain an understanding of a family's basic rhythmic patterns. Within a family's daily experience, getting up in the morning, getting out to daytime locations, the returning of members back home, the gathering to eat, and the putting to bed are all important recurring events. Similarly, in the course of the week, the cyclic passage of weekdays and weekends—work times and play times, busy times and leisure times—is basic to family life. . . . Family members erect temporal boundaries as well as the spatial ones and regulate access to one another and to the world at large. . . . [M]embers establish whether their rhythms are in phase or out of phase with each other, and with the movements of the world at large. The term "in phase" suggests a considerable overlap or similarity in the clock and calendar schedules among family members or between members and outsiders. "Out of phase" is a condition in which there is very little overlap or contact. (p. 43)

Thus, the temporal equivalents of "close" and "distant" are "in phase" and "out of phase." When time is added to three-dimensional space, they make up the four-dimensional spatiotemporal matrix of family actions, interactions, and transactions. As we have already indicated, however, the opportunity matrix has two additional components. The first we have called the *material milieu*. It is a factor of great importance that is nevertheless omitted from most discussions of these matters. The second is the *social milieu*.

The Family Material Milieu and Its Meanings

How family life is patterned is enormously affected by the presence or absence of certain facilities such as hot and cold running water, gas, or electricity; the availability and placement of appliances such as television sets, personal computers, washing machines, microwave ovens, refrigerators, and central heating; and the accessibility of various vehicles, tools, toys, and weapons. A few examples will suffice to make the point.

- Although it may be a passing fad, we now have a generation of boys and young men who spend hours each day deeply engaged in video games and who are thereby unavailable for other interaction within or outside the family.
- Studies have shown that one-half of all the time now spent together by American families is spent on watching television together (Eccles, Timmen, & O'Brian, 1986).
- Whether married couples own twin, double, or king-sized beds affects their sexual interaction.
- The availability of a gun on the family premises is one of the best predictors of family members' risks of dying from gunshot wounds.
- Analyses of the impact of technological innovation on the family have shown that the automobile's mass availability permanently altered courtship behavior in the United States. Similarly, each object in a family's environment has some attached set of meanings. Some objects are especially freighted with significance: engagement rings and wedding pictures, baby books and teddy bears, graduation tassels and family heirlooms. In Chapter 7 we will consider the particular place of such symbolically loaded items in the lives of families.

Anthropologists refer to our "material milieu" as *physical culture*. Many from that discipline have attempted to evaluate comprehensively the interactions between the overall physical culture of certain preliterate tribes and their family structures. In our own culture, an entire branch of psychology deals with these matters, and even a *Journal of Environmental Psychology* is available to scholars. Unhappily, too little cross-fertilization has taken place between family process scholars and researchers from these complementary disciplines. Environmental psychologists often write as though they were struggling to reinvent family systems theory, and family process researchers most often conduct their observations of family interaction in sterile laboratories or in therapists' interview rooms, isolated from the environments that shape and are shaped by families themselves. Progress in understanding the interaction between family processes and family environments awaits a greater investment in observing families in their natural habitats.

The Family Social Milieu and Its Meanings

Chapter 5 considers the importance of the family's placement in various social networks and also the importance of its members' co-membership in various other formal systems such as school and the workplace. Chapter 6 will discuss the significance of a family's placement in its community's hierarchal stratification system. Here we wish only to note that one of the most influential elements in every family's opportunity matrix is the presence or absence of certain categories of people.

Earlier we cited Felson's work on the accurate prediction of certain categories of crime based solely on knowledge of the routine daily activities of the potential criminal, potential victim, and potential guardians. When the path of the potential criminal (or criminals) crossed the path of the potential victim in the absence of any potential guardian, the probability was high that a crime might be attempted. In this formulation, no effort is made to account for variations in levels of motivation to commit a crime; a sufficient level of motivation is taken for granted. The relevance of this work for family theory is that the effective guardians in the Felson model are usually not police officers or security guards. Most often they are family members. Thus, unsupervised children are more likely to become involved in delinquent behavior than are supervised children, and gang members are far less likely to become involved in street crime after they have married. Of course, the general principle is not restricted to the explanation of criminal behavior. Every family experiences the shift in probabilities of a wide variety of behaviors when, for example, the in-laws visit, the neighbor children are in the house, the teenage son's girlfriend spends the evening, the children leave for their every-other-weekend visit with their father, or the mother's boyfriend moves in.

Strengths of the Opportunity Matrix Model

The opportunity matrix model has three major strong points:

1. The model explicitly uses a crucial component of the patterning of family behavior that is not focal in the standard cybernetic model (although the component might be seen as articulating with the cybernetic model through the environment-monitoring component) and which is also largely ignored by the other models we have reviewed. The importance of spatio-temporal configurations and material and social stimuli as determinants of individual and family actions is supported by research and theory from a variety of disciplines.
2. Like the psychopolitical and reflexive spiral models, the opportunity matrix model incorporates the premise that family behavior patterns are emergent in real time. These patterns are seen as growing from the interactions of individual members' behavior patterns, which are in turn the products of individual intentions interacting with individual opportunity matrices.
3. The model also explains the regularities of family behavior patterns as a function of the regularities of family opportunity configurations. It is not a static model, however, because it also is sensitive to how changes in one pattern are reflected in changes in another.

Weaknesses and Limitations of the Opportunity Matrix Model

The model, however, also has the following three drawbacks:

1. Although it provides for the influence of intentions, it relegates goal seeking to the periphery of the model, giving center stage to opportunism instead. On the one hand, this shift may be seen as a correction to the original cybernetic model, which places more emphasis on goal seeking than observers have been able to discern in actual family interaction. On the other hand, it overemphasizes passive or reactive elements.
2. The opportunity matrix model does not specify any family life-course sequencing as does the developmental model, but it does offer an explanation of how changing life circumstances may influence family behavior.
3. The model provides for neither purposeful psychopolitical processes nor unmediated reflexive spirals as determinants of family directionality. In summary, the opportunity matrix model tilts toward what psychology calls "field dependency" rather than toward a cybernetic "field independence." Presumably, just as no individual's choices are entirely dependent or independent of his or her environment, so no family is entirely goal-oriented or entirely opportunistic. Rather, this element should be seen as a dimension along which individuals or families move over time. Also, at any given time, the model is able to compare any particular pair of individuals or families according to their relative positions on this continuum.

Toward a Unified Transcybernetic Model
of Patterned Family Action

Having reviewed these approaches to the explanation of how family behavior is patterned, we return to the question raised in the first section of this chapter: How well does the family fit the cybernetic model? Does it meet the criteria of a goal-seeking, self-regulating system? The answer that has emerged is that it shares some but not all features of cybernetic systems. It is a far more complex entity than any electronic-guidance system. It is more complex than any individual organism. Yet, in all of this complexity, order persists and systemic principles can be helpfully applied to simplify that complexity.

We have seen the importance of avoiding four common errors when explaining family patterning and directionality:

- the error of personifying the family system;
- the error of assuming that all family members share the same values, perspectives, or goal commitments;
- the equal and opposite error of assuming that individual agendas are developed in a developmental or social or situational vacuum; and
- the error of ignoring unmediated, reactive cycles that may regularly propel the family in counternormative directions.

Having reviewed both the insights into complex social structure that are provided by cybernetic theory and also the pertinent contributions of several other models of social action, the challenge is to construct a unified model that integrates all of their crucial elements. The chief postulates of such a unified *transcybernetic model* might include the following:

1. The cybernetic functions of goal selection, goal seeking, and self-regulating behavior, are elements in the patterning of family action. In every case, their influence interacts with the ongoing influence of the family's opportunity matrix. The relative importance of these two antipodal sets of factors varies both across and within a family over time. Some of the time, some families may fit well into the cybernetic model; other families (or those same families at other times) may operate opportunistically, with little evidence of cybernetic function. This is a continuum along which families vary at any given point of time.
2. Members of family systems may be observed to interact with each other (and with elements in the external world) in patterned and predictable ways. Some of these patterned behaviors seem to be directional—that is, they move the family from a starting place toward some predictable

destination. These directional patterns of interaction and transaction are of two types: goal-directed behaviors and reflexive vectored behavior.

    a. *Goal-directed behaviors.* As a result of psychopolitical processes, one or another family member (or a coalition of family members) may succeed in imposing his or her own hierarchy of goals on other less influential members. Barring this, members with different views may achieve a compromise position. In either case, members are fully aware of this politically achieved set of family priorities. Most discussions of the family as a goal-seeking, self-regulating system assume the existence of this type of consciously held and prioritized group objectives.

    b. *Reflexive vectored behaviors.* In the course of psychopolitical confrontation, a directional pattern may emerge that is not the result of members' purposeful goal seeking but which an external observer would recognize as having many of the characteristics of goal-directed behavior; that is, it is a recurring and persevering pattern of behavior that leads reliably toward a given outcome. As with goal-driven behavior patterns, efforts to modify the course of these response cycles, either from within or without, are met with resistance—despite the fact that the predictable outcome may not be congruent with any member's values or intentions. This type of unintended but stubbornly directional behavior deserves a terminology of its own to distinguish it from goal-seeking behavior. As suggested previously, the term *vector* implies directionality but is free of any connotation of intentionality.

3. From the discussion of reflexive vectored behaviors, we may conclude that both the family executive and the status-monitoring functions are emergent by-products of the psychopolitical process. No specialized subsystems dedicated to these functions need be posited. Therapists have sometimes referred to the parental dyad as the family's executive subsystem. But even if *every* family unit had two parents, this inaccurately describes how the family system operates. Different members may have different effects on the final direction the family takes; this is the "political" part of *psychopolitical*. But the entire family is involved.

4. Also following from the discussion of goal-seeking and reflexive vectored behaviors is the family *archival function,* which is the family's ability to store its array of hierarchically ordered goals so that they may shape the system's actions over a period of time. This function can exist only in one of two forms: shared memories or preconditioned reflexive responses.

    a. *Shared memories of individual family members.* Each family member has an independent version of the family's hierarchy of goals stored in his or her own memory. Archival retrieval in this circumstance is scarcely an automatic procedure as the cybernetic model implies. Rather, it requires the same psychopolitical processes as are described above for goal-seeking behavior. In some families, the results of certain of these deliberations may be committed to paper, but this is a rare event and only effective if it influences the individual players' behaviors on subsequent occasions.

   b. *Preconditioned reflexive responses.* By their very nature, vectors are not suited for storage in the shared memories of family members. Yet vectors recur from time to time as if they were stored and available for instant retrieval when cued. Some scholars have argued that this factor can be fitted snugly into the psychopolitical model by assuming that not all motivations are conscious. According to this view, these reactive spirals are intentionally pursued even though the intentions are shielded from awareness, hidden away in the individual's unconscious. My own view is that no such construct is needed to explain the phenomenon. As Rapoport's equations demonstrate, all that a family requires to achieve a runaway spiral is a high level of reactivity, a relative absence of thoughtful evaluation, and a grievance. My observation is that these conditions are commonly met in family relationship dyads of every sort. We do not need to posit an unconscious motivation.

5. Individual needs, developmental factors, social pressures, and shifts in the family opportunity structure all have their effects on family patterns through psychopolitical encounters. Even unmediated reflexive spirals are initiated and maintained through such encounters. In other words, according to this model, no mechanism exists for any influence to affect the operations of the family system directly except through its impact on the agendas or response patterns of individual members who in turn introduce them into the family's psychopolitical processes.

6. The preceding point having been made, it remains true that a great deal of the patterning that occurs in family interactions and transactions reflects patterning in either family members or the immediate environment. Scholars from various disciplines have found it profitable to trace these effects in either developmental or real time.

   a. *Developmental time* has three sets of interacting factors that are known to have significant effects on family patterning: (1) individual developmental imperatives and associated shifts in normative pressures, (2) changes in family membership, and (3) life-course-related shifts in family economic and domestic circumstances.

   b. *Real time* family patterning grows out of the psychopolitical process that automatically factors in such issues as power differentials, individual needs, individual reflexive responses, and the four components of the family opportunity matrix.

In reviewing this attempt to summarize how family systems *do* operate, I am struck by how clinicians spend a good deal of energy trying to get families to operate as they believe a good family system *should* operate

—that is, by establishing joint goals and monitoring progress toward them. These clinicians work hard to make family members more aware of the dynamics of their previously unmediated escalating cycles so that they can bring these cycles into line with their intentions. In short, such clinicians do all they can in their power to make families more cybernetic, less reflexive, and less opportunistic.

Little wonder then that the field has been so slow to acknowledge the obvious flaws in the cybernetic model; it has been and remains the model of the officially blessed, *well-functioning* family. For students of the family whose primary purpose is understanding rather than healing, I recommend this transcybernetic model as a closer approximation of how families actually work in the real world.

PART II

Exploring Relational Space

CHAPTER 4

Distance Regulation Within the Family System

The Nature of Relational Space

From family process theory's very beginning, the regulation of relational space within the family has been an issue of central concern to theorists. Hess and Handel listed "establishing a pattern of separateness and connectedness" as one of the five basic processes that constituted family process (1959, p. 12). Kantor and Lehr list this question—"How does a family regulate distance among its own members?"—as one of the two core questions that a family must address with respect to its internal relational space (1975, p. 41).

Even family scholars who are not identified with the family process perspective have noted the issue's centrality. For example, in his article on conflict theory in *Contemporary Theories About the Family*, Jetse Sprey posits as a basic quality of family relationships "a perpetual confrontation between the quest for autonomy and jointness" (1979, p. 141), and Ammons and Stinnett in their discussion of successful marriages refer to the necessity of finding a balance in the "individuation-mutuality see-saw" (1980, p. 41).

In our discussion of the family opportunity matrix in the last chapter, we noted the importance of the configurations of physical space (not to mention temporal patterning and the material and social milieu) in shaping family behavior patterns. As important as they have been shown to be, however, they have been less central to the concerns of family process theorists than *relational space*. Relationships may be described using the spatial metaphor, but the distances involved have little to do with inches, feet, or miles. A couple may feel "close" when separated by half a world and "distant" when both members are going through the motions of having sex with each other. In this chapter and the next, we wish to focus on the dynamics of distance regulation within what might be termed the *horizontal* dimension of this metaphorical, relational space.

This process of regulation involves the ever-shifting balancing of two opposing forces: the centripetal forces that link each member to every other member, which we shall call *bonding processes*; and the centrifugal forces that separate each member from other members, and which we shall call *buffering processes*. In Chapter 5 we shall consider a parallel pair of opposing processes—*bridging* and *boundary maintenance* —that are involved in distance regulation across family boundaries. Relational space also has a *vertical* dimension whose dynamics of regulation will be treated in Chapter 6.

As we prepare to examine the regulation of relational space within the boundaries of the family system, we must recall just which relationships are defined as included or excluded from membership in the system. In Chapter 2, I argued for the utility of following the traditional census guideline that a family is two or more persons who share a common residence and are related by blood, adoption, or marriage.

Some reviewers of early drafts of this text have urged me to adopt a broader definition, one that would be less evocative of the judgmental, exclusionary values of the traditional establishment. Although I am sensitive to this issue and to its political ramifications (see the accompanying box on political correctness), I have elected to stick with the narrower definition on pragmatic grounds. In my opinion, it makes more sense analytically (if not politically) to start with the substantial body of theory and research that concerns the three basic familial relationship units: coresidential married pairs, parent-child dyads, and sibling dyads. Although many families may lack one or another of these sets of relationships, nearly all are based on one or more of them. Second-order relationships such as stepparent-child, grandparent-child, and half-sibling fit the definition if the relationship is coresidential.

ON POLITICAL CORRECTNESS AS A FAMILY SCHOLAR

I am painfully aware that the decision to proceed with a restrictive, traditional definition of the family will cause many to question both my currency and my political perspective. Perhaps some comfort may be gleaned from the fact that, at least, this is a familiar charge. It has been my lot to be perpetually out of synch with the politics of the field for nearly 40 years. In the '50s I was considered a radical because I objected to presentations at professional meetings on the relative merits of premarital chastity or sexual involvement. In the '60s I was labeled a Communist for being an activist in the sex education movement. In the early '70s, I was nearly impeached as editor of the *Journal of Marriage and the Family* for devoting two issues to the new, raw, militant, feminist scholarship of that period. Paradoxically, it was during that same period—that others pigeon-holed as a chauvinist reactionary for refusing to endorse the doctrine that the family was a failed institution hopelessly enmeshed in a crumbling political order. (I remember writing in its defense that the family was like crab-grass and cockroaches; you didn't have to admire everything about it to believe that it was an ancient, hardy, evolutionary form that would survive into the foreseeable future.) In the '80s I lost status with my scholarly peers by failing to publish a single research-based article in a refereed journal and getting too involved in writing textbooks and training clinicians. And now this.

The family system as defined here includes neither members of the household who are not related to any other members by blood, adoption, or marriage nor relatives who do not share the same residence. Such research as we have on family-like systems shows not only significant similarities between these units and families, but also significant differences. This holds true whether the unit in question is a mixed household system that includes unmarried heterosexual or homosexual couples or close friends living together in communal arrangements, or a kin network that includes closely related persons who do not share a common residence. Of course, we have no intention of ignoring these significant categories of relationships. They are of signal importance to family members, and we will consider what we know about their impact in subsequent sections.

For a quite different approach to family dyads that makes fewer restrictive assumptions, see *The Sexual Bond: Rethinking Family and Close Relationships*, a fascinating alternative model from John Scanzoni, Karen Polonko, Jay Teachman, and Linda Thompson (1989).

Distance Regulation in the Coresidential Marital Dyad

Fluctuations in Real Time and Trends in Developmental Time

For more than 75 years, researchers by the hundreds have asked the question, "What forces hold men and women together in the marital union, and what forces work in the opposite direction to separate them?" Mostly these researchers have surveyed couples at a single point in time, thus ignoring the question of how these forces might vacillate over time. When the question was addressed at all, it was cast in a developmental time frame and looked at shifts in the degree of mutuality or stability over the marriage's life course. One unique contribution of the family process approach has been to focus attention on the normal, rhythmic alternation of connection and separation between spouses in real time. In doing so, the attention also has shifted the meaning from connection and separation as equivalent to good and bad relational moves to a metaphoric comparison to the action of the heart in contracting and relaxing: Each phase of the process is requisite to its normal functioning (Hoffman, 1981, p. 91).

Seldom has a single set of scholars even attempted to investigate either the ebb and flow of marital morale and stability over developmental time or the ongoing rhythms of marital approach and avoidance in real time. The challenge of figuring out how the two are tied together is intriguing and full of promise. With the help of strategic, longitudinal process research by Gottman and others, I intend to suggest a model for bridging between the two time frames. First, a brief review will illuminate the separate conclusions of those who have studied marital bonding and buffering in both real and developmental time.

Marital Distance Regulation in Real Time

At least one researcher has suggested that each of us has a more or less built-in daily quota of social interactions and withdrawals (Chapple, 1970). Farley (1979) broadened the concept by suggesting that each of us develops a certain range of tolerance for separation and for connection—a comfort zone—outside of which we are uneasy. When the relational pulsations of marital life carry us outside of that zone, we are strongly motivated to do what we can to regain the safety of our preferred parameters. A long history of clinical reports such as John Byng-Hall's 1980 article "Symptom Bearer as Marital Distance Regulator" suggests that individuals and couples may even exhibit dysfunctional behavior if it restores the relational equilibrium. Currently, support for this concept is clinical and anecdotal rather than systematic. Perhaps future researchers may give us more information about how couples negotiate mutually acceptable definitions of the marital comfort zone. Meanwhile, my own clinical observation is that the matter is dealt with in one of three ways: (1) The couple has the good fortune of bringing well-matched comfort zones to the marriage, (2) one member (the woman in a patriarchal culture) is normatively elected to yield to the other, or (3) with a combination of good wills and good skills, the matter is negotiated through the psychopolitical process. Failure to achieve a mutually acceptable accommodation through some means will lead to a systematic erosion of the relationship's intimacy over developmental time.

Marital Distance Regulation in Developmental Time

Over the years, many studies have tracked the course of marital relationships over developmental time. The first long-term longitudinal study (Burgess & Wallin, 1953) started out with a survey of 1,000 engaged couples who were then recontacted 3 to 7 years later. By that time, the number had dwindled to 666 couples because of breakups, deaths, and inabilities to locate. Fifteen years later, another follow-up was able to locate 400 survivors (Pineo, 1961). Two-thirds of these remaining couples scored lower on marital adjustment after 20 years of marriage than they did after 3 to 7 years. They reported communicating less, being less in love, doing fewer things together, having a less satisfactory sex life, and being less certain that they would marry the same person if they had to do it over again. In short, in these marriages the long-term, overall balance between bonding and buffering had shifted in the buffering direction.

Not all marriages had followed that pattern; some had actually grown closer over the years, but the general pattern was one that Pineo called *disenchantment*. A further analysis of these same data (Dizard, 1968) revealed that, during the 15-year interval, partners had gradually withdrawn from the practice of joint decision making, either dividing the responsibility for decisions in particular areas between them or, more often, shifting the entire burden of responsibility in family decisions to one or the other. They also shifted further in the direction of establishing a traditional division of labor in other family tasks, retreating from the more challenging strategy of joint participation.

Other longitudinal and retrospective studies have suggested the developmental processes through which these systematic disengagements occurred. The two chief stimuli appear to be competing involvement with children (Feldman & Rogoff, 1968; Ryder, 1973; MacDermid, Huston, & McHale, 1990; Whyte, 1990, p. 140) and competing involvement with work. On the latter point, one of the most carefully controlled studies was done by Greenstein (1990), who followed a national sample of more than 5,000 young women through a series of interviews that spanned the 15-year period of 1968 through 1983 (70% of the women in the 1968 sample were still available to be interviewed in the 1983 follow-up). Greenstein found that, among employed wives, 80% of those who averaged 1 to 20 hours per week at a job away from home during their marriages were still married at the end of the study, while only 57% of those who averaged more than 35 hours per week remained married. This finding may have many possible explanations, including the perception of substantially sounder postdivorce financial prospects for those wives who had full-time jobs. But the conclusion is hard to escape (and is supported by a series of other studies): Being all things to all people is not easy. We shall have more to say about this general principle later in this chapter and in our discussion of competing loyalties in the next chapter.

The good news is that considerable support exists for the observation that when the children finally leave, couples tend to reinvest in the relationship with each other, and the balance shifts a bit back toward the bonding side of the equation.

All of these conclusions, of course, are based on group averages. Individual couples may have quite different developmental experiences. Remember also that because relational space exists in the minds of the participants and has no objective existence, we cannot assume that he feels as close to her as she feels to him, and vice versa.

This point was illustrated in a study of newly married couples who were randomly selected from the list of marriage license applications in a Pennsylvania county recorder's office (Broderick & Hicks, 1970). The newlyweds reported having reached marriage through several different courtship processes. Some had experienced what we might call *scarcely buffered* courtships. From these newlyweds' independent reports, the researchers determined that the couples were reciprocally attracted from the beginning and that the relationship had only grown closer since that time. Their bonding process was short, smooth, and symmetrical.

Other newlyweds, although equally symmetrical, had an opposite courtship experience. Their relationships were hard to get off the ground in the first place and then had bumped along through many a breakup or other crisis, each partner plagued with recurring bouts of cold feet. Interviews suggested that they ended up married less because of enthusiasm for a lifelong companionship and more because they had run out of excuses. We might label this the *mostly buffered* courtship. Still others had *lopsided* courtships with one or the other doing the pursuing and persuading while the other dragged his or her feet. In these cases, one partner was long on bond, the other on buffer. Of interest to note was that the courtship patterns continued into the marriage, at least for the first year. Twelve months after the wedding, the scarcely buffered group reported high levels of intimacy and satisfaction with their relationship; the mostly buffered group reported low levels of intimacy and satisfaction with the relationship; and the lopsided group remained lopsided, with the more enthusiastic partner reporting higher levels of intimacy and satisfaction than the more reluctant partner reported.

Bridging Between the Time Frames

In a series of longitudinal studies of couple process, John Gottman and his associates established a strong link between certain observable real-time patterns of interaction between newly married husbands and wives and their eventual breakup in developmental time (Gottman, 1989). These data were collected by getting newly married couples to agree to debate a "hot" topic (that is, some unresolved difference of opinion in which they had some emotional investment). These discussions were recorded on videotape while simultaneously each individual had his or her level of physiological arousal monitored (for changes in palm moisture, blood pressure, and pulse). Similar sessions were recorded each year for 4 years in one study and for 9 years in another. At the close of each study, Gottman and company attempted to determine whether they could retroactively identify patterns of interaction in the earliest years that accurately predicted eventual breakup. Somewhat to their surprise, they found that level of emotionality of debate did not predict marital demise, particularly if the negatives were balanced by a great many positives (the optimal ratio of positives to negatives was 10 to 1). Overcompliance on the part of the wife (what Gottman called "stuffing it") did not predict a positive outcome, because such behavior tended to eventuate in resentment and distancing by her. But the most lethal pattern they found involved the husband's "stonewalling" the wife's efforts to engage him in "meaningful discussion." Gottman summarized the process of alienation as follows:

> The first stage begins with marital conflict in which the husband becomes very physiologically aroused and [in an apparent attempt to relieve the discomfort] stonewalls his wife [i.e., his eyes glaze over, fixed, not on her, but perhaps on a point just over her left shoulder]. Then, finally, [he] emotionally withdraws from the conflict. Over time he becomes overwhelmed by his wife's emotions and avoidant of any conflict with her.
>   The husband's stonewalling is very aversive for the wife and leads to her physiological arousal. She responds by trying to reengage her husband.
>   The second stage is marked by the withdrawal of the wife. She expresses criticism and disgust. Their lives become more parallel [read "buffered"] and he is fearful. In short the husband's withdrawal from hot marital interaction is an early precursor of the wife's withdrawal. When both withdraw and are defensive, the marriage is on its way toward separation and divorce. (Gottman, 1989, p. 41)

This is a vivid example of an unmediated reflexive spiral of escalating hostility and withdrawal. No single round of the cycle is responsible for the final decision to abandon the relationship, but each round adds to the archived grievances of the participants and, over a period of time, unmediated repetitions finally exceed the limits of tolerance and destroy the marital system.

Astute readers may have noted that the foregoing discussion has focused entirely on the emotional or expressive component of the marital relationship, ignoring the pragmatic and normative or obligatory components. It is not uncommon for the family process literature to err in this direction. Perhaps if the theory had its roots in a sociological perspective rather than a psychiatric perspective it would have had different biases. In this case, however, the blind spot is a consequential one.

Perhaps the most significant finding of sociological studies of marital stability over developmental time is that many couples stay together even when their emotional bonds have substantially atrophied.

As early as 1945, Burgess and Locke contrasted the companionate aspects of the marital union (which incorporated the affectional, sexual, and associational elements) with the institutional aspects (which included the pragmatic and obligatory elements). Over the years, the evidence has accumulated that marital stability depends at least as much on these less romantic components of the marital bond as on the more heavily researched emotional components (Levinger, 1965; Lewis & Spanier, 1979). This requires us to broaden our conceptualization of the processes connecting (and separating) the connubial pair. They are more complicated than we have previously considered. Not only may they be asymmetrical, with the relational distance between him and her differing from the distance between her and him, but also the distances may vary by sector. That is, the bonding-buffering balance in the emotional sector may vary independently from the balance in the pragmatic or obligational sectors. In the following pages, we will at- tempt to explore the various components of the marital connection and the implications of each for developing a more comprehensive model of the bonding-buffering processes in that relationship.

Bonding and Buffering in Various Sectors of the Marital Domain

The marital bonding process is unique, at least in part because it involves the unique combination of three distinguishing characteristics: (1) It involves an adult, nonkin, heterosexual couple; (2) this couple shares a common residence and economy; and (3) the partners have made personal and public commitments to each other through the ceremony of marriage. By virtue of the first of these characteristics, the couple must deal with a host of gender differences and sexual and reproductive issues; by virtue of the second characteristic, they cannot escape an unending array of pragmatic interdependencies and confrontations; by virtue of the third characteristic, they have accepted a formidable list of long-term, reciprocal expectations and obligations toward each other.

Bonding and Buffering in the Heterosexual Dyad: Gender, Sex, and Fertility

Gender. One may argue that gender shapes the marital relationship in more ways, subtle and obvious, than any other single factor. Although this fact has been recognized by all, none have developed the matter as fully as have feminist scholars. In recent years, an entire literature has arisen on the process of gendering.

Both in their families of orientation and in their marriages, males and females establish and continually re-create their identities as persons of their own gender. Rooted in biology, community, and sexual politics, this process influences the way men and women relate to each other in every possible venue. It influences the ways they perceive and negotiate differences of opinion, sexual relations, parenthood, money issues, and the division of labor.

Perhaps a brief summary of the findings of a single recent study (Tornstam, 1992) will serve to illustrate the point. The general subject under investigation was loneliness and what caused it. The survey included a representative sample of almost 2,800 Swedes of both sexes ranging in age from 15 to 80. The findings were as follows:

1. On the average, women were substantially more likely than men to report being lonely.
2. This entire effect was the result of the high degree of loneliness reported by one subgroup of married women in the 20-to-49-year-old age bracket.
3. The subgroup consisted of women with low self-esteem and high expectations of intimacy. Their surplus of loneliness could not be explained by any relative deficit in their social networks.

No explanation for these data can be found that is not rooted in the differences between men's and women's calibration of the optimal balance between togetherness and apartness.

Researchers such as Janet Lever (1976), Carol Gilligan (1982), Alice Rossi (1984), and Barie Thorne (1992) have been among those who are documenting the developmental life experiences that engender such differences. As we shall see, the consequences of these gendering experiences are evident in each of the several aspects of marital bonding and buffering discussed below.

Sex. If anything in the affectional bonding of mates differentiates that relationship from others in the family, it is sex. The sexual dance, while by no means restricted to the marital bond, is only fully sanctioned and even obligatory there. It adds a flavor to the relationship that sets it apart from all nonsexual bonds. Because sexual space is the most private sector of the generally private space of families, it has not been easy to study in a systematic manner. Our clearest view of it has been through the window of clinical inquiry, and much of what we know about the dynamics of sexual process has been learned through observing the results of attempted clinical interventions. The major conclusion of these investigations is that sexual interaction is, in most ways, not very different from other types of social interaction and communication. It is a compound of messages and, more particularly, metamessages. Its patterns are governed by only partly conscious and only partly shared sets of expectations and meanings and rules. For each partner, the ever-changing balance of positives and negatives in the experience shapes his or her own responses (see Scanzoni et al., 1989, Chapter 8, for an expansion of this point).

But if sexual interaction mostly partakes of the qualities of other types of interaction, it is all the more interesting to note its unique qualities. In some aspects, sexual interaction differs only in degree from other interactions. For example, even more than other mediums of social exchange, sex is dependent on the management of suitable opportunities. A modicum of privacy and physical comfort are required. In particular, sleeping arrangements (such as whether the couple sleeps separately from the rest of the family, with visual and aural privacy, perhaps with locks on the door, or with strong house rules about not being disturbed; whether they routinely share the same bed; whether they wear nightclothes; whether they habitually go to bed at the same time; and so on) may have important consequences for the frequency and quality of sexual interaction.

A second important set of differences between sexual and nonsexual interactions derives from what might justly be called the *sexual dilemma*. This dilemma grows out of the intersection of three biological and social realities:

1. By virtue of their biological makeup, men and women are endowed with some degree of sex drive that varies widely, not only among persons but also from time to time within the same person; therefore, it is highly probably at any given moment that a couple's sex drives are out of synch with each other.

2. In many cases, this drive is notably insistent and persistent, but in no case is individual survival dependent on its gratification (unlike some other biological drives, such as hunger, thirst, and the need for rest); therefore, to decline sex on any particular occasion is an ethical option.

3. Although every other biological need may be met without reference to a particular partner, society continues to prescribe that sexual needs should be met within the marital relationship; therefore, to the extent that they observe that prescription, each partner holds the other's sex drive hostage.

The dilemma resulting from these interacting factors is that sexual encounters can neither be avoided nor taken for granted in a marital relationship; and each encounter carries an element of risk.

A third set of particularly pertinent issues includes the matters of exclusivity, possessiveness, and jealousy. These issues are not unique to the sexual bond, but in that context they take on a distinctive coloration. Even a casual observer of family interactions may note that this subsystem of the family expends a significant amount of emotional energy defending its own immediate boundaries, above and beyond the energies that it expends in defending the integrity of the larger family system. The norms of our society support the marital pair in defending its sexual monopoly against intrusion from other family members as well as from outside competitors. Also supported are the partners' investments of energy and priority in their sexual relationship, that is, for keeping the two of them in as well as interlopers out. Once again, however, we know more about the norms governing these matters than about the dynamics of these protective processes in real families. The dynamics of spousal interaction when these norms are discovered to have been violated (as occurs with some frequency in contemporary society) are also underinvestigated.

Clearly, clinical experience shows that not only is an intriguing choreography performed around the ongoing balance of bonding and buffering within the sexual relationship, but also the whole sexual subsystem is typically involved as one of the important elements in the regulation of the larger marital system. That is, seduction, coercion, avoidance, and rejection in the sexual arena may be responses to (or stratagems intended to influence) events occurring in other sectors of the family system. Clinical observations remind us also that the sexual arena is one of the chief venues for psychopolitical contests of will.

Fertility: The reproductive potential. If the ongoing sexual relationship imparts a coloration to the marital relationship that differentiates it from others, so also does the potentiality or actuality of coparenthood. In addition to the pragmatic issues inherent in coresidential coparenthood and to the weight of normative prescription associated with those responsibilities, reproduction also triggers an observable shift in the gendering of the marital roles, with each partner likely to assume a more traditional posture and a more conventional division of labor (Entwisle & Doering, 1981; La Rossa & La Rossa, 1981; Cowan, Cowan, Cole, & Cole, 1978; Cowan, Cowan, Heming, Garrett, Coysh, Curtis-Boles, & Boles, 1985). I have observed an equally significant transformation in the quality of the marital affectional bond, but I know of no research that directly addresses the issue. Most studies comparing child-less couples with those who had children have found that the childless couples tended to score higher on standard marital adjustment inventories than did those with children (see Houseknecht, 1987, for a critical evaluation and summary of these studies). However, one particularly careful study (Houseknecht, 1979) found that of the four components of marital adjustment measured on Spanier's Dyadic Adjustment Scale (marital satisfaction, dyadic consensus, affectional expression, and dyadic cohesion), only the latter—which mostly reflected the greater opportunity to do things together—actually discriminated between the two sets of couples. Clearly, one reality of becoming a parent is that an infant is a new source of competition for the partners' limited resources of time, space, and energy. The result may often be a reduction in the amount of each of these scarce commodities that are dedicated to the marital relationship—and a corresponding reduction in marital morale. None of this research, however, would appear to have been designed to capture the shift in couple definition that accompanies childbearing. None has explored the qualitative transformation in the couple bond that occurs when that couple has produced a child. The topic awaits investigation.

Pragmatic Interdependencies

Because they share a common domicile and a joint economy, coresidential married couples are bound to each other by a whole range of pragmatic ties. When they also are parents of the same children, the interdependencies multiply. These pragmatic interdependencies have not received the same attention as emotional ties in either the family process literature or in mainline family studies. In part, this may result from the long tradition in sociology of contrasting families and their enduring emotional bonds with businesses and their more transient ties based on the division of labor. This forced dichotomy traces back at least to Tonnies, who used the German term *Gesellschaft* to refer to the practical interdependencies of the business world and then contrasted it with *Gemeinschaft*, which referred to intimate interpersonal bonds based on similarity and affection. Clearly, however, marital ties incorporate both varieties of bonding. Certainly, this duality stands out in bold relief when marriages are dissolved. Even when the bonds of love have withered away and left the relationship emotionally bankrupt, it remains a challenging task for lawyers to disentangle the couple's coresidential, coeconomic, and coparental ties.

Every couple develops its own unique scripts for the division of labor between the partners, its own unique sets of expectations as to what they may count on from each other. Yet the incontrovertible fact remains that gender plays a major role in shaping those expectations. Many scholars have attempted to sort through the various facets of this issue. For example, when women enter the work force, they increase their total workload many hours per week, partly by virtue of the fact that in most cases their husbands seem to be unwilling to pick up an equitable share of the housework and child care. It is, perhaps, understandable that men might lack enthusiasm for increasing their own workload; a more perplexing question is why women themselves do not seem to be as dissatisfied with this inequity as the normal rules of justice would dictate. Feminist scholars researching the issue found that although patriarchal reluctance was surely a factor, an even more important factor was that housework and child care for many women were not just unpaid labor, but also core elements in their definitions of themselves as competent women. Some writers even began to refer to these as "gendering activities," that is, activities that define and reaffirm gender (Berk, 1985; Ferree, 1990, 1991). Thus, even pragmatic interdependencies between husband and wife are colored by meanings that go far beyond the pragmatic.

As in every other case, where bonds are found, so are buffers. In the pragmatic sector, these come in the form of backup arrangements to cover the spouse's part in the division of labor or as assertions of one's own freedom from cross-sex dependencies: "Fine, if you won't listen to me, I know someone who will," or "I don't need you to support me or fix my car, thank you; I can do both very well myself." In short, the opposite of pragmatic interdependence is pragmatic independence. Many marriages have survived the death of devotion because the cost of pragmatic disengagement was so great.

Public and Private Commitments

Pledging to keep a marital commitment, is, of course, only a special case of family goal seeking and self-regulation. Sociologists are likely to focus on the public aspect of these commitments, the solemn vow taken to keep the terms of the marital contract "of your own free will and choice, before God and these witnesses." Making such a declaration in public rather than on some altogether private occasion might be seen as having two important social functions: first, to impress the participants themselves with the seriousness of the commitments made, and second, to mobilize community support for the norms of primacy, exclusivity, and reciprocity that are associated with the marital contract. The social processes involved in community support for the marital contract have been studied in actual operation in certain contained communities. For example, one group of sociologists (Bellah, Madison, Sullivan, Swidler, & Tipton, 1985) have studied how this process works among a community of fundamentalist Christians. Such investigations lend support to a normative model of marital self-regulation. Social processes can be observed that seem well calculated to instill feelings of guilt, shame, and fear should either partner violate the marital agreement.

As we saw in Chapter 3, however, the normative model, despite its attractive features, is not adequate to represent the complexities of marital self-regulation as it occurs in real life. The transcybernetic model developed in that chapter was designed to approximate actual family processes more closely. To the extent that the transcybernetic model provides a more accurate representation of marital self-regulation, we must assume that marital commitments exert their influence on the real-time bonding and buffering processes through the mechanism of psychopolitical negotiations. We may also assume that these commitments, like other family goals, are subject to evolution in response to changing life circumstances. As Brickman (1987) would have it, the commitment to one's marital partner typically evolves through three stages in the course of developmental time: from the passionate commitment of youth, through the quiet commitment of the middle years, to the integral or balanced commitment of old age. Clearly, this example is one of those idealized oversimplifications that gave developmentalists a bad name, but it serves well enough as an illustration of how the commitment process might evolve within one relationship.

Howard Becker, a sociologist, has noted that commitment relates to one's hierarchy of values. "What kinds of things are . . . wanted, what losses are feared? What are the good things of life whose continued enjoyment can be staked on continuing to follow a consistent line of action?" (1960, p. 39). If these are the issues, then obviously the marital commitment, especially the commitment to primacy (that is, putting the spouse's welfare ahead of any other consideration), must sooner or later come into direct conflict with competing values and priorities. We noted earlier that long-term marital disenchantment was, at least in part, the result of competing demands from children and careers. The broader principle is that marital bonding and buffering never occur in a vacuum; they are always contextual, always embedded in an infinite array of ongoing triangular competitions.

The Triangular Context of the Marital Bond

Perhaps the most systematic modeling of this reality has been offered by Stephen Marks (1986, 1989) in what he calls his "three-cornered" approach to the marital bonding-buffering process. Drawing on the work of George Herbert Mead, Henry Bowen, and others, Marks views the relational world through the eyes of the individual, subjective self (Mead's "I"). He conceptualizes this "I" as existing in a state of perpetual flux, darting about among three aspects of his or her social or reflexive self (Mead's "me"). In one corner of this triangular self-space is found what Marks calls the "interior me," "laden with diverse strivings, impulses, and energies, a center of intentionality that is informed by the long record of its total life experiences" (1989, p. 16). A second corner is occupied by the "partnership me," which "ongoingly takes notice of, coordinates with, and attends to a primary partner" (ibid.). The "third-corner me" "represents any recurring outward focus of the self in addition to a primary partner," such as "children, jobs, relatives, friends, recreational interests, and religious commitments" (ibid.). Marks summarizes his image of the self-system as follows: "The 'I' of the self, then, is that whirl of conscious human energy which attends to these 'me's' and carves out courses of action" (1989, p. 17).

The point of Marks's argument is that pair bonds always occur in a context; without taking that context into account, much of the dynamic of the relationship is lost. Figures 4.1 to 4.4 are his graphic representations of four different bonding configurations. He chooses to represent the triangular self-space as a circle in these figures in order to highlight the "whirl of the 'I' " between the three corners. He uses heavier arrows to represent the investment of greater time, energy, and attention to that sector of life (1989, Figures 4-7). In Figure 4.1, the energy devoted to the relationship overshadows the energy devoted by either partner to their interior selves or to outside interests (here shown as divided between shared and unshared interests). In Figure 4.2, the strongest element in the relationship is the couple's shared connection to an outside interest such as the children, a family business enterprise, common friends, or recreational interests. In Figure 4.3, the strongest investments of energy and attention are on unshared outside interests such as may occur in dual-career families or in highly role-segregated traditional families where her focus is the home and children while his is his career. Finally, in Figure 4.4, Marks depicts the perfectly balanced family.

As each of us knows from observation, however, most marriages are not as symmetrical as these diagrams suggest. Indeed, Marks includes

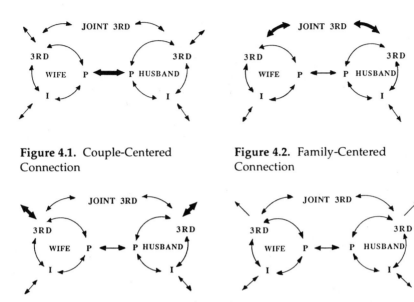

Figure 4.1. Couple-Centered
Connection

Figure 4.2. Family-Centered
Connection

Figure 4.3. Loose Connection

Figure 4.4. Balanced Connection

The Triangular Context of the Marital Bond: Four Configurations of Husband-Wife-Other Interests.
SOURCE: Reprinted with permission from Marks, 1989.

another set of diagrams in his 1989 paper that depict various lopsided and nonreciprocated arrangements, including some in which one or both partners shows an obsessional level of investment in one or another of the corners to the detriment of the entire system.

Distance Regulation in the Coresidential Parent-Child Dyad

In contemporary American culture, several periods occur when parents and children share the same residence. First is the traditional period of childhood dependency, although it may be complicated by shifting marital and custodial arrangements. In many families, episodes of varying length take place when adult children, with or without spouses or children of their own, live in their parent's house. And, finally, in a substantial number of families, an aging parent may live with his or her child in a situation of reverse dependency. Most of the research and theory on space regulation in the parent-child relationship has focused on relationships in the family with two natural parents and their dependent children. Only sporadic attention has been given to each of the other situations, particularly the cases of stepparenting and an aging dependent parent. We will consider several of these less frequently examined situations after reviewing the larger body of work on intact families with young children.

Natural Parents With Dependent Children

Just as separate literatures exist on distance regulation in marriages in real time and in developmental time, so separate literatures can be found on parent-child relationships in those two time frames. Curiously, family process scholars have not been much involved in research on real-time interactions between parents and their young children. More often they have been content to extrapolate backward from the interactions they observe after the child has become an identified patient. Happily for us, others have been active in observing and analyzing the real-time processes of bonding and buffering in this dyad, especially for children of very young ages.

Parent-Child Distance Regulation in Real and Developmental Time

Perhaps the most systemic research on distance regulation between young children and their parents is the work of Elizabeth Fivaz-Depeursinge (1991), a Swiss developmental psychologist. She conceptualizes the parent-child dyad as one example of a "coevolutive system" (other examples she has studied include teacher-student and therapist-family systems). The roles of the partners in such systems are reciprocal but not symmetrical, because one is mentor to the other. Fivaz-Depeursinge calls the person in the mentoring role the "framing party," and the other the "developing party."

The distance regulation behavior she investigated among infants and their parents was coordinate gazing (that is, looking deeply into each other's eyes for a protracted period). The particular study reported in this reference involved 16 infants ranging in age from 5 to 13 weeks. Each was paired in turn with its mother (half of whom had suffered postpartum depression, while half were free of such symptoms), its father, and a stranger. Each adult attempted to establish a communicative episode with the infant involving reciprocal gazing. The main findings are of interest to family systems theorists:

1. The first move in the process consisted of the adult picking up the infant, orienting the infant's body relative to the adult's own face, and

attempting to engage the infant in a reciprocal gaze. The researchers called this the "adult holding offer." The response was called the "infant's gaze counteroffer." Observers were able to identify three distinct patterns of emergent interaction; they labeled these *consensual engagement, paradoxical engagement,* and *conflictual engagement.*

2. Consensual engagement resulted when the adult oriented his or her body to face the infant's body, positioning the infant initially at a distance and angle that allowed for comfortable eye-to-eye contact and flexibly adjusting both on cue from the infant as to its own preferences. In these circumstances, the infants were highly likely to return the adult's gaze at least when the adult was a parent. Most of the mothers and fathers in the nonclinical sample were successful in achieving consensual engagement; most of the parents in the clinical sample as well as the strangers were not.

3. Paradoxical engagement consists of an ambiguous adult offer and an equally ambiguous or negative infant response. For example, while persistently soliciting the infant's attention vocally and attempting to engage its averted gaze, the adult may position the infant's body at an awkward angle or too close or too far for comfortable dialogue. In such situations, the infants' responses were to avert their eyes or to assume a glazed, unfocused look that was perhaps directed at the adult's overly close forehead. These types of response cycles occurred most often in the clinical families.

4. Conflictual engagement most frequently occurred when the adult was a stranger. These women knew how to hold a child and were usually successful at initiating a mutual gaze, but the infant's initial counteroffer was often withdrawn when it recognized that the partner was a stranger. Among the younger infants (5 to 9 weeks), this dawning awareness was typically manifested by breaking the gaze and starting to cry. Older infants (10 to 13 weeks) were more likely to interrupt the mutual gaze by looking away temporarily and then back but without crying.

5. The author argues that as these patterns are repeated many times in the child's early weeks and months, consistent experience with consensual engagement enlarges not only the child's sense of trust but also its sense of autonomy because the consistently enabling parental move leaves the form of the countermove in the child's hands. By contrast, ambivalent engagement confuses the child and also takes the matter of participating in a reciprocal dialogue out of the child's hands, because he or she has no way of influencing the inept adult holding offer. Thus, this experience undermines the development of both trust and autonomy.

The term used most frequently in the research literature on early bonding is *attachment.* This use of the term originated with Bowlby (see *Attachment and Loss,* Vols. 1 and 2, 1969 and 1973), but some of the most interesting longitudinal studies of it have been done by Ainsworth and her colleagues (Ainsworth et al., 1978; Ainsworth, 1979). These studies have focused on the quality of the attachment, whether it was secure or anxious, and have hypothesized that the nature of these early attachments will largely determine the person's interpersonal style later in life. This research shows that mothers who provide neither too much nor too little interactive attention to their infant and whose responses are sensitive to the infant's immediate needs are most likely to produce a sense of secure attachment in the child. In other words, mothers who appropriately balance bonding and buffering in their interaction with the child get the best results. This point is specifically reinforced by the work of Brazelton and his colleagues (1974, 1979), who have studied the young infant's need for regulating the alternation of connected, attentional phases with disconnected, nonattentional phases in his or her relation with the caregiver.

Another set of scholars has focused its attention on the difference that gender makes in the quality of parent-child interaction at these early ages. Without attempting to review this large and complex literature here (but for such reviews, see Steinmetz, 1979; Peterson & Rollins, 1987) we can assert that the gender of both the parent and the child are significant and that significant interactive effects are seen (that is, the mother-daughter dyad is different from the mother-son dyad, and both differ from the father-daughter and father-son dyads). And some interactions vary with the age of the child (that is, for example, father-son and father-daughter dyads show distinctly different differences at 10 days, 10 weeks, and 10 months).

Perhaps the most central tenet of the early versions of family process theory was the belief that personal dysfunction was a product of an unhealthy parent-child bond. Exactly what made the bond unhealthy was defined variously by different theorists, but most agreed on at least two elements: (1) the child was *overconnected* with and *undifferentiated* from its parents (particularly its mother); and (2) the quality of the bond was toxic in that it imposed "crazy-making," contradictory, nonnegotiable demands on the child.

The first of these points was argued most forcefully by Bowen (1960, 1971a, 1973) and Minuchin (1974; and Minuchin, Baker, Roseman, Liebman, Milman, & Todd, 1975). While still at the Menninger Clinic in the early 1950s, Bowen began to observe what he then called *symbiosis* between the disturbed children in his care and their mothers. Eventually, he built his theory of mental illness around the notion that the dysfunctional child's ego was suspended in a state of undifferentiated enmeshment with the mother's. The achievement of maturity and mental health depended on the child's beginning to recognize and act on its own separate feelings, needs, and perceptions—in short, to differentiate from the mother. Actually, the term *enmeshment* was Minuchin's and was coined to expand Bowen's concept to permit the inclusion of multiple relationships in the family that were characterized by being (to use our terminology) overbonded and underbuffered. As we shall see in a later section, enmeshment between the child and one parent was often accompanied by a "cutoff" (Bowen) or "disengagement" (Minuchin) from the other, which resulted in the formation of what Haley (1971) called the *perverse triangle*.

The second of these points—that the roots of personal dysfunction lay in the toxicity of inconsistent and even paradoxical parent-child interaction—was most persuasively introduced into the early process literature by Bateson and his associates (1956) with their concept of *double-binding* and by Wynne and his associates (1958, 1963) with their concepts of *pseudomutuality* and *pseudohostility*. (See Broderick and Pulliam-Krager, 1979, for a fuller analysis of these early theories.) As we have seen in the review of the Fivaz-Depeursinge study, some evidence suggests that this principle holds true even in the first few weeks of life.

Even in the healthiest families, the constant renegotiation of the parent-child relationship required by a child's normal development can prove to be challenging and stress-producing. Olson's survey of 1,000 nonclinical Midwestern families found that navigating the turbulent waters of graduated emancipation during the child's teenage years was the most difficult of all developmental challenges (Olson et al., 1983, chap. 7; for a more broadly based review of this subject from a systems theory perspective, see Preto, 1989). In *Leaving Home: The Therapy of Disturbed Young People* (1980), Jay Haley argues that in families that are unusually rigid, overconnected, and paradoxical in their bonding patterns, a young person's attempt to make the transition from adolescence to young adulthood can be dangerous to his or her mental health. In view of the high level of general interest in this age group and the strategic importance of this transition for process theory, I find it strange that so little research has been done on the real-time interactions of adolescent children and their parents.

Normative and Pragmatic Aspects of the Coresidential Parent-Child Bond

No other human relationship is so heavily freighted with normative prescriptions and proscriptions as the relationship between a parent and his or her dependent child. And no other human relationship is so asymmetrical in its pragmatic interdependencies; from a strictly practical point of view (omitting the emotional elements), there could scarcely be a less balanced exchange. Parents support and nurture and educate and protect children with very little compensating benefit in return. Perhaps this imbalance is somehow connected with the strong normative controls over parental behavior. Emotional bonding is a powerful centripetal force, but one suspects there are times in every parent-child relationship when normative constraints have played an important part in restraining parental impulses to escape the sometimes unrewarding demands of their role.

As in so many other matters, the norms that tie adults to their parental obligations seem to be gender-skewed. Approximately half of all children (more in some ethnic groups) experience separation from their natural fathers for at least part of their growing-up years. An extended separation from a living natural mother is relatively rare.

In the transcybernetic model developed in the last chapter, norms were seen as entering the equation of family interaction through their effects on individual actors in the psychopolitical process. That conceptualization is not intended to minimize the importance of norms in shaping behaviors among family members. One example, which currently is receiving a good deal of attention in the normatively oriented family literature, is the phenomenon of child sexual abuse.

The norms that govern family relationships define sexual interaction as a strongly valued and recommended component in the bonding process of the marital pair. Related norms concern sleeping and dressing arrangements that appear to be designed to optimize the opportunity for sex to occur. On the other hand, few family norms are more strongly held than those that prohibit sexual activities between parents and children. Given this fact, we may note the circumstances surrounding such activity when it does occur. First, the occurrence of incest is gender-skewed. Male parents are far more likely to be the offenders, and female children the victims. This appears to reflect not only the previously noted general tendency for females to be more fully socialized into the parental role than are males, but also the well-documented fact that males are more ambivalently socialized with respect to restraining their sexual impulses. Research on the subject (such as that by Finklehor, 1980a, 1980b) allows us to draw four conclusions about the matter:

1. Males in a paternal relationship to a child are restrained by incest norms in direct proportion to their identification with the parental role. Thus, natural fathers are five times less likely to force sexual attentions on a child

than are stepfathers or foster fathers, while mothers' boyfriends are still more likely to become perpetrators.

2. As outlined in the discussion of opportunity structures, one important element in the protection of any potential victim is the role of guardian. Thus, children living without the protection of a mother because she is either physically or emotionally absent are at higher risk of being victimized by the father or father figure in the home. Also, children are less likely to be victimized by male friends of the family visiting in the home if their own father, rather than some other father figure, is in the role of guardian. Studies of Japanese families where mother-son incest is many times more common than in the United States suggest that the extensive, work-related absence of the father as a potential guardian is a key factor in predicting its incidence.

3. Anything that attenuates the operation of the mechanisms of normative reinforcements of guilt, shame, or fear in a father figure increases the risk of his becoming a perpetuator. For example, being socialized in a family where incest occurred, living in a socially isolated environment, having a network of friends who are sexual abusers of their own children, and being an alcoholic or drug user are associated with greater incidence.

4. Having a hierarchy of values that subordinate the value of protecting children from sexual exploitation to other, potentially conflicting values such as a rigidly held view of patriarchal dominance also increase the chances of such abuse.

Norms related to the prohibition of incest apply equally at every age, even into adulthood, but many of the other rules governing parent-child interaction change with the child's developmental stage. A mother who never bathed her healthy 2-year-old would be disapproved of, but so would a mother who continued to bathe a healthy 12-year-old. The disapproval would be even greater if the parent were a father. Developmental scholars spend their careers tracing the interactions between biological and societal factors that shape the developmental evolution of such norms. For our purposes, we need only acknowledge that whenever we refer to the normative component of the bonding-buffering process between parents and children, we implicitly understand that these norms are gender-skewed and developmentally shifting.

The Father-Mother-Child Triangle

In an earlier section, we noted that the marital bond can be strengthened or weakened by triangular involvements. Certainly this is true in the case of triangular involvement between two parents and their child. Unhealthy permutations of this basic family triangle have fascinated clinicians since Freud targeted the Oedipal complex as the chief dynamic in personality development. According to psychoanalytic theory, resolution of competition between son and father for the mother's love (and, to a lesser extent, competition between daughter and mother for the father's love) is the crucial step in achieving emotional competence. Children who fail to accomplish this task at the appropriate age become fixated at this developmental level and manifest a wide range of dysfunctional behaviors.

The family therapists who helped found the family process approach were not overly impressed with Freud's triangular dynamics, but they did have strong ideas of their own about the potential for trouble inherent in the core family triad. Three configurations have received the most attention: the child as scapegoat, the child as mediator, and the perverse triangle.

The child as scapegoat. In this situation, the marital pair seeks to preserve its conflicted relationship by deflecting tension to the parent-child bond (Vogel & Bell, 1960). The child is identified as the source of all family and marital problems. When two or more children are present, the weakest, most sickly, or least conforming is selected. Minuchin calls this a *detouring coalition* (Minuchin, Rosman, & Baker, 1978), because its function is to detour stress from the marital relationship. Bowen (1971b) called this *triangulation.* By whichever name, the process victimizes the child and transforms the parent-child bond into a toxic rather than a nourishing relationship. In a sense, the child may be seen as a co-conspirator in this arrangement if he or she accepts the role and plays into it in a reactive manner. Thus, the therapeutic goal in such a case is to help the parents take responsibility for their own relational agenda and to address it within the marriage while helping the child to differentiate from the toxic system.

The child as mediator. In this situation, the marital relationship also is stressed, but here the child is cast in the role of mediator. This role is similar to that of the "parentified" child, who, in effect, inverts the parent-child relationship, taking responsibility for guiding and counseling the parents and monitoring their irresponsible behavior. The therapeutic goal is the same in this case as when the child is cast in the scapegoat role.

The perverse triangle. In this situation, a crossgenerational coalition forms between the child and one parent (usually the mother) against the other parent (Haley, 1971). For Bowen and Minuchin, the child is *undifferentiated from* (or *enmeshed with*) the one and *cut off* (or *disengaged*) from the other. The therapeutic goal in such a case is to help the parents mend their own fences and reconnect the child to the cutoff parent while assisting him or her to differentiate from the enmeshed parent.

The Coresidential Step Relationship

If one were to design an experiment whose object were to discover the various dimensions of family structure and function, one could do no better than to invent the stepfamily. Each year, hundreds of thousands of families with dependent children lose a parental member to death, divorce, or separation. Each year, hundreds of thousands of families graft a new substitute parent in the place of the missing member. Every imaginable set of variations in this scenario is played out. Every variety of family size and composition and social circumstance is represented; every degree of emotional and pragmatic bonding and buffering with the lost natural parent is included; every conceivable strategy of incorporation is enacted. Seldom has a natural experiment offered a richer treasure of understanding, yet remained unmined, or nearly so.

However, a few points may be tentatively made, based on a scattering of research finding and a smattering of clinical wisdoms that are beginning to accumulate. (For a review of the former, see Ganong & Coleman, 1984, or Ahrons & Rogers, 1987; for an example of the latter, see Visher & Visher, 1979, 1982, 1987.)

Bonding and Buffering in the Step Relationship

Step relationships vary in all the ways that natural families vary, such as age(s) of child(ren), gender configuration, ethnic and social status placement, and so on, as well as in several ways that are unique to this circumstance. For instance, stepfamilies and the bonds within them vary by the age of each child when the stepparent was grafted into the family, by the quality and frequency of contact with the non-custodial natural parent, and by the presence or absence of new half-siblings brought into the family system on either a continuing or intermittent basis.

One approach to these questions is to note which circumstances seem to be associated with the greatest (or the least) amount of stress in the stepfamily system. McGoldrick and Carter (1989) summarize several studies that suggest the importance of the following factors:

elapsed time, gender, developmental stage, binuclear connections, and prior experience with system complexity.

Elapsed time. Relational tensions are greatest at the beginning and gradually relax over the ensuing months. A study by Stern (1978) suggests that a stepfather usually needs approximately two years to establish himself as a comanager of the children.

Gender. Stepfathers seem to be accepted more easily than stepmothers, and in either relationship, stepsons seem to adjust more easily than stepdaughters. Because males are *not* the gender with the greater social or coping skills, their apparent advantage in adjusting to step relationships probably derives from their greater marginality to the core family processes; that is, to use Marks's model of the three-cornered self, more of their selves are invested in the nonrelational corners. Thus, a substitution in the father role is less perturbing to family functioning than a discontinuity in the more central role of mother, and sons are less affected by stresses in the family relational system than their more invested sisters.

Developmental stage. Young children seem to adapt to step relationships most easily, preteens seem to profit most from continued contact with the noncustodial parent, and teenagers have the most difficult challenges (they also have the most conflictual relationships in natural families). A young person has particular trouble in resolving the boundary ambiguities, conflicting loyalties, and unscripted relationships of the blended or binuclear family while simultaneously attempting to establish an independent identity, one that is differentiated from any and all family claims. A noteworthy interaction between gender and developmental level also is seen: For teenage males, the natural father-stepmother parental dyad seems to be more effective, while for every other age and gender combination, the natural mother-stepfather dyad seems to have the advantage. This presumably follows from the tendency of teenage males to test the limits of parental authority, and in this society, the norms invest natural fathers with more legitimate authority than either mothers or stepfathers.

Binuclear connections. Stepparents do better when they are not simultaneously playing the role of noncustodial parent to natural children living elsewhere. Apparently, trying to meet both of these competing role obligations at the same time is stress-inducing. Paradoxically, children, especially preteen children, do better when they are able to maintain regular and warm contact with their noncustodial parent.

Previous experience with system complexity. Children without their own natural siblings have a more difficult adjustment to the challenges of blending families than do children who have had experience with sibling competition and relational complexities.

Any attempt to develop a model of family bonding and buffering in the stepfamily would need to take these factors into account.

Normative Issues in Step Relationships

The norms that govern parent-child bonds and buffers are attenuated in step relationships. This fact is evidenced by the substantially higher levels of counternormative behavior on the part of both parents and children in this situation. Parents exhibit a substantially higher incidence of neglect, abuse, and incest. Children show more rebellion, defiance, and running away.

Triangulation in the Stepfamily System

Unlike the natural family in which the husband-wife bond is typically well established before it is confronted by competing parent-child bonds, the parent-child bond in the step relationship substantially predates the husband-wife bond and presents a substantially greater challenge to the normatively prescribed primacy of that bond. As a result, these families are more susceptible to the formation of perverse triangles are than natural families. Virtually all of the increased hazard of divorce in second marriages is a function of the presence of children from a former marriage (White & Booth, 1985).

Other important qualitative differences may exist in the parent-child triangle, as suggested by Buhr's finding (1974) that children suffer more ego damage at the hands of abusive natural fathers than equally abusive stepfathers. Buhr attributes this partly to the different meanings attached to the two relationships, but, more particularly, to the difference in the mothers' actions in the two cases. When natural fathers engaged in conflict and even abuse, mothers showed a great reluctance to intervene. When the abuser was a stepfather, however, many mothers seemed to assume a maternal duty to act as protectors and buffers.

Crossgenerational Space Regulation in the Family
With an Adult Child in Residence

According to traditional wisdom, the family is supposed to raise its children to young adulthood and then launch them into marriage or careers—and independent living arrangements. Survey studies on marital morale over the life cycle have tended to find an upswing during the so-called empty nest period after the children leave home. According to the usual explanation, now that the distractions of raising and launching children are over, the couple is free to reinvest in the marital relationship and that most partners do so and with good results. But what of those couples who, for whatever reason, find it not so easy to empty the nest? This might occur for a great many reasons, including children who cannot seem to find a place for themselves in the adult world of committed relationships and self-sustaining jobs and others who launch forth bravely into that world only to return ingloriously as casualties of the hazards that lurk there. Whatever the reason, do these middle-aged parents, finding themselves without the traditional empty nest, fail to reinvest in their marriage? The answer is, we do not know. Despite the notable increase in the number of young adults who remain in or return to the parental home (Glick, 1988), we know next to nothing about the dynamics of this counternormative arrangement except that they tend to be riddled with conflict (for an example of one of the few studies on this group, see Clemons & Axelson, 1985).

A second, quite different arrangement involving adult children living in their parents' home occurs when middle-aged children come to live with their aging parents, at least in part to care for their parents in their waning years. One recent study of families in this circumstance found them to be relatively conflict-free in contrast to the not-so-empty nest arrangement mentioned above (Suitor & Pillemer, 1988). This finding probably reflects that these arrangements are not considered counternormative in our culture, although we might also see this as merely another example of how family conflicts of all sorts tend to diminish with age over the adult life-span (Straus, Gelles, & Steinmetz, 1980; Pillemer & Suitor, 1988). An observation that is consistent with this latter interpretation is that conflict among these aging parents and their middle-aged children tends to be associated with the adult child's age; the younger the child, the greater the probability of conflict. Another provocative finding: Conflict was least when the marital status of the aging parent matched that of his or her coresidential adult child. These sparse findings offer food for thought, but we are far short of having enough information to generate hypotheses at the process level.

Crossgenerational Space Regulation in the Family With an Aging Parent in Residence

Most aging parents live independently (Glick & Lin, 1986), but as health problems, frailty, and sometimes emotional and cognitive disabilities become too difficult, one of the options is to move in with adult children. Studies have suggested that the warmth of the parent-child bond is not the best predictor of whether one or another child will volunteer to bring an aging parent home (although it does help to predict how happy the arrangement will prove to be). Rather, such a decision will be made by weighing a sense of duty (in our terms, internalized social norms about caring for one's own) plus pragmatic considerations such as degree of perceived need, availability of adequate space and time, and lack of other alternatives. Women are many times more likely than men to accept the burdens of this responsibility. Those employed outside the home are less likely to volunteer than those who are at home, and those who are married are less likely than those who are living alone (Stoller, 1983; Lang & Brody, 1983). Those already emotionally burdened with a recent divorce or widowhood may also feel less able to handle the added responsibilities of caring for dependent parents. Cicirelli (1984) found that, in such cases, other siblings often took over to protect the recently "wounded" brother or sister.

Little is known about the bonding and buffering patterns of families with dependent aging parents except that the caretaking child is likely to feel overloaded and that if the aging parent is male, he is particularly likely to resent the dependency. We are not aware of any systematic data on day-to-day family processes in these circumstances.

Bonding and Buffering in the Coresidential Sibling Relationship

Observational research on sibling relationships dates back to the 1930s when Levy (1934, 1936, 1937) and others set up a series of experiments to study sibling rivalry. These investigations predate family process theory and were inspired by psychoanalytic theory. Freud was impressed by the possessive love that children feel for their mothers during the 4- to 6-year-old age period and the seriousness of the threat to this emotional hegemony that is posed by the birth of a baby brother or sister. Adler, for whom the driving principle of personality formation was power rather than libido, wrote of the childhood trauma of being "dethroned" by the infant rival.

At least two sets of conclusions from this early literature seems worthy of note by contemporary scholars. First, the most consistent finding of the perhaps two dozen studies of sibling rivalry from this period is that the degree of rivalry expressed is largely a function of the way the mother handles the two children. In our terms, this is a triadic rather than merely a dyadic matter. Second, a staggering array of structural variables must be contended with in attempting to draw any conclusions at all about sibling relations. Even if one limits one's investigation to two-child families (a Draconian restriction, in itself), one still must address issues of gender, birth order, and birth interval. That is, we must consider the structure of the pair and whether it is older brother-younger brother, older brother-younger sister, older sister-younger sister, older sister-younger brother, twin brothers, twin sisters, or mixed twins. For the nontwins, the number of months that separate the births of the siblings should be taken into account, because it may vary from less than a dozen months to more than a dozen years.

If the sibling dyad is permitted to be from families of varying sizes, the range of structural permutations arises geometrically. Despite this bewildering array of possible configurations, some reliable empirical generalizations have emerged from the research that has been done in the years following the early rivalry studies. Cicirelli's comprehensive review of the sibling literature (1985) has been of particular value in preparing this overview.

The Quality of Interaction in the Sibling Dyad

Various strategies have been employed to impose order on this complex relationship. The three-dimensional approach used by Stocker and McHale (1992) in their analysis of 103 preadolescent sibling pairs is perhaps as good a place to start as any. They did not observe these pairs in real-time interactions, but they did get ratings from each sibling separately. Their three dimensions are affection, rivalry, and hostility. The decision to treat hostility as a separate variable rather than as the opposite of affection was a wise one, because the correlation between the measures of each were small. (Orden and Bradburn, 1968, had found the same thing among married couples many years earlier.) Siblings tended to rate the level of affection in their relationship similarly, but their ratings of the level of rivalry and hostility tended to be uncorrelated. One of the most interesting findings, from a systems perspective, is the degree to which the sibling bond was influenced by the quality of the parent-child bond. Warmth in the parent-child relationship (as reported by the children) was a moderately good predictor of higher levels of affection and lower levels of rivalry and hostility among siblings. In particular, children of both sexes who reported the most one-on-one, positive interaction with their fathers reported the most positive sibling relationships.

Earlier studies have also found that gender and parenting style, together with birth order, tend to be the main determinants of the quality of the sibling bond. Girls are more likely to be involved in positive, mutually supportive or even nurturant relationships, and boys are more likely to engage in negative, competitive styles of interaction. Thus, on the average, pairs of sisters get along better than pairs of brothers, with brother-sister pairs in the middle. In the younger, largely preverbal years, rivalry and conflict may take the form of hitting, pinching, shoving, taking toys, and so on. But as the children mature, additional tactics such as damaging each other's property, arguing, interfering with each other's activities, and getting each other in trouble with their parents become more common. By adolescence, direct physical attack becomes rare, and the arena of conflict shifts almost entirely to the verbal level. At every age, the range of responses to aggression vary from counterattacks to submission to attempts to appease or negotiate. At every age, first-born siblings exhibit more aggressive feelings and behaviors than their younger competitors, but they also exhibit more prosocial and helpful interactions.

Schachter and her associates (Schachter, Shore, Feldman-Rotman, Marquis, & Campbell, 1976; Schachter, Gilatz, Shore, & Adler, 1978; Schachter, 1982) have identified one common sibling buffering tactic that they call *deidentification*. To reduce comparison and competition, siblings may describe themselves as at the opposite poles from each other on a series of personality descriptors. The researchers found that, in three-child families, this tactic was used most often in one dyad—first born-second born—and used least in another—first born-last born. This fact suggests that the need for defense against comparisons and competitions is greatest in the first of these pairings and least in the second.

Parents who attempt to be even-handed and fair in their treatment of their children have less conflicted relationships among their children than those who display favoritism or inconsistencies. Sibling conflict is also reduced when parents explain their policies and behaviors rather than merely call the shots on a case-by-case basis without explanation (Cicirelli, 1985).

The Frequency-Intensity Dimension of Sibling Interaction

The small handful of studies that have looked at the frequency-intensity dimension have concluded that, within families with more than two children, often dramatic differences are seen in the frequency of interactions among the possible pairings. Consistent with the Schachter findings on sibling rivalry (cited above), studies find that, in general, closely spaced siblings are likely to have more intense relationships, both positive and negative, than those who are more separated by age and interests.

Sexual Interaction Among Siblings

Sexual interaction is one aspect of sibling bonding and buffering that has received more attention in recent years. Few data are available on the dynamics of the incest taboo as it plays itself out among children in families. Common observation would indicate that families differ in their degree and use of spatial buffering (i.e., separate bathing and sleeping arrangements at various ages), modesty norms, and supervision, but we are aware of no systematic study of these matters. Finklehor's survey of New England college students (1980a) found that 15% of the females and 10% of the males were willing to report some sexual interaction with a sibling. At younger ages, looking and touching were the most common activities; however, beginning in the preteen years, intercourse becomes more frequent, accompanied by force in approximately one-quarter of the cases. Bank and Kahn (1982) make the observation, based on clinical data, that the consequences of sexual interaction among siblings may vary enormously, depending on the degree of mutuality or coercion involved, but that, at best, this counternormative behavior generates stress in the participants if only from the fear of being discovered.

We might reasonably assume that stepsiblings are more likely to violate the norms governing sibling relationships (including incest prohibitions) than are natural siblings. They have virtually the same opportunity for sexual stimulation and access without the history of familial identification and behavioral shaping.

Future Directions for Process-Oriented Research
on Sibling Dyads and Constellations

All of this falls far short of either observing or attempting to explain the processes of sibling interaction in the matrix of the family system. No systematic studies are available of the management of relational space in these dyads. The issues of bonding and buffering, of privacy and sharing, of nurturing and subverting in real time in natural settings has scarcely been touched. Understandably, the enormous range of possible structural variations has been intimidating. One strategy for making the analytic task more manageable might be to set up a 2 by 2 matrix based on the dimensions of frequency and intensity. One would start with as widely varying a set of families as possible, sort all of the sibling pairs into the four quadrants of the design, and then examine the correlates of both structure and process.

To broaden the analytic framework to include more than a single pair of siblings, perhaps Stephen Marks's three-cornered approach (discussed earlier in the chapter) may prove fruitful. This approach directs our attention not only to the impact of parents or other siblings on the dyadic relationship but also to the importance of other competing concerns and outside influences.

These days, a very substantial number of families include stepsibling and half-sibling relationships. On the one hand, evaluating the scattered findings on these is quite difficult without a more solid understanding of the basic sibling relationships of which they are variants. On the other hand, these millions of natural experiments in melding the elements of disparate families together provide a treasure of opportunity for social scientists interested in the investigation of family dynamics. In each instance, the process of renegotiating family rules of every sort reveals those rules with a clarity rarely achieved in the natural family setting. We anticipate that comparative studies of natural and stepsibling relations—and especially longitudinal studies tracking families through the process of shifting from one to the other—will throw unparalleled light on the physiology and anatomy of family systems.

Relationships Among Coresidential Secondary Kin
and Nonkin

At the beginning of the chapter, we defined three kin relationships as primary: husband-wife, parent-child, and sibling-sibling. Secondary relationships include uncle-nephew, grandparent-grandchild, step-parent-stepchild, half-sister-half-brother, mother-in-law-son-in-law, and brother-in-law-sister-in-law. The inclusion of secondary kin within a family's living arrangements, for at least some extended period of time, are not at all rare. Many families also have nonkin living with them from time to time. These may be boarders who are taken in for the additional income, unmarried lovers of some member of the household, or dispossessed friends or friends of friends who are taken in out of a sense of compassion for their circumstance. Plays and novels have occasionally focused on how such relationships are negotiated, but we are aware of no systematic research or theory on this fascinating topic, other than the studies of stepfamilies that we have already noted and a few interview-based studies of three-generation families.

Summary of Distance Regulation Within the Family System

In this chapter, our subject matter has been the management of the family's immediate spatial environment, both literal and metaphorical. First, we began by noting that family interaction shapes and is shaped by the opportunity structure in which it is embedded. The family opportunity matrix comprises the configurations of space in the physical environment, the established temporal patterns, the material milieu, and the meanings attached to each aspect of these elements by each family member.

Second, we considered the management of metaphoric or relational space in the family, restricting the discussion to bonding and buffering processes and deferring consideration of transboundary bridging, boundary maintenance, and management in the vertical or power dimension to later chapters. Insofar as previous scholarship permitted, we examined empirical generalizations and theoretical issues that are pertinent to bonding and buffering processes in each of the family's primary dyads: husband-wife, parent-child (except for reviewing the socialization literature, which requires a later chapter of its own), and sibling-sibling. Finally, we noted that families frequently include other members and relationships, but that almost nothing is known of the interaction patterns involving them.

CHAPTER 5

The Regulation of Transactions Across Family Boundaries

Boundary Maintenance: Clarifying a Murky Concept

One defining characteristic of a living system is its capacity to maintain a selectively permeable boundary between its interior elements and its environment. If the boundary were not permeable, the system could neither access the resources it requires for survival from its environment nor rid itself of its own toxic waste products. If the boundary were not selective, it could not avoid taking in toxic elements from the environment, and the system could neither protect itself from attack nor hold on to those internal elements that it needs to maintain its own organization.

Social systems such as families also require selectively permeable boundaries. At the most fundamental level, they also must be able to access from the environment those resources needed for survival of their members and rid themselves of their toxic wastes. (Social scientists are generally too refined to acknowledge the necessity of toilets and garbage-disposal systems and even mortuary services for the survival of groups, but families understand these basic issues.) But, as we have noted in earlier chapters, the family is also a *semiotic* system that deals in symbols and their meanings. Thus, families and other social systems, unlike biological systems, can maintain their boundaries even when their members separate in the regular social rhythms of *assembly* and *dispersion* that are intrinsic to the life of groups (a concept first introduced into the social science literature by Parsons, Bales, and Shils in Chapter 4 of their 1953 volume). As we shall use the term, then, *family boundaries* enclose not only the actual spatial territory that the family claims as its own but also a more expansive symbolic territory that we shall call the *family domain*. Included within this domain are six conceptually distinct components. Four of these parallel the four components of the family opportunity matrix described in Chapter 3 (i.e., the family spatial and temporal territories, the meanings attached to them, the family's material and personal assets, and the meanings attached to those). The other two components of the family domain, as defined here, are the family's life-style and the family's world view.

Before turning to a consideration of the family processes involved in maintaining boundaries in each of these six aspects of the family domain, we will consider one more distinction. The maintenance of selectively permeable boundaries involves two distinct classes of processes: (1) those that function to keep threatening or unwanted external elements out (while at the same time admitting needed or wanted elements), and (2) those designed to maintain member loyalties and preserve valued family assets from being lost to the system (while at the same time providing for the elimination of waste, the launching of mature children, the banishment of unacceptable members, and, more mundanely, the regular, necessary, and desired excursions of members into the outside world). The first of these sets of processes might be called *protective territoriality*; the second, *possessive restrictiveness*.

Defending the Family Domain: Protective Territoriality

Defense of the Family's Spatial Territory

Families may defend their territory with physical as well as symbolic barriers. The "property line" may be marked by a wall or fence, embellished perhaps by a "NO TRESPASSING" or "NO SOLICITING" sign or a guard dog. The actual family living space is almost always completely enclosed, with curtains at the windows and a lock on the door. One might argue that the more efficacious protections are not the physical barriers themselves, but the social rules, many of them incorporated into law, that define the rights of families vis-à-vis their places of residence. In most Western democracies, even the government itself is prohibited from trespass onto private property without a warrant from a judge that is obtained on the basis of evidence that the intrusion is necessary and within legal guidelines. The degree of physical protection a family feels it needs to erect around its living space is a direct inverse function of how safe it perceives its environment to be. In a neighborhood in which experience has shown that rule breaking is common, the fence around the property may be high, the windows barred, the doors double-locked and provided with peepholes, and the householder armed. In a more benign neighborhood where people know one another well and have reason to trust that their neighbors respect the rules, most doors remain unlocked, most property unsecured, and neighbors enter one another's living space with little formality. Depending on how much space a family claims, there may be progressive zones of defense against intruders. Some outsiders are not even permitted on the property (or in the apartment complex or in the restricted neighborhood), others may converse with family members at the door but are not invited inside, and still others may come into the "public" part of the house (the living room or kitchen) but not into the space designated as "personal" or "private" (such as bedrooms, certain bathrooms, closets, and so on).

I remember being invited home over a long weekend by a college roommate who belonged to an old established New England family. I had never been in such a lovely home before in my entire lower-middle-class life, and I'm sure I gaped at all of the art on the walls and the elegant antique furniture, much as the tourists did who visited the home by the busload during certain seasons of the year. Having toured the garden and the downstairs guest room (where my own luggage had been placed)—plus the drawing room, music room, sun room, dining room, and kitchen—I put my foot on the lowest step of the grand marble staircase that led to the unimagined marvels of the second floor and suddenly *felt* the social temperature in the room drop. Without anyone having to explain it to me, I was able to discern this family's rule that outsiders simply did *not* venture into the private family space of the second floor without a specific invitation.

Of course, just as there are zones of differential access, so there are individuals with differential degrees of "security clearance." A few close relatives or friends may have keys to the house or be expected to enter at any time without invitation or prior warning. Others need to knock or even call ahead if they want to gain full entrance. Still others may be denied any access to the home at all. And within the home, various levels of clearance may be needed for the various zones of privacy. In fact, as noted earlier, certain zones (such as the bathrooms or the parents' bedroom) probably will be off limits even to some members of the family at particular times. This brings us to the issue of temporal territoriality.

Defense of the Family's Temporal Territory

Just as a family identifies a specific physical space as its own preserve and is willing to defend it against intruders, it may also identify certain blocks or categories of time as under its protection. The most obvious example of protected time is the period allotted to sleep. Probably each of us has inadvertently called someone in a different time zone or with different sleep patterns from our own and recognized the error immediately on being greeted with some variation of "This is who? What the hell time is it?" Other inopportune times that, in various degrees, may be declared off limits to intruders, include dinner time, television time (during which period certain valued programs, sports events, or video movies are viewed), family ritual occasions, or times when guests are being entertained. Some families exhibit much more temporal territoriality than others, and, just as in the case of space protection, they may have zones with various degrees of privacy attached to them and friends, neighbors, and relatives who have various degrees of permission to intrude on those blocks of time. For example, a close relative with health problems may be encouraged to call "any time of the day or night, if you need us," but a teenage daughter's schoolmate may be restricted to a 2- or 3-hour slot in the early evening.

Defense of the Family's Material Possessions

We are not aware of research on the family's material possessions and how ownership rights over various assets are conceptualized by family members. Common observation suggests that, in this culture, valued items usually may be viewed as the property of one or another individual family member rather than as communal property. The Toyota may be Mom's; the Ford, Dad's; the old beat up Volkswagen, the teenage son's. Within the house, the PC may be Mom's; the tool box, Dad's; and the stereo system and video games, Johnny's. For another family member to give an outsider permission to borrow one of these except in the most unusual emergency would be seen as a gross violation of family norms.

Common observation also reveals that not all family possessions are protected with the same vigilance. Just as family space and time may be divided into private inner sanctums and outer, more public zones, so possessions can be sorted into those with more or less restricted access. At the most protected core are items whose uses are very personal to individuals, such as lipstick, toothbrushes, hairbrushes, and contraceptive devices; items of great symbolic significance, such as wedding rings or family heirlooms; items that are secret, sacred, or associated with worship or with secret rites; financial and other records that are held to be private to the family; items that are dangerous, such as weapons or explosives; and items that are themselves illicit or that constitute evidence that at least one family member is involved in illegal or counternormative behavior, such as an illegal still, street drugs, or pornographic materials. Highly restrictive societies often have long lists of books or communication devices (such as shortwave radios or dish antennas) that are considered contraband and must therefore be prohibited. Radiating out from this core of closely guarded possessions are zones of accessibility that would even include the household garbage, which has been disowned by the family and may be available to be rummaged through by vagrants.

One frequently overlooked but important category of material possession in discussions of boundary maintenance is the family's financial resources, both cash and credit. Recent years have seen an upsurge of interest in the matter as illustrated by two recent volumes: *Warm Hearts and Cold Cash: The Intimate Dynamics of Families and Money* (1991) by Marcia Millman and *Money in the Family: Financial Organization and Women's Responsibility* (1987) by Gail Wilson. Each examines the symbolic and pragmatic uses of money as an element in family interactions and transactions. Among the factors that most influence the patterns of financial ebb and flow within the family and across its borders are gender, generation, and social class. Although financial predation has not been studied by family scholars (to the best of my knowledge), any comprehensive discussion of family boundary maintenance ought to consider it. Clinicians regularly encounter families who are struggling to cope with this experience.

Defense of Family Members at Home and Abroad

To defend family members at home is one thing, but what can the family do for them when they are outside the perimeters of protected family space and time and may be beyond the range of easy communication with one another? First, the social norm is that very young or very old or incompetent dependent members are not to be left alone or sent away from home without appointing a responsible protector. This guardian need not be a family member: It may be a baby-sitter, a practical nurse, a child care center, a school, a relative, or a neighbor. Regardless of who assumes this responsibility, the family has not abandoned its protective function, it has only delegated it. Almost without exception, the guardian has some means of contacting the responsible family members in case of an emergency that requires more immediate family action. Second, even fully responsible adult members would ordinarily not leave home without taking some family protective links and resources with him or her, particularly if the excursion into the outside world takes one far from home and among strangers (that is, among those with whom one has no meaningful relationship or no operational alliances). The importance of certain symbolic and material ties to the family and its resources may be of paramount importance: a means of transportation, money, identification, credit cards, insurance, or phone numbers where family members can be reached. Anyone who has found themselves far away from home and in a strange place without such resources knows what it is to feel naked in the world. In such circumstances, nearly all of us feel an overwhelming desire to contact a family member who can mobilize family resources that are sufficient to rescue us. Like E.T., the little abandoned alien in the popular movie of the same name, we want to go home. Third, family members generally stand ready to respond to a call for help from another member, whether it involves attempting to assist them physically, financially, or even spiritually. In summary, the family attempts to extend its protection to members even when they are dispersed, partly through preventive measures (such as baby-sitters and credit cards) and partly through protective outreach in time of threat to a member.

Defense of the Family's Life-Style

In protecting its *life-style*, a family defends its rights to protect (1) its established patterns of interaction and transaction (including their pace and style) from disruption by outsiders and (2) its internal operations from outside surveillance and evaluation. These are respectively known as the *principle of local control* and the *principle of privacy*.

The principle of local control. This principle dictates that the rules of family behavior be extended to any outsiders who accept the family domain's hospitality. Visitors, especially frequent visitors, may be directed to remove their shoes at the door or at least to wipe their feet, to pick up after themselves, to turn down the volume on the stereo, to turn off the television or to switch channels, or to watch their language in this house. The object of attempting to enforce all such rules is to establish the family's control over its own experiential environment. Outsiders (or even family members) whose activities endanger the family's peace, tranquility, and safety—or, in a word, its *ambience*—are restrained if possible and, in extreme cases, may be excluded from family territory altogether.

The principle of privacy. This principle dictates that the family protect its self from surveillance or intrusion into its intimate, informal life space. Social historians such as Barbara Laslett (1973) have attempted to demonstrate, through an analysis of changes in architecture and household composition over the past few centuries, that family privacy is a relatively recent accomplishment among Western nations. Not many generations ago, only the very wealthy lived in houses with hallways, which permit access to bedrooms without the need to pass through other rooms. Commonly, no room was dedicated entirely to sleeping or bathing. Most households of any size included live-in apprentices, hired hands, or servants. Modern concepts of privacy were a luxury few could afford and perhaps few sought.

Be that as it may, privacy is clearly a value in contemporary American family life. Just as families may wish to restrict outsiders' access to objects that have intimate, sacred, or counternormative associations, so they may wish to shield family actions or interactions that have these qualities from outsiders' view. Erving Goffman (1973) has noted that, in every ongoing social group, a striking difference is seen between public or "frontstage" behavior and private or "backstage" behavior. His own systematic observations were of employees in a rural British inn that catered to tourists, but, in spirit if not in detail, the description fits any group (including the family) that operates in both a public and a private arena. Goffman wrote:

> Throughout Western society there tends to be one informal or backstage language of behavior, and another language of behavior for occasions when a performance is being presented. The backstage behavior consists of reciprocal first-naming, cooperative decision making, profanity, open sexual remarks, elaborate griping, smoking, rough informal dress, "sloppy" sitting and standing posture, use of dialect or substandard speech, mumbling and shouting, playful aggressivity and "kidding," inconsiderateness for the other

in minor but potentially symbolic acts, minor physical self-involvements such as humming, whistling, chewing, nibbling, belching, and flatulence. The frontstage behavior language can be taken as the absence (and in some sense the opposite) of this. (Goffman, 1973, p. 128)

In the family, we may speak of putting on "company manners" as contrasted to being able to "let our hair down." We can easily appreciate the difference when we see the two styles in close juxtaposition; for example, when the telephone rings in the midst of a family feud and the adult member answers with a "phone voice" that is civilized, calm, and polite—and in almost comedic contrast to the tone and vocabulary of his or her most recent utterances. Similarly, the family member who, glancing out the window, discovers that some important outsider (the pastor, the boss, the mother-in-law) is about to make an unscheduled visit, may trigger a flurry of picking up, moving unsightly debris—and even informally dressed (or undressed) persons—from the frontstage to the backstage portions of the house. The designated door answerer may be thrust into a frenzy of personal preparation, "throwing on something decent," brushing his or her hair, and the like. At the door, one is virtually required to express polite pleasure at the visit while apologizing for "the way the place looks." Some households would consider it an almost unforgivable gaffe for an insensitive guest to make an uninvited excursion into the disarrayed backstage portion of the house (or for an insensitive member of the household to invite them into this region). Goffman cites a paragraph from Henry's *Madeline Growing Up* to illustrate the fact that part of boundary maintenance is setting up what he calls "staging cues," that is, warning signals that a family's backstage is about to be converted to frontstage status.

On the way past Gennaro's I became filled with apprehension about our lunch, wondering how my mother would take to Scotty [a manicurist colleague she was bringing home to lunch for the first time] and what Scotty would think of my mother, and we were no sooner on the staircase than I started to talk in a loud voice to warn her that I was not alone. Indeed, this was quite a signal between us, for when two people live in a single room there is no telling what kind of untidiness can meet the unexpected visitor's eye. There was nearly always a cooking pan or dirty plate where it should not be, or stockings or a petticoat drying above the stove. My mother, warned by the raised voice of her ebullient daughter, would rush around like a circus dancer hiding the pan or the plate or the stockings, and then turn herself into a pillar of frozen dignity, very calm, all ready for the visitor. If she had cleared up things too quickly, and forgotten something very obvious, I would see her vigilant eye upon it and would be expected to do something about it without exciting the visitor's attention. (Henry, 1953, cited in Goffman, 1973, p. 184)

To preserve the family's privacy and protect its public image, Goffman identified three defensive strategies that insiders use with outsiders, namely *loyalty*, *discipline*, and *circumspection*. Children may be systematically excluded from discussions of private family matters between the age when they are old enough to understand what is being discussed and their achievement of sufficient maturity and mastery of these three strategies to be trusted with the secrets (Goffman, 1973, pp. 212ff). To reciprocate, responsible outsiders will support the family's privacy protection efforts by exercising *tact* (i.e., overlooking lapses and leaks).

Defense of the Family's World View

When Hess and Handel (1959) wrote their pioneering essay on the psychosocial interior of the family, one of their major topic headings was "Establishing Boundaries of the Family's World of Experience." Under that heading they wrote,

A family constitutes its own world, which is not to say that it closes itself off from everything else but that it determines what parts of the external world are admissible and how freely. The family maps its domain of acceptable and desirable experience, its life space. . . . Limits to experience—broad or narrow—are established. . . . How deep or how shallow experience is . . . how much of the world it is important to know about and be interested in. (Hess & Handel, 1959, pp. 14-17)

Hess and Handel's concern seems primarily to be with the process that we have called "the defense of the family's world view" rather than with any of the other aspects of boundary maintenance we have discussed to this point. Similarly, David Reiss seems to focus on this part of the family bounding process in his discussion of the *family paradigm*, which he defines as the "central organizer of its shared constructs, sets, expectations, and fantasies about its social world" (1981, p. 2). A detailed discussion of this matter will be deferred to Chapter 7 (Family Meanings and Shared Realities), with the brief exception of noting in a later section of this chapter certain strategies that families may use to protect their members from being seduced away from family beliefs and perspectives when they are abroad or otherwise outside the immediate influence of the other members of the family.

Maintaining Family Loyalties and Assets: Possessive Restrictiveness

We have attempted to spell out some of the main processes involved in *protective territoriality*, that is, in keeping threatening or unwanted external elements out (while at the same time admitting needed or wanted elements). A second set of bounding processes, which we have called *possessive restrictiveness*, is the reciprocal of the first set and of equal importance. These processes function to maintain member loyalties and to preserve valued family assets from being lost to the system (while at the same time providing for the elimination of waste, the launching of mature children, the banishment of unacceptable members and, more mundanely, for regular, necessary and desired excursions of members into the outside world).

Spatial, Temporal, and Material Restrictions

Restrictions on a family member's freedom in space and time vary by his or her developmental level and gender. All other factors remaining constant, the older that children get, the farther they are permitted to roam without supervision, the longer they are permitted to pursue their own interests without having to check in with a parent or parental surrogate, and the later their curfew for being back in family territory. In most cultures, including our own, female children have been more restricted on all three counts, presumably because of the greater risk of sexual exploitation by outsiders. In recent years, increased sensitivity to gender inequities in our own society have stimulated a reevaluation of this and other gender differences in children's growing-up experiences. I am not aware of any reliable data on the degree to which this pattern of differential protectiveness may have changed as a result of this heightened sensitivity. Adults also have had a traditional gender bias in the social rules that govern the freedom to range away from home without accountability. As with boys, men have tended to be less restricted. Probably few family members of any age or sex are entirely free to come and go as they wish without any accountability or constraint.

One set of societal changes that have affected children's freedom from restrictions are those related to reduced parental supervision. Both the increased number of single-parent families and the increased participation of mothers in the work force have reduced the availability of adult guardians (to use the language of the opportunity matrix model).

As mentioned earlier, the restrictiveness of the rules varies from family to family, partly because of objective differences in the level of threats lurking "out there" and partly because of the family's own perceptions and projections. As many researchers have pointed out, given the same degree of objective danger, some families habitually invest far more energy into defensive and protective measures of every kind than do others. This matter will be discussed more fully in a later section when we consider some of the typologies of family operating styles that have been put forward by various family process scholars.

Possessive tracking. One means to extend the family's protective influence, especially during its dispersed phases, is by requiring members to check in with one another and to make sure that every member's whereabouts and activities are known (or at least that some mechanism is available to find them). This general strategy, which we have called *possessive tracking*, may take many forms. Included would be husbands and wives calling each other during the workday just to "check in" (that is, having no specific family business to transact other than touching base). Letters between family members who are separated for a more extended period serve the same function. In everyday interactions, members may hold one another accountable for the time spent out of the family's purview. Straightforward attempts are made to extend the family boundary in time and space by asking such questions as "Where will you be?" "How can you be reached?" "How long will you be?" and "Who else will be there?" together with after-the-fact reporting questions such as "Where have you been?" "How did it go?" "Why did it take so long?" and so on. Other examples of common questions serving this function might be "Call me if you are going to be late," "Who was that on the phone?" and "What on earth do you two find to talk about that takes two hours?"

Monitoring family assets. Boundaries are intended to protect family assets as well as family members. The family's well-being requires that these valuable resources be conserved and protected not only from outside thieves and interlopers, but also from the irresponsible actions of family members. Often enough, investigation shows that what was believed to have been an outsider's rape or plunder of the family treasury actually involved an insider as confederate. In other cases, such violations turn out to be entirely inside jobs. Every family therapist sees cases regularly that involve children's using their parents' bank card ruinously or parents' siphoning off their children's inheritance from a grandparent in order to support their own or another's

spending patterns. Other examples of the failure to guard family possessions would be a member loaning or giving valuable family assets to
a "buddy" or relative without consultation or consent, a child giving
away (or selling) her bicycle to a neighbor, a teenager hocking the family
silverware to support his drug habit, and a parent gambling the
family assets away or making impulsive, improvident investments or
expenditures.

In any of these cases, the loss is likely to be perceived as a violation
of the family's self-protective rules and a threat to the family's welfare.
In at least some families, the monitoring program may be passive,
while in others (usually those with a history of abuse), it may be quite
active and intrusive: "Where did you get that sweater?" "What is this
charge on our Visa card?" "Who made these withdrawals on the auto-
matic bank machine?" "Who took my mother's antique pearl necklace
that I kept hidden in my underwear drawer?"

So far as we are aware, no serious scholarly literature has tackled the
processes involved in the family's protection of its assets from the
improvidence of its own members. The subject has remained at the
anecdotal level of analysis.

Relational Restrictions

An important part of possessive restrictiveness in families is the set
of rules that restrict certain classes of relationships between members
and nonmembers. Members' relationships may be monitored for a
variety of reasons, such as concern for the family's social placement in
the community ("I don't want you running with that crowd; they are
not our kind of people!"); concern for a member's personal safety
("Don't you *ever* get in a car with a stranger again! I don't care if you
have to walk five miles!"); concern for his or her morals ("I know those
kids are into drugs and sex and I don't want you hanging out with
them!"); and, of course, concern for the exclusivity of the marital bond.

Of all of these, scholarly interest has focused most on the question
of marital infidelity. Several surveys have attempted to identify its
incidence as well as its chief sociological, psychological, biographical,
and situational precursors and correlates. Among the more reliable
findings are the following:

1. Fidelity is more likely to be successfully maintained when the spouses are
   (a) satisfied with their marriages, (b) religious, (c) conservative in their
   personal life-styles, (d) relatively inexperienced with sexual liaisons before
   marriage, and (e) relatively insulated from opportunities to interact inti-

mately with attractive members of the opposite sex in the community or workplace.

2. Men are more likely to become extramaritally involved in the first 5 years of marriage (possibly, in part, as a response to the disruption of their marital sex life because of pregnancy, childbirth, and infant care).

3. In contrast, women are more likely to become involved in their late 30s or early 40s, possibly, in part, as a response to their increasing freedom from child care responsibilities. (For a more extensive discussion and documentation of this topic see Broderick, 1992, pp. 326-328.)

The divorce rate is higher among couples who have experienced infidelity than among those who have not. One study (Buunk, 1982) found that the most frequent (and least healing) response to a spouse's infidelity is to confront him or her (and possibly the outside partner) and threaten to leave. The next most common response was to attempt to normalize the situation: "This happens in lots of marriages and they survive." The third most likely response—attempting to talk it through with the spouse and perhaps the outside partner—was the most likely to restore a full marital commitment.

All of this falls far short of illuminating the real-time family interaction involved. We know little or nothing about the boundary mechanisms by which families attempt to defend against infidelity, the spirals of marital interactions that lead to it, the couple dynamics that lead to discovery and confrontation, or the interactive sequences that may follow and their various consequences. The work of discovery lies yet before us.

One area that has received scholarly attention is parental involvement in their children's selection of friends, especially of dates and mates. As might be expected, this is a gender-skewed matter. Young women's choices are more carefully scrutinized than their brothers', and mothers are more involved in this activity than fathers, a finding that is consistent with the widely observed tendency for women to be more invested than men in every aspect of familial relationships. They also are more invested in the social-placement aspects of courtship, playing a more active role in applying the standards of social, racial, and denominational eligibility to their children's potential mates.

For their part, children, especially partly emancipated college students, are liable to postpone a full disclosure of their potential mate's background and values to the family until the latter stages of the courtship process. Apparently, the process of having his or her suitability analyzed before the relationship seems as if it might be the real thing is just not worth the hassle. We also should note that, even at this point, serious parental disapproval may have a real impact, especially with young women. Negative evaluations by family members is among the most common reasons given for breaking engagements. (For a more detailed review of this literature and documentation, see Broderick, 1992, chap. 6.)

Protecting Family Life-Styles and World Views Through Restrictions on Members

In an earlier section, we discussed the family's defenses against outsiders who threaten local control of the family's life-style or challenge its values. Clearly, in most cases, such potentially disruptive outsiders enter the family domain at the invitation of a family member. But often enough, the challenger of family peace and certainties is no outsider. It is a member who violates the boundaries by introducing disruptive, inappropriate, or illegal behaviors, substances, language, or sensory images (such as explicit sexual materials by way of prohibited magazines, videotapes, music, or "pay for porn" telephone calls on the one hand, and forbidden political or religious literature or icons on the other). With some justification, most families attribute such aberrations and disloyalties to the unwholesome influences of particular outsiders or unmonitored outside experiences on the errant member. A case of falling in with bad companions and adopting their ways, perhaps, or, more generally, a manifestation of the "How ya gonna keep 'em down on the farm, once they've seen gay Paree?" syndrome.

As a specific prophylaxis against such defection, many families become very invested in the strategy of channeling. As used in this context, *channeling* is the practice of attempting to maintain some degree of control over the quality of experience and the content of the values that a member is exposed to in the dispersed phases of family life. We will explore the topic more in Chapter 8 (The Socialization Process). Here we briefly note that the process involves attempting to exercise some control over member's away-from-home experiences by channeling them into "safe" settings.

A setting is considered safe to the extent that the family has cause to hope that its own most cherished values and beliefs will be reinforced rather than challenged there. Thus, some parents go to great lengths to get their children enrolled in the "right" schools, camps, and youth groups, and they do all within their power to keep them away from the "wrong" ones. Children may be permitted, even encouraged, to invite certain friends over and to reciprocate by attending "slumber parties" at their friends' homes, while other relationships are actively discouraged or even forbidden. Although the concept of channeling is encountered mostly in the literature on socializing children, clearly it applies also to the efforts that families make to limit the exposure of adult members to potentially threatening situations. For example, certain relationships and associations are encouraged and sponsored, while others are not.

Typologies and Styles of Boundary Maintenance

In their 1959 statement about the importance of establishing and maintaining family boundaries so as to protect a common world view within the family, Hess and Handel went on to note that " Families differ . . . in how insistently they will impose their images on their children" (p. 17). Fifteen years later, Kantor and Lehr (1975) empirically investigated this dimension of family process as part of their intensive observational studies of 19 Boston families. They were immediately struck by the differences among the families in their styles of relating to the outside world. Some families kept very much to themselves, seeming to view outsiders as a serious threat to their safety and integrity; Kantor and Lehr labeled them as *closed* families. "Locked doors, careful scrutiny of strangers in the neighborhood, parental control over the media, supervised excursions, and unlisted telephones are all features of a closed-type family" (p. 120). At the other end of the spectrum, the researchers observed *random* families who "deemphasize the territorial defense of the family. Indeed, they have a tendency to extend entry and exit prerogatives broadly, not only to members, but to guests and strangers as well" (p. 134). "Each person develops his own bounding patterns in establishing and defending his own and his family's territory. . . . 'Do your own thing' is perhaps the most important family slogan" (pp. 134-135).

Between these extremes, Kantor and Lehr labeled a third type of family as *open*. In these families, "Individuals are allowed to regulate the direction and destination of their incoming and outgoing traffic as long as they do not cause discomfort to other members or violate the consensus of the group. . . . In general open bounding fosters the desire for beneficial interchange with members of the community, since guests are not only welcome but made to feel important for the contributions they make to the family" (p. 127). We can see that the open family style of dealing with outsiders is more than a midpoint between closed and random.

The three styles do not lie on a single line; instead, they form a triangle. Two qualities lift open families from the closed-random axis. The first is their penchant for communication and negotiation; the second is the energy and forethought they invest in selectively co-opting those elements from the outside world that are calculated as reinforcing the family's world views and values, or which are seen as potentially helpful in forwarding the family's goals. These families are the consummate channelers. (See Cox, 1982, for an empirical documentation of this second dimension in the Kantor and Lehr typology; and Constantine, in press, for a persuasive theoretical rationale.)

In my view, the nomenclature Kantor and Lehr introduced in this typology is unfortunate, particularly because it has been so widely adopted by writers in the field. By definition, all social systems are open and hierarchically ordered; none could be rightly characterized as either closed or random. Still, the characterizations of the three styles, however labeled, has provoked a great deal of research and theoretical refinement. Among the most thoughtful and creative attempts to re-conceptualize and restructure the Kantor and Lehr model is Larry Constantine's soon to be published pyramidal model (in press). It does scant justice to his contribution to note that, in addition to the three familiar types, he argues for the logical necessity (and empirical reality) of a fourth type of family, which he calls *synchronous*. Just as the closed family is in some senses the antithesis of the random family, so the synchronous is the antithesis of the open family. "Instead of utilizing communication and negotiation, [the synchronous family] relies upon tacit understanding and unstated rules for regulating its operation" (1992, manuscript pp. 6-7).

Other typologists also have had difficulty in developing a nomenclature that is both systemically sound and simple to remember. One noteworthy effort is by David Reiss (1981). In summarizing 20 years of experimental research on patterns of family interaction, Reiss concurred with Kantor and Lehr in concluding that families choose from a relatively small array of styles (he called them *family paradigms*) when relating to the outside world. He called the first type *consensus sensitive*. These bore some resemblance to Kantor and Lehr's closed families in that they viewed the outside world as unpredictable and uncontrollable and hence tended to close ranks against it. A second type, *distance sensitive*, bore a resemblance to the random family in that each member stood alone in his or her relation to an unfriendly and chaotic outside world. A third type, *environment sensitive*, corresponded in some degree to the open family in that its members had congruent values, worked well together, and saw the outside world as "a universe they can understand and master" (Reiss, 1981, p. 334). In his more recent work, Reiss has also identified a forth type, the *achievement sensitive*, which has no counterpart in the Kantor & Lehr typology but bears some resemblance to Constantine's fourth category, the synchronous family. The achievement sensitive family shares with the "environment sensitive" family the view that the world can be conquered, but its members approach the challenge as individuals in a competitive rather than a cooperative mode and without much sense of mutuality or common cause with other family members.

At least one dimension in each of these typologies is concerned with the permeability of the family boundary. Not much research has been done on why some families adopt a more open style than others, but, as noted earlier, at least one important element has been identified. This *principle of perceived threat* holds that any system (whether an individual, a family, or a nation) defends itself against outside influences when it perceives them as threats to its well-being. Nothing novel is in this principle. In fact, it is the embedded moral of the ancient human morality tale about the contest between the Sun and the North Wind, who try to get a man to release his cloak. As every school child knows, the North Wind's effort to blow the cloak off merely increased the man's determination to clutch it about himself as a protection against the raging storm, but when the Sun came out and warmed him, he readily laid it aside. The applications of this principle are easy to see in everyday life. People who perceive their neighborhoods as unsafe are more likely than others to lock their doors and bar their windows. The inverse is equally true; that is, defenses are relaxed when an outside influence is perceived as benign. Almost a century of clinical practice has documented that the willingness of individuals or families to open up their inner selves to therapeutic scrutiny is a direct function of their perception that the listener is nonjudgmental and trustworthy.

One might reasonably assume that this principle of perceived danger not only is a determinant of a given family's general posture toward the world as reflected in Reiss's or Kantor and Lehr's typologies, but also is useful in explaining selective openness (for example, being relatively open to those of one's own faith or ethnicity, while maintaining defensive barriers against others). At least some ethnic groups' levels of "clannish" behaviors are certain to be a function of how safe they feel in their position in the larger society. Clearly, at least two separable components are at work in the operation of this principle: (1) the objective degree of real danger to the system (however measured) and (2) the system members' perceptions of the danger posed. Any given family may hold a range of opinions as to the level of threat by a particular external influence. We get some insight into the dynamics of this type of perception from the series of studies on the correlates of such ethnic clannishness cited by McGoldrick (McGoldrick, Pearce, & Giordano, 1982). She concludes that the data support the generalization that "if people are secure in their identity, then they can act with greater freedom, flexibility, and openness to others of different cultural backgrounds" (p. 5). We would assume that this principle applies to all boundary issues, not just ethnic exclusivity. The full statement of the principle of perceived danger, then might be as follows: Any system defends itself against outside influences when it perceives them to be a threat to its well-being. The perception of threat has two components: the objective danger to the system and the perceptual sets of the system members making the judgment. The perceptual sets of the system members will tend to be open and trusting to the degree that they are secure in their own sense of identity.

Bridging Across Family Boundaries

The previous section's premise holds that family systems survive only to the extent that they are successful in defending the integrity of their boundaries. The reciprocal premise of this section asserts that family systems survive only to the extent that they are successful in providing for essential transactions across those boundaries. These families require the exchange of goods, services, and information with other families and institutions. In the process of acquiring these, families must send their members out into the world—to the workplace and marketplace, the school, the church, the theater, the hospital, and the polling booth. They are likely also to both need and want to permit selected outsiders into protected family space: close friends, relatives, and children's playmates, not to mention various delivery or repair or salespersons, social workers, pastors, and the like. Sociology has a long tradition that considers *informal* and *formal* transactions separately. By informal transactions, we mean social contact with relatives, neighbors, friends, co-workers, romantic partners, and acquaintances. Formal transactions are those between family members and other formal organizations such as businesses, churches, and government agencies.

Informal Networks of Transaction

Family members' informal social networks have been the subject of lively scholarly investigation and debate in recent decades, but family systems theorists have not participated much in the process. Nevertheless, social network theory and research articulates well with family process theory: Both are concerned with the patterning of transactions between family members and various categories of outsiders in real time. (For a useful selection of review articles, see Robert Milardo's 1988 volume of readings, *Families and Social Networks*.) Many of the empirical findings and conceptual clarifications of network scholars contribute directly to understanding how families function outside their own boundaries. One of the most helpful conceptual contributions is Granovetter's (1983) distinction between *strong-tie* and *weak-tie* networks. Strong ties involve those kin and close friends who are most trusted and most relied upon in time of real need. This network never constitutes a large number of persons, and in some cases may be limited to only one or two—or even *no* outsider who will qualify. Weak-tie networks, on the other hand, are those extensive and amorphous collections of casual associates and acquaintances who know us and whom we know with varying degrees of intimacy. Included in this category are our more distant relatives and in-laws, present or former college roommates, neighbors, co-workers, classmates, members of the same congregation, business acquaintances, and friends of friends. These people may number in the hundreds, and although they may not be relied upon for the kind of immediate response to need that one hopes for from those in the strong-tie network, they are a crucially important resource for the family, as we shall see below.

Strong-Tie Networks

We are tempted in both informal speech and scholarly writing to speak of the *family system* itself as the unit in strong-tie networks. We are accustomed to saying things such as "Our family is very close to their family," and scholars commonly draw diagrams of networks in which a single line connects family A to families B and C but not to families D and E. Research on the actual, real-time dynamics of networking does not support this conceptualization. In real life, the basic unit of network bonding is the individual family member. Rarely is every member of one family symmetrically bonded to every member of another family, even if the two families are closely related. "Hey, she's *your* sister, not mine," or "Honey, you know I would do anything for your mother, but I don't have to like her new husband," would be typical expressions of less-than-uniform closeness between members of kin-connected families.

The same sort of selective bonding occurs with the families of close friends. For example, one study of Chicago housewives found that most of them interacted daily with their closest friends, either in person or on the phone, but entertaining or visiting these friends in the company of their respective husbands occurred far less frequently, typically less than once a week (Lopata, 1971). Another study (Tognoli, 1980), which focused on husbands' friendship patterns, found that they were even less likely than their wives to bring their closest friends into the family circle. Similarly, children's closest confederates and intimates may be quite loosely connected to the rest of the family. Apparently, just as we have his and her marriages, we have his and her (and the children's) networks of intimates.

The degree to which these individual networks overlap varies from family to family. As early as 1955, Elizabeth Bott suggested the existence of a correspondence between the internal structure of family-interaction patterns and the degree of overlap in their intimate networks. Based on her observations of a small set of working-class families in East London, Bott hypothesized that the more segregated the couple's internal role structure, the more segregated their networks. Specifically, she saw that when husbands and wives were flexible in their definitions of what was men's work and women's work in the home and cooperated in performing the labor required to keep a household going, they were likely also to prefer joint activities outside the home, interacting as a couple with other couples. In the language we have used here, their individual social networks tended to be overlapping. By contrast, those who maintained a rigidly traditional division of labor in the home typically went their separate ways when they sought social interaction outside the home, the women gravitating to their female relatives and the men to their cronies at the local pubs. As often happens when a study comes up with a tidy finding that makes good common sense, subsequent research has failed to support Bott's hypothesis. The relationship between internal family structure and external network structure appears to be more complex than Bott first imagined (for reviews and examples of such studies, see Bott, 1971, pp. 248-330; Gordon & Downing, 1978; Lee, 1979; Richards, 1980; Morris, 1985; and Rogler & Procidano, 1986).

In another, quite differently conceived investigation of the links between family structure and network structure, McAllister and his colleagues (1973) examined the impact of having a developmentally retarded child on the extrafamilial transactions of the parents. They found that the presence or absence of a retarded child made no difference at all in the family members' relationships with formal systems, but that it did influence informal visiting patterns. The parents of retarded children maintained considerably less contact with neighbors and somewhat less contact with relatives and co-workers than did other families. They observed that a gradient seemed to operate so that families withdrew from social contact most in the neighborhood "where the retarded child is most visible" and least in formal settings where the fact of having such a child may be kept literally out of view (pp. 97-98).

A similar phenomenon was observed by Zimmerman and Broderick (1954, 1956). In a decade that assigned only slightly less stigma to divorce than to arrest, these researchers found that families who had suffered either humiliation had smaller networks than did stigma-free families. In the case of the Zimmerman and Broderick findings, only longitudinal investigation could determine whether the smaller network contributed to the family deviance or the other way around, but in the McAllister study, the sense of shame undoubtedly prompted the social withdrawal.

Despite these intriguing and scattered findings, the complex interactions between the characteristics of particular family systems and the characteristics of their intimate networks remain poorly understood. One approach adopted by those investigating the matter has been to examine the apparent *functions* of close networks for families— shades of Parsons's structural functional analyses! By comparing families with rather full networks to relatively isolated families, researchers adopting this conceptual mode have identified at least four functions of the intimate network: (1) They typically provide family members with opportunities for *relaxed, nonjudgmental companionship*; (2) somewhat paradoxically, they appear to provide *protective and regulatory surveillance* by checking up on the family member's welfare and on his or her conformity to the network's standards of taste and conduct; (3) they are an important source of *emotional and material support* in time of need; and (4) they provide *linkages with the resources of the larger community*.

Providing opportunities for relaxed, nonjudgmental companionship. In a fascinating series of studies, Reed Larson and Mihaly Csikszentmihalyi, together with their colleagues, have tracked the quality of shared experiences over the family life cycle. They were able to convince a substantial sample of adolescents and adults to carry electronic beepers for two weeks and to record not only what they were doing but also their subjective states (i.e., how they were feeling) every time the beepers sounded (approximately seven times a day at irregular intervals).

From the data collected (see Larson & Bradney, 1988), they were able to draw several provocative conclusions about the quality of interactions with friends as compared to interactions with family members at various ages. Adolescents managed to spend two or three times as many hours in leisure pursuits with their network of peers as their older married siblings and parents were able to arrange. Probably no one was surprised to discover that these experiences with their friends were associated mostly with feelings of openness, freedom, common goals, positive response, humor, acceptance, and excitement. Although these feelings were not entirely foreign to the family environment, they were experienced far less frequently there and were balanced with virtually equal incidence of discord and disharmony. What may have been a less expected finding was that exactly the same pattern was observed among the adults. For them also, the intimate network was a far more frequent setting for experiencing openness, sharing, acceptance, and excitement than was the family. Larson and Bradney write:

> There are undoubtedly long-term satisfactions in being a parent, but they are not visibly manifest in the immediate moment. . . . [As for the husband-wife relationship in later life, the] average state of older adults when they are alone with their spouses is remarkably low; it is not that much different than they report when they are completely alone. (1988, pp. 119, 122)

At any age, then, in the company of friends, one's thoughts are wont to transcend the mundane problems and limitations of everyday life, indulge in playfulness, consider ideas, and explore the wider scope of human affairs.

Another finding of this study, informally observed for millennia but never before scientifically documented, was that weekend teenage peer interactions often escalate into a runaway spiral that Larson and Bradney called *careening enjoyment*:

> Freedom, openness, and mutual supportiveness provide the structure of a positive feedback system. . . . [Figure 5.1] shows [the] increasing excitement as the night progresses, but it is coupled with the increasing loss of any feeling of control. . . . Continual positive exchange fuels enjoyment, and without moderating feedback the group careens without limit. Thus it is not surprising that delinquency, unanticipated sexual intercourse and other spontaneous actions evolve out of interactions among adolescent friends. (1988, pp. 113-114)

This pattern was not observed among the adults in their sample, but most observers of the human scene would agree that the phenomenon of careening enjoyment is not restricted to a single age group.

Providing protective and regulatory surveillance. Paradoxically, the first function of the intimate friend network is nonjudgmental acceptance

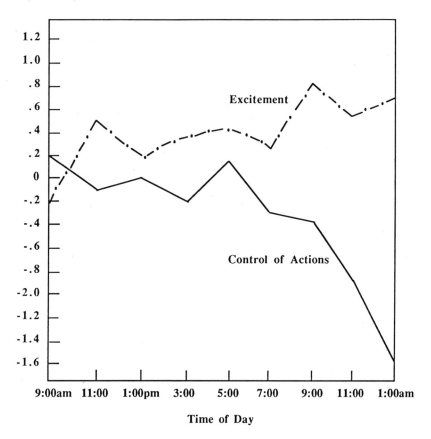

Figure 5.1. The Path of Experience With Friends on the Weekend
From Larson and Bradney (1988, p. 113) with permission

and the mutual expression of relatively untrammeled backstage behaviors, while the second function is regulatory; that is, enforcing the
norms of the group (together with looking out for one another's
welfare). One foundational truth of human interaction, however, holds
that agents of social control—whether they be parents, teachers, therapists, or friends—cannot expect success in their attempts to influence
anyone until after they have established rapport with them. And the
key steps in establishing rapport with anyone are (1) paying attention
to them; (2) accepting their behavior, feelings, and perceptions non-
judgmentally; and (3) expressing warmth toward them. Only when these
steps have occurred and a bond of rapport is established will anyone be

likely to respond to attempts to influence or change them. (See Broderick, 1983, for a full exposition of this principle as it pertains to therapeutic interventions.)

Of course, in the case of teenagers, the values and standards of their peer group are likely to be in conflict with those of the mainline adult culture. One ought not expect youth networks to demand adherence to society's norms, but to demand it to their own. The measure of their success is the extraordinary level of conformity in dress, language, opinion, and behavior that is achieved among them. Recognizing the power of peer influence, parents work hard to channel their children into settings where (they hope) their own core beliefs are prevalent. Good evidence suggests that the desired outcome (children's effective incorporation of their parents' values) depends almost entirely on whether the approved setting does indeed provide peer reinforcement rather than mere institutional indoctrination.

The impact of peer influence on the important life decisions of youth is further illustrated by the series of studies that have found that the probability of a young person involving themselves in some activity counter to the adult norm increases approximately 10 to 15% for each intimate friend who participates in that activity. (See, for example, the Schulz et al., 1977, study of premarital sexual behavior among college students.) Mutual reinforcement and monitoring is, of course, also a fundamental part of the fabric of adult networks. The same close friends and relatives who joke, laugh, and play with them also *check* on them, in both senses of that word. That is, these friends and relatives check not only on how one another are faring in the world (as in "Hi! Just dropped by to see how you were doing"), but they also check on whether they are operating within the acceptable range of behavior. In short, they tend to be nosy and interfering as well as caring and helpful. Only they have the standing to say out loud what others may think to themselves, sometimes with tact and sometimes as bluntly as a hammer. "Alec, I hate to butt in, but you've got that little boy terrified of you. There's just no need to yell at him like that," or "Michelle, honey, have you ever tried your hair pulled back like so? Why don't you check it out in the mirror and see if you don't think it thins your face down a little." Sometimes the negative observation is coupled with an offer to help, "I know, I know, some days are just like that. Listen, why don't we get the boys in here to give us a hand. We've got just enough time to get this place picked up before Terry gets home."

With respect to their functions of monitoring, maintaining, and, where necessary, restoring the family's social conformity and well-being, networks may be rated as *more effective* or *less effective*. Almost four decades ago, Carle Zimmerman, Lucius Cervantes, and I began a series of studies of urban networks (Zimmerman & Broderick, 1954, 1956; Zimmerman & Cervantes, 1960; Cervantes, 1965). All of us found that both the number of close friends of the target families and the degree to which they shared their values and backgrounds predicted the effectiveness of the network. Friends who came from quite different religious and regional backgrounds and who shared few political or economic perspectives had virtually no effect on the family's probability of getting a divorce, having a child drop out of school or become delinquent, and so on. Also, close associates who themselves had experienced these problems were less "protection" against them than others. These observations led Zimmerman to the socially and ethically objectionable recommendation that families who wished to avoid these problems should shun the company of those who had them. This rhetorical posture probably explains, at least in part, why these rather substantial pioneering studies of family networks went out of print quickly and are virtually ignored in reviews of the research on the subject.

Reiss and Costell (1976) provided a less provocatively packaged finding: The effectiveness of networks is enhanced if the members are richly interconnected with one another, which provides more coherence and focus to their influence. Although close friends' and relatives' efforts to bring the family back into line with community values may sometimes be experienced as noxiously intrusive rather than helpful, on balance, the evidence shows that families whose network connections expose them to this type of surveillance are better off than families without strong ties. One series of studies (reviewed by Broderick, 1992, pp. 320-321) showed that socially isolated parents tend to be far less effective in their parenting skills, more likely than others to be involved in incest and child abuse, and to have children who drop out of school or become delinquent, even when socioeconomic factors are controlled. They also are more likely to indulge in spouse abuse, to experience stress and depression, and, eventually, to divorce.

But one also can be *overly* involved with the members of one's network to the detriment of relationships inside the family. Also possible is that high levels of network involvement are correlated with antisocial behavior such as violence and incest if the core values of the network itself are antisocial.

One final point: We should not assume that all networks or network members share the same point of view on important matters. Ample evidence suggests that when people find themselves flirting with some behavior that may be contrary to the values of some members of their established network, they are quite likely to restructure their network and enrich it with friends who *are* supportive of the intended behavior. This process has been observed in a wide variety of circumstances, such as an individual anticipating intentional childlessness, adultery, divorce, or, change of religion or life-style. Family members may also develop specialized subnetworks for specialized subsectors of their lives. Alcoholics may have their drinking or Alcoholics Anonymous buddies (or both); the genealogists, their coenthusiasts; the athletes, their teammates; and so forth.

Emotional and material support. One curiosity of the history of research on family-kin-friend networks is that, without the benefit of communication among the investigators, the three pioneering studies of the 1950s each focused on a different but complementary aspect of the phenomenon. As we have seen, Bott (1955) addressed the question of husbands' and wives' leisure companions, while Zimmerman and his colleagues (1954, 1956, 1960) were concerned with the regulatory and support functions of close family associates. The third set of pioneering researchers in this field comprised Marvin Sussman (1953) alone and with his associate Lee Burchinal (Sussman & Burchinal, 1962a, 1962b). Their interest was in mutual help patterns between parents and their married children. These and later studies (for example, Adams, 1964, 1968; Wellman, 1979; Cheal, 1983; Rossi & Rossi, 1990) demonstrated that kin turned first to one another in time of need. Their help included physical assistance (for example, in baby-sitting, providing transportation, or giving a hand in moving, redecorating, or maintaining the homeplace), material support (loans and gifts of money and needed items, cosigning notes for large purchases, and so on), and emotional support.

As Cheal (1983) and Rossi and Rossi (1990) have demonstrated, the rule is that intergenerational help is reciprocal but sharply asymmetrical over nearly the whole course of the life cycle. As long as the older generation has the resources, it will give more often and more generously than it receives. The net flow reverses only toward the very end of life and then only in those areas of giving that are beyond the aging parents' resources and capacity. Two families are more likely to exchange support if they live near each other, if the interactions between them are positive in tone rather than conflicted, and if they have an established visiting pattern. Such exchanges occur among families of every social level and ethnicity, although the details of the pattern may vary. Poor families may trade food stamps, tools, rent money, and clothes

(Stack, 1974), while families at the other end of the social scale may provide a close relative the down payment for a home (Wellman, 1979).

The importance of a safety net of supportive friends and relatives in time of real need can scarcely be overstated. In Kay McChesney's in-depth study of street families (1987), in many cases, little difference was seen between their backgrounds and original circumstances and those of comfortably housed blue-collar workers—except that when financial reverses came they had no effective support network that was accessible to them. One of the most involving patterns of reciprocal help is for relatives or intimate friends to move in with one another, to pool virtually all of their resources. Although we have no good records of how common this pattern may be among friends, Beck and Beck's 1989 paper on their longitudinal study of family living arrangements reported that between one-fourth and one-third of white households and fully two-thirds of black households included extended kin at some point over the study's 15-year life-span.

Linkages with the resources of the larger community. Carle C. Zimmerman (1947) has suggested that the great civilizations of the world seem to have a natural sequence of formats for families to relate both to one another and the larger society. Early in its history, a civilization tends to be organized into clans, large groupings of related families that regulate their own internal affairs and relate to the outside world as a unit. Zimmerman called this the *trustee* family mode, because each individual family viewed itself as a trustee for the welfare of the entire clan, not only for its current incorporation but also for its previous and later forms. Gradually, the growth of central government and state religion encroached on clan's the authority, and a second type of relationship between families and external systems emerged; Zimmerman called this the *domestic mode.*

As its name implies, the key unit in this modality is the independent domestic household, which consists generally of an older male head, his wife and dependent children, and perhaps other dependent relatives such as spinster sisters and widowed mothers-in-law, as well as, in many cases, hired hands, apprentices, house servants, and the like. Because the father held such power in this arrangement, the domestic mode is also called the *patriarchal* mode.

Gradually, this family format yielded also to a still less restrictive arrangement. The growing powers of the state encroached upon the powers of fathers. Human rights derived directly from the state and not from particular family membership. Fathers' behavior toward their wives and children became the subject of law and public surveillance. Women's rights and children's rights increased dramatically. Free marriage (or union without marriage), birth control, abortion, and no-fault divorce put individuals in charge of their own affairs. Wives and children could get jobs in the economy or find support through the welfare system, independent of patriarchal control. Zimmerman called this the *atomistic* mode in reference to the freedom of each individual or "atom" to determine its own fate and to make its own way in the outside world. Although the shift in modalities from trustee to atomistic is far advanced in Europe and North America, clan organization is still prevalent in many Third World societies and therefore may still be encountered even in the West among immigrant populations. In their classic study of French Canadian workers at a turn-of-the-century New England cotton mill, Hareven and Langenbach (1978) found the following:

> Textile work was family work. . . . Workers often tended to bring in members of their family or ethnic group to fill job openings in their work rooms. Even after the opening of a centralized employment office, hiring through kin continued. . . . Most new workers learned their jobs from friends or relatives. [They] would act as translators and would often protect the new arrivals from abuse by bosses or fellow workers. Moreover, once one family member was established in a particular department, others would follow. For example, if one family member was a weaver, the others tended to flock to the weave room; if one was a spinner, others were likely to become spinners. (p. 118)

Exactly the same pattern has been observed in studies of contemporary immigrant groups from Asia, Latin America, and the Near East (see, for example, Kibria, 1987, 1989). Immigration and resettlement from Third World countries to the United States continues to be structured by clan and village ties.

Once the hardy pioneers have settled in, virtually all subsequent immigrants come as compadres. They may receive financial help and be put in contact with the proper authorities or illegal smugglers; they may be passed along from "station" to "station" in the clan network and then move in with clan members at their destination. Through clan connections, they find a more permanent residence, extract a driver's license from the state bureaucracy, and find work with the employers of other relatives or perhaps take their place in the informal, extralegal economy as a part of an immigrant-run enterprise. What is observed in full flower among these immigrant groups with their quasi-trustee types of patterns of family organization can also be observed on a more limited basis among the domestic cum atomistic family networks of the predominant culture. Thoroughly acculturated American parents still give their children jobs in the family business or arrange their summer employment through kin-friend networks.

In summary, then, studies of the functionality of strong-tie networks have found evidence that they may perform an impressive variety of important functions for their members. Small wonder that the family without such a network is severely disadvantaged. But as important as they are, intimate networks of close friends and immediate kin are by nature far too constricted to bridge well to the more distant reaches of the surrounding social world. For this purpose, research has shown that a family must marshal the resources of its far more extensive weak-tie network.

Weak-Tie Networks

Although family members seldom can count on more than a handful of truly committed, intimate friends and relatives (and sometimes none at all), virtually every member of every family has an extensive network of more casual friends and acquaintances. In "The Strength of Weak Ties," Granovetter (1983) demonstrated that these loose webs of association provide each family's chief connections to the surrounding larger world. These webs provide the medium of rumor; of fashion in speech, clothes, and opinion; and of social influence. Most often, through this network rather than through direct exposure to print or video media, people learn of job openings and government programs that are pertinent to their welfare. Through this network, rather than through listings in the Yellow Pages, they are most likely to choose their doctor and car mechanic and hair dresser, their bookie or housekeeper or therapist or divorce lawyer.

All networks are not equal, although they may be equally important to all. Among the poor, survival may depend on well-functioning connections. Among the affluent, power and influence and professional or business success may depend on the quality of the carefully nurtured "old boy" or "old girl" network. But, by nature, weak ties are not restricted to a single social level. In many cases, they cross the barriers that separate social strata and ethnic groupings.

In addition to the natural, complex matrix of acquaintanceships that grows out of everyday interactions among people of all sorts, some individuals specialize in providing an effective linkage between, for example, the Latino and the African-American community, or between the new Asian immigrant community and the city fathers and mothers, or between Catholics and Jews. By becoming recognized as the person who can arrange contact with the "other" group, such specialists accrue power and influence. In fact, one could argue that one of the chief requirements for power and influence in any community is a well-cultivated access to others who control valuable information or resources. The old saw may be true: "It is *who* you know, not *what* you know that matters most."

In a very real sense, all family systems are connected to one another through the medium of weak ties. Some theorists have estimated (and partly demonstrated) that no family on earth is more than 12 links away from any other family (see, for example, Killworth, Bernard, & McCarty, 1984).

Transactions With Formal Systems

There is no dearth of research on family transactions with formal organizations such as the workplace, the marketplace, or the school. Much of it is at the macrolevel of analysis, but excellent integrative reviews also have focused on microlevel exchange (for examples, see Piotrkowski, Rapoport, & Rapoport's 1987 comprehensive survey of the research on the reciprocal influences of family and work, and Bronfenbrenner's 1979 systems theoretic analysis of the intersection of family and school). In the following paragraphs, we will be able only to outline some of the more pertinent contributions of these substantial literatures.

The Family and the Workplace

Perhaps no two sets of social systems in our society have more obvious mutual impact upon each other than the family system and the various occupational systems in which its members are involved on a daily basis. At least three types of reciprocating effects have been identified. First, family and occupational systems compete head on for the limited time, energy, and loyalty of the same individuals. How family members are affected by these tensions at both home and work has been the subject of many studies and also has generated a great deal of rhetorical comment. Second, we have *spillover*, which is the transfer of mood, style of interaction, and acquired skills between work and home settings. Third, in addition to these two types of direct effects, we have indirect effects that are of at least equal importance. The family living space, material possessions, life-style, educational opportunities, and social standing in the community are all substantially determined by family members' occupational placement and income; these in turn influence that placement and that income. In the traditional domestic family, the father's employment was preeminent in setting the economic and social level for the entire family. In today's more atomistic world, that level is more likely to be set by the joint incomes of both parents or the wages of a single mother, perhaps augmented by child-support payments or welfare.

Competition for Time, Energy, and Loyalty

Time. The competition between work and family does not take place in a zero-sum system—that is, a system in which all hours are allocated *either* to work *or* to family and where every additional hour allocated to one necessarily requires one less hour for the other. We also spend time in sleeping, eating, and grooming; in leisure pursuits; in socializing with friends; in church activities; and in athletics and night school. When work or family demands fluctuate, at least some of the impact is absorbed by adjustments in the time dedicated to some of these other activities. For example, studies show that mothers who accept full-time employment must reduce their time commitments to sleeping, eating, gardening, socializing, watching television, and, of course, housework. But both research and common observation affirm that major changes in the time demands of work also significantly affect the availability of time for family relationships and activities.

Dramatic shifts in the temporal demands of families also echo in the workplace. For the most obvious example, women tend to drop out of the work force for some period following childbirth, and observers have noted that the reabsorption of unemployed or retired husbands into the domestic routine is often challenging. Perhaps the largest number of studies on this matter has focused on the personal and interpersonal strain induced by this competition. Each relationship that involves individuals who are members of the two competing systems must negotiate the division and allocation of their limited resources of time. In their review of this literature, Greenhaus and Beutell (1985) note the wealth of empirical evidence that suggests that when either system is particularly intrusive or demanding, the level of strain, both within the individual and within involved relationships, is certain to increase.

On the work side, stress has been shown to increase in occupations that require long and irregular hours, unconventional scheduling (as with shift work), travel, or regular intrusions into family space (as with ministers, on-call physicians, and people who conduct business from their homes). On the family side, families with a surplus of dependent members (young children, ailing parents, handicapped or ill members), or a deficit of competent adults (single parent families with no effective strong-tie backup) are at special risk. Uncertain schedules and ambiguous expectations are particularly challenging because of the difficulty in designing family or workplace rules that are flexible enough to accommodate these schedules smoothly. Within each system, each person's allocation of time and experience of overload is affected by the time allocations of other members of the system. At work, the newest employee may have to work weekends and holidays so that others with more seniority can participate more fully in family activities at these specially valued times. Or an aspiring young professional may have to work extra hours to compete for a limited number of senior slots. Or the proprietors of a "mom and pop store" may have to work much longer and harder to replace the son or daughter who has left the family business to pursue a higher education, let alone earning enough extra money to cover the child's tuition.

In the home, a woman's level of stress has been shown to be as much a function of her husband's work schedule as her own (Keith & Schafer, 1980). Evidence also suggests that when both husband and wife are engaged in demanding careers, neither is likely to compete well with men who have a full-time, unemployed wife to support them in their demanding life-style.

Energy and loyalty. If time is a limited commodity and thus the object of competing demands, then energy and loyalty are even more so. We lump energy and loyalty together because our loyalty is generally judged by how we spend our energy. The consequences of overextended demands on these finite resources are tension, anxiety, fatigue, depression, apathy, and irritability. Most studies have confined themselves to examining the impact of stress generated in one setting on the other. Thus, Greenhaus and Beutell (1985) reviewed several findings that showed that both conflict at work and dissatisfaction resulting from unchallenging employment or career blockage generate tensions in the marital and parent-child dyads. Similarly, family troubles have been identified as a major factor in absenteeism and poor work performance.

On the other hand, research also shows that support in one sphere may translate into better performance in the other. For example, when spouses of either sex actively support their mates' careers, both the mate and the career prosper. Similarly, employment settings that are flexible and responsive to the demands of family emergencies have

been shown to promote higher morale, at least among female employees. Unfortunately, only a few studies have attempted to examine the
reciprocal processes that surge back and forth between the two settings
as they compete for the energy and loyalty of their shared members.

Spillover: The Transfer of Mood, Style,
and Competencies Between the Workplace and the Family

One of the fundamental assumptions of sociologists since the time
of Tönneis and Weber has been that interactions in the family are
governed by rules that are the polar opposites of those that shape
relationships in the occupational sphere. The culturally prescribed
coping mechanism for those who must shift back and forth between
these opposing styles nearly every day of their lives is to interpose a
sort of air lock between them so that the incompatible atmospheres
will not pollute each other's environment. Pearlin and Schooler (1978)
found this strategy, which they call *disengagement*, to be the most
effective available to commuters between the two worlds. Yet as we
observed in the previous section, real life offers a continual intermix-
ture and confrontation between these two supposedly segregated
realms. This well-documented point is nicely illustrated by Bolger and
his associates (1989), who found that, for both sexes, the best predictor
for getting into a quarrel with one's spouse was having already had a
quarrel with co-workers that same day. They also found that whereas
both sexes were equally likely to bring work-generated tensions home
with them, it was husbands, not wives as some might have supposed,
who were more likely to bring home-generated tensions to work with
them. One of the most interesting of their findings was that when men
experienced increases in tension at work, women's tension around
housework increased, which led the researchers to conclude that women
under these circumstances attempted to relieve some of their husband's
emotional load by taking an increased responsibility for the work he
might ordinarily feel responsible for at home. Some authors have
called this *crossover* rather than spillover because the effect is indirect,
transferring the stress from one partner to the other.

The transfer of other moods and styles of interaction besides those
that reflect stress also have received some research attention. In most
cases, the researchers have traced the spillover from the workplace to
the family, but a few have also investigated the flow in the other direction.
The empirical evidence strongly supports this observation: No matter
what the category of behavior studied, how people act at work and
how they behave at home are mutually contingent. As Rosabeth Kanter

wrote in 1977, "if the emotional climate at work can affect families, so can a family's emotional climate and demands affect members as workers" (p. 56). Crouter (1984) has elaborated the concept of spillover to include not only the transfer of mood, energy level, and interpersonal style between the two systems, which he calls *psychological spillover*, but also a second category of exchange that comprises technical and interpersonal knowledge, perspectives, and skills, and which he calls *educational spillover*. Although no thoughtful person would disagree with the premise that the chains of influence between these systems are reciprocal and circular, as we have noted, convention has led to the study of *either* psychological spillover from the workplace to the home setting *or* spillover in the other direction (see Piotrkowski et al., 1987, for a comprehensive review of the two approaches). Thus, we have had studies of the consequences of marital tensions and conflict for job performance and other studies of the effects of job-related tension and dissatisfaction on marital morale, but no study of the reciprocal process that links these two sets of variables.

Similarly, the impact of fathers' (Kohn, 1977; Coburn & Edwards, 1976) and mothers' (Morgan, Alwin, & Griffin, 1979; Piotrkowski & Katz, 1982) working conditions on their styles of parenting has been extensively investigated by one set of scholars, while the consequences of certain parenting styles on the career paths of both men and women have been studied by an entirely separate set of researchers. What is true for studies of psychological spillover is equally true for the smaller set of studies on educational spillover. In effect, Crouter (1984) argues in favor of a linear model for the family-to-workplace transfer of skills and disciplines. He points out that most of a worker's job-relevant resources were acquired many years earlier in the process of socialization in the family of orientation. Because of the time lag, a truly reciprocating process would not seem to apply.

Although Crouter's argument has some merit, we prefer the model developed by Ulrich and Dunne (1986), which focuses equally on the relevance of workers' childhood and contemporary family experiences. This conceptualization leaves room for both time-lag effects and current exchanges. Less research has been done on the other half of the exchange, the transfer of skills and disciplines from the workplace to the home. Although it is proverbial that the shoemaker's children go barefoot and that marital therapists have the rockiest marriages, reciprocal transfers seem evident. The boundary mechanisms by which some people insulate the two spheres more completely than others have not yet been identified.

Family Business and Family Businesses

We have discussed the workplace and the home as though they were mutually exclusive. This approach is the most common one taken by family process theorists in their discussions of linkages between the two systems. In reality, the situation is more complicated. Families may engage in at least five different types of economic activities as they struggle to meet the challenges of economic survival: (1) *earning wages,* the category that is least likely to occur in the family home; (2) *market sales,* which may take place anywhere and in many cases may be home-based; (3) *rent* or *investment* (i.e., money generated by ownership of assets rather than by production or exchange), which also is often managed directly by the family from its own premises; (4) *transfers* (sometimes called *grants* or *gifts*) from public or private sources, which also are received directly by the family in its own territory; and (5) *subsistence*— that is, the economic productivity and provision of services by family members that is dedicated directly to the maintenance of the household, such as growing one's own food, making one's own clothes or furniture, and building or remodeling one's own home (also included are ongoing tasks such as home management, home nursing, child care, home and car repairs, yard work, food preparation, shopping, and so on); by definition, these important economic activities take place in the home.

One special case deserves particular mention because it defines the limits of family-workplace boundary sharing. For a substantial number of families, the bills are paid through the joint operation of a family business. (For a full discussion of family businesses, although not from a systems perspective, see Rosenblatt, De Mik, Anderson, & Johnson, 1985; Ward, 1987; and current issues of the *Family Business Review,* published by Jossey-Bass.) The exact dynamics of such organizations vary. One very common pattern retains the structure of Zimmerman's domestic family style. It features a patriarchal head or a partnership of brothers with wives assigned to vital but often subordinate positions in the financial, public relations, or office-management side of the business. Children are motivated by the promise of eventual inheritance, and from their earliest years are directed to "learn the business from the ground up." As youths, they may end up doing much of the common labor in the organization, rising to more responsible positions only as they are judged ready for it. Whether organized in this patriarchal format or according to some more egalitarian or female-centered model, the stress points tend to be found where familial and business rules of interaction come into confrontation.

The Family and Other Formal Systems

This volume's scope cannot include a review of all of the work that has been done by scholars from a wide variety of disciplines on the connections between family systems and other social systems such as the school, the church, and the community.

First, most research and theory on these connections do not employ a process perspective. Exceptions certainly exist, and we may instructively look at a single example of the sort of work that holds great promise for the future of this part of the theory. Urie Bronfenbrenner (1979, 1986) is perhaps the most felicitous example of a scholar who has developed a systems-based theory of transactions between a family member (in this case, the developing child) and non-family systems. He concerns himself with how children's development is reciprocally related to all of the elements in their *ecosystem*, that is, in their environment. He develops separate propositions for their interactions within their *microsystems* (face-to-face relationships in their families or peer groups), their *mesosystems* (face-to-face relationships in more formal organizations such as schools, scout programs, churches, and employment settings) and their *exosystems* (significant external systems in which they do not directly participate but which have significant indirect effects on them—and which they may also indirectly affect— such as their parents' places of employment or government agencies).

Bronfenbrenner has the rare capacity to discuss complex multi-system transactions without losing his reader. For example, in his reanalysis of Ogbu's 1974 ethnographic study of the school system in one of the poorer sections of Stockton, California, Bronfenbrenner (1979, pp. 250ff) makes the following observations:

- Students' performance at the school is partly a function of their parents' relationship to the school. Parents who are members of low-status minorities have little influence on school policies or practices; as a result, there is a poor fit between these and their perceptions of their children's needs.
- Low-status parents have little influence because (1) they are less likely than middle-class parents to visit their children's schools or local meetings of the school board; and (2) when they do attempt to participate in the school system, they find their opinions ignored, partly because they are viewed as "nontaxpayers" (i.e., not property owners) and partly because their representation is inevitably female because of the values of the ethnic groups they come from, which hold that school business is "women's work" (in contrast to "taxpayer" groups, which frequently include males, a power advantage in a society with deeply rooted patriarchal biases).

- School authorities, believing that these low-status mothers have little of interest or importance to say, make their communication with them unidirectional.
- Unlike their middle-class counterparts, these parents thus come to believe that school policies and practices are decided at a level remote from their influence. Even if school rules and curricula are sometimes ill-suited to their children's interests or needs, nothing can be done about it. The research shows that these parents do urge their children to attend regularly, mind their teachers, and try to do well, but they unwittingly also communicate to them that the schools are a foreign institution in which they are fortunate even to hold their own, let alone excel.
- The children meet the expectations of their parents (and their teachers).

This sequence, although based on actual observations and interviews in the community, is doubtless an oversimplified outline of the relations that link children's performance and their family's position in the larger social system. Nevertheless, in the language Bronfenbrenner has adopted, this outline still identifies some of the events in the child's exosystem that help shape his or her transactions with the school mesosystem. (For another approach to investigating the real-time experience of mothers as they attempt to negotiate the parent-child-school triangle, see feminist scholar Dorothy Smith's, *The Everyday World as Problematic*, 1987, Chapter 5).

The Family and the Media

Without question, the media are among the most pervasive purveyors of ideas, information, and images from the external world into the interior of the family. Newspapers and all of the other print media, radio programs, and all of the other audio media each have their influence. But every study affirms that watching television is the chief joint "activity" of families at each stage of the life cycle. Ninety-eight percent of American families own a television set (67% own more than one), and the set is turned on an average of seven hours per day (Broadcast/Cable Yearbook for 1989 as cited in Andreasen, 1990). As Goodman succinctly stated, "The family system can be seen to include the family unit and the television. Family members interact with each other and with the television, both individually and as a family unit" (1983, p. 408). A wealth of data are available on this topic, most gathered by students of the media rather than by students of the family. Excellent reviews of this literature are available in sources such as Bryant's edited volume, *Television and the American Family* (1990) and Huston and associates' collection of review articles in *Big World, Small Screen* (1992).

Television (and, to a lesser extent, other media) occupy a peculiar position with respect to family boundary maintenance. The usual selective vigilance that most families exercise in excluding external influences that challenge family values and world views seem to be substantially relaxed in the case of many media. Moreover, the selective *zonal defense* by which families admit strangers only into the outer frontstage arenas of family activities and restrict the inner backstage sanctuary to trusted intimates is rendered altogether inoperative in this case. Media products are received directly into the heartland of the family, into the most intimate zones of interaction. In view of this, studies show the most remarkable fact: Supervision over who watches what is absolutely minimal. In fact, studies of children's viewing habits show that they see more violence and sex while watching with their parents than when watching "unchaperoned" (McLeod, Atkin, & Chaffee, 1972).

Television's impact on family consumer attitudes and transactions in the marketplace have been the most frequently studied issue, followed by investigations of whether and under what conditions television violence engenders violent behavior in children. A host of other topics that might be of greater interest to family process scholars have been less thoroughly investigated, among them, the suppression of alternative family interactions. As Bronfenbrenner once wrote:

> Like the sorcerer of old, the television set casts its magic spell, freezing speech and action and turning the living into silent statues so long as the enchantment lasts. The primary danger of the television screen lies not so much in the behavior it produces as the behavior it prevents—the talks, the games, the family festivities and arguments through which much of the child's learning takes place and his character is formed. (Bronfenbrenner, 1979, p. 242)

Whether one shares Bronfenbrenner's implicit disapproval of the preemptive role of television watching as a family activity, clearly study of this phenomenon offers much opportunity as a window into the dynamics of family bounding and bridging.

Summary of the Bounding-Bridging Dynamic

Like all living and social systems, families are selectively open systems. They expend energy in the *bounding* process, protecting family space, time, and possessions, as well as family members at home and abroad, family life-styles, and family world views. As part of this process, they also invest energy in attempting to maintain the loyalties of their members and the integrity of their assets.

Families differ in the styles of operation they adopt in these matters. Some, for example, may give high priority to defending their boundaries with a plethora of quite detailed and unbending rules about who or what may enter or leave and under what conditions. Others seem to be very relaxed about these matters and impose few restrictions on either members or outsiders. Some may be in a continual process of negotiation and debate about their bounding rules, while others take them entirely for granted.

In dynamic opposition to the bounding function, families also expend energy in selectively sponsoring transactions with external systems, the process we have called *bridging*. Many of these vital transboundary exchanges are with other members of informal networks. Through participation in *strong-tie* networks of close kin and intimate friends, family members are most advantageously positioned to receive nonjudgmental companionship, protective and regulatory surveillance, emotional and material support, and restricted but significant linkages to other important systems. Through participating in *weak-tie* networks of more casual friends, neighbors, co-workers, and acquaintances, they are advantaged in gaining ready access to the opinions and resources of the larger community. Other crucial transactions link the family to the formal worlds of employment, business, the marketplace, schools, churches, other organized groups, and the media.

The scope of these transactions is so vast and the bodies of scholarship concerning them so extensive that we explored only a few of them. The purpose of these brief excursions was primarily to indicate the promise that a more comprehensive exploration holds for the further development of family process theory.

CHAPTER 6

The Regulation of Vertical Space and Vertical Placement

The Vertical Dimension in Social Space

According to the observations of pioneering sociologist Max Weber, all societies are stratified; that is, in each society, some members are more powerful, control more property, and have greater prestige than others (1946). As the emergent barnyard leaders in Orwell's *Animal Farm* put it, "All pigs are equal, but some pigs are more equal than others." The three components of high status that Weber listed—power, property, and prestige—ordinarily go together. An individual, however, may be endowed with an abundance of one and, for various reasons, be lacking in the others. One thinks of the second-level general who may have enormous power over his troops but little property and fame, of the old and infirm widow who inherited enormous estates but has neither power nor recognition, and of the citizen videotaped risking his life to rescue a small child from a collapsed well, whose name became a household word for a brief time, but who had little power and less property.

Families relate to stratification in two ways. First, like other groups, they are internally stratified; at any given point in time, certain members are accorded more influence, have more ready access to valued resources, and receive more respect. Variations in the vertical structuring of families figured prominently in the theories of many of the early family therapists who helped give shape to process theory. Theodore Lidz and his associates (1957), Jay Haley (1971, 1976a, 1976b), and Salvador Minuchin (1974), for example, all granted vertical relationships among family members great significance as an explanation for how well the family functioned. The therapeutic interventions recommended by these pioneers involved challenging, and if possible, rearranging dysfunctional hierarchical patterns, empowering the parents vis-à-vis the children by strengthening the parental coalition and, if possible, by eliminating the parent-child, revolutionary coalition. (We shall have more to say about family coalitions later in the chapter.)

We should note that Gregory Bateson, one of the most influential of the founders of the family process movement, took exception to this approach on theoretical grounds. He argued that families are *not* hierarchically structured in any stable fashion and that the emphasis thus placed on the vertical structuring of family relationships by these therapists was ill-advised and antisystemic (1972). As we shall see, some evidence suggests that static models of family stratification may, indeed, be problematic from a process perspective. However, *how* family members are positioned on the vertical dimension has proved to be a generative issue in the family process literature. The next section of this chapter will concern itself with this issue.

Second, a family relates to stratification by occupying a particular place in the strata of the larger society. Over time, a family may improve its standing in the community, exhibit downward mobility, or maintain its place. Its own behaviors and transactions partly determine how it is ranked, and matters outside of its control also have influence, such as economic booms and busts, wars, natural disasters, changed political circumstances, and plant closings. This family relationship will be the focus of the final section of the chapter.

The Internal Stratification of the Family

At the core of the transcybernetic model of family decision making developed in Chapter 3 is the psychopolitical process. As noted there, this is the process by which individual members negotiate family action and policy. In the presentation of that model, any detailed consideration of the dynamics of inequalities, of the enactments of power and privilege, were explicitly deferred to this chapter. Here we must look not only at the hierarchical structuring of family rules that govern precedence, but also beyond them to the hierarchical structuring of the family membership itself. Is there a "pecking order" in families? If so, is it stable or changeable? Does it permeate all family interaction or is it manifested only under certain circumstances?

In families, as in other social groups, vertical structuring is revealed by observing what happens when the system confronts (1) conflicts of opinion or of interest (these correspond roughly to Weber's *power* issue), (2) competing demands on the limited resources of the family (these correspond roughly to Weber's *property* issue), and (3) struggles over the allocation of those less-tangible resources of esteem, respect, and affection (these correspond roughly to Weber's *prestige* issue).

Power in the Governance of Families

Power may be most simply defined as the ability to win contested decisions. A broader definition might include such issues as who is charged with carrying out decisions, who monitors this process, and who is accountable to whom.

Literally hundreds of studies have been done on family power, who wields it and at whose expense. The matter has turned out to be complicated and elusive. As a result, the scholarly literature on family power is voluminous, complex, and often contradictory (see Szinovacz, 1987, for a comprehensive review). The great majority of these studies are based on questionnaires that ask the respondent to report on who wins the most contested decisions in his or her family. Critics have noted several problems with this approach.

First, where two or more members have been asked to fill out the same questionnaire, an impressive correspondence in their reports has not been seen. Partly this results from each reporting from a different perspective and with a distinctive perceptual bias. Partly it results from the well-documented fact that people tend not to be accurate observers of the social processes in which they participate. Second, critics have noted that most of the questionnaires measure power by asking who usually makes decisions in a set number of areas. No consensus has emerged, however, as to whether the areas sampled in the various instruments actually represent the domain of significant family issues. Third, and more damaging still, is that the questionnaire format apparently is not flexible enough to capture the complex dynamics of actual decision-making processes.

Family process scholars have attempted to address these limitations through both methodological and conceptual contributions. They have avoided reliance on self-report and instead used a variety of observational or mixed observational and self-report approaches (Gilbert & Christensen, 1985). These more process-oriented observations have led to the conclusion that power is an emergent rather than a static quality of family interrelationships. The long-held premises that family members are vertically stratified in a stable, well-established pecking order is called into question by these data.

Process-oriented research seems to indicate that, in an ongoing system, the exact vertical positioning of any two members with respect to each other is constantly in flux in both clock and calendar time. New positioning is created in each interaction. To this extent, Bateson's concern that the family power structure tended to be overreified in the literature may be well founded. Of course, families vary as to their actual degree of vertical fluidity. In particular family dyads, the habitual dominance of one member over another across a variety of situations may indeed be observed. However, the assumption that such stable patterns of domination are characteristic of family relationships seems to be unwarranted. An enormous body of research based on this premise has failed to yield a coherent body of results. This systematic failure suggests a systematic flaw in the logic of the approach adopted by most investigators.

One important methodological and conceptual weakness in the power literature is shared by both questionnaire and observational approaches. In their attempts to get at the issue of relative power, researchers almost uniformly require family members to focus on incidents in which differences of opinion occurred *and were resolved*. This approach makes two implicit assumptions: (1) that significant differences of opinion are a frequent and universal feature of family process and (2) that these differences are routinely addressed and resolved. Both of these assumptions may be questioned. Families vary enormously in both the frequency and style of their conflicts (Klein & Hill, 1979). Also, the various dyads in the family are not equally prone to direct contests of will. This fact not only is evident through common observation, but also has been documented in several research studies. For example, in their study of 1,000 Midwestern families, Olson and his associates found that 50% listed family conflict as a major stressor during the stage of the family life cycle with preteen children and only 10% during the empty nest stage (Olson et al., 1983, p. 123).

The second assumption, that most cases of family conflict are seen through to some conclusion (which would permit the assessment of relative influence of the family members involved), has also been brought into question. The key to putting this matter in naturalistic perspective is to observe families in naturalistic settings rather than in contrived situations that require them to resolve a contested issue in a just a few minutes. Vuchinich (1985), for example, left an open microphone on the dining room table through the dinner hour in several homes and was successful in identifying 200 instances of naturally occurring family conflict. He found that fully two-thirds of them ended in *standoffs*, in which neither party yielded to the opinion of the other and the topic was finally and simply dropped. Of the remaining one-third, the most frequent response was *withdrawal*, in which one member of the conflicted pair refused to continue the discussion, in some cases leaving the table. By far the least common responses were *submission*, in which one party acknowledged being wrong or at least yielded to the other's demand or opinion, and *compromise*, the solution that all textbooks recommend. Only in these less common cases do we have even a basis for assessing the vertical ordering of family members on these occasions, much less in the general case.

I believe that any effort to resolve the problem of power in families must start with an analysis of the hierarchies of rules that undergird the stratification of the family membership. Chapter 3 suggested that these rules are organized into a four-level pyramid. At the bottom of the pyramid are *concrete rules and immediate goals*; at the next level, *metarules and goals* specify the conditions under which particular first-level rules and goals are implemented; above them are still more general *midrange policies* that govern family interactions in whole sectors of their joint life; and at the top is the most general, overarching *family paradigm*, which shapes all of the family's shared assumptions, expectations, and commitments. Let us consider each of these levels, starting with the most abstract level.

The Family Paradigm:
Defining the Family's Overall Style of Interaction

At the top of the hierarchy is that more or less integrated set of shared assumptions, expectations, and commitments that constitute each family's operational philosophy of governance. The entire tone and texture of family life are affected by this basic orientation (Reiss, 1981). Different authors have developed different typologies of family paradigms. For example, as discussed in Chapter 5, Constantine's model of the family universe (in press) includes four: random, closed, open, and synchronous. Reiss's 1981 typology also includes four paradigms (which are roughly comparable to Constantine's): consensus sensitive, distance sensitive, environment sensitive, and achievement sensitive.

At the risk of cluttering the conceptual marketplace, I should like to add my own quite different top-of-the-pyramid typology of family paradigms. In considering specifically the styles of family governance, 35 years of clinical practice has persuaded me that families employ three distinct approaches that correspond to Lawrence Kohlberg's three levels of moral reasoning: the competitive paradigm, the policy-governed cooperative paradigm, and the principled interaction paradigm (Broderick, 1975, in press; Kohlberg, 1969; Kohlberg & Turiel, 1973).

The Competitive Paradigm

In this style, each individual looks to his or her own welfare without concern for the welfare of other family members. Game theory distinguishes two different approaches to pursuing one's own benefit:

1. *Zero-sum* strategies, which are based on the assumption that any other player's gain is a loss to one's self because all are competing for the same limited resources and the total winnings across all players is always zero; and

2. *Mixed motive* approaches in which strategic cooperation with certain other players is seen as advantageous when pursuing one's own goals.

The Policy-Governed Cooperative Paradigm

In this style, individual family members consider themselves under the rule of policies that transcend individual will. Competition in limited arenas may be permitted and in some circumstances encouraged, but these are not no-holds-barred clashing of independent wills but rule-governed contests to see who can, for example, get their chores done first. Some policies specify directly the governing sets of rules and metarules that apply in each case. For example, "In this family there are bedtime rules for children according to their age. You are six; your bedtime is 8:30" or "In this family we are considerate of each other; it is considerate for each member to let the others know if he or she will be late for dinner." Some policies specify the rules for negotiating differences. "There is no need to yell at each other. Let's all take turns speaking" or "We'll talk about that later when everyone is here." And still others allocate authority for adjudicating differences. "It's Bobby's bike. You have to ask Bobby if you can borrow it" or "That's up to your mother. If she says you can go, you can go."

The Principled Interaction Paradigm

This style requires a fairly advanced level of personal maturity on the part of family members, because it depends on internalized principles of mutual respect, empathy, and equity rather than specific rules. Because the style is so demanding of family members, few families are likely to operate consistently at this level, although this style of interaction has been observed and must be included in any list of available formats for family governance.

Chapter 2 suggested that every set of rules (even metarules and policies) have finite ranges of circumstances within which they can operate with requisite variety. As we shall see in this chapter, outside of that range, family systems must modify existing rules and policies, generate new ones, or "punt"—that is, execute a default response.

One form of punt may be to kick the system up or down the styles-of-governance staircase. For example, when a principled family encounters a situation that does not yield to a principled solution even after its full range of available responses has been exhausted, its punt response might be to fall back on an earlier strategy of governance, namely, policy enforcement. Suppose an aged, incontinent parent is taken into the home and does not respond to the principled strategies of family governance typically employed there. Finding the entire range of principled approaches ineffective in eliciting the parent's cooperation, the beleaguered caretaker might resort to a regimen of rules, similar to the style of governance that, in earlier years, was effective in dealing with young children. Similarly, a policy-bound family, on discovering that its processes of rule making and rule enforcement are foundering in the face of intransigent willfulness, might be tempted to resort to a more primitive competitive or even coercive approach. (See Broderick, in press, for a fuller discussion of this cascading default or "punt down" process.)

On the other hand, some evidence suggests that families stuck in a never-ending competitive conflict may finally "punt up" to a more effective set of policies. Many years ago, Spiegel (1960), based on his clinical observations of families in conflict, noted that paired sets of competitive tactics and countertactics (such as attempting coercion and defying coercion, offering a bribe and refusing it, misrepresentation and unmasking the deceit, and negative evaluation and replying in kind), virtually always ended in standoffs. But some families eventually escaped these futile deadlocks through shifting to one or another of the following, more effective approaches: role-reversal (i.e., putting oneself in another's place), nonderisive humor, and mediation (inviting a third party to mediate the difference). Each tactic elevates the perspective of the participants to a metalevel and out of the valley of the contest of wills. This shift from competitive to cooperative tactics seems to be an example of a punt up.

Midrange Policies

Normative and emergent policies are midrange, sector-specific guidelines for governing family interaction in that sector of the system. They are *midrange* in that they are less generic than the overarching family paradigms discussed in the previous section, but they are still broad enough to subsume a wide range of specific sets of metarules and their derivative concrete directives. They are *sector-specific* because they pertain to only one of the several sectors of the family process domain (such as parent-child distance regulation or family fiscal policy).

Most discussions of policy imply a family consensus around some *normative* agreement. Normative policies may have been uncritically incorporated in their entirety from the larger society or they may have been hammered out in the psychopolitical crucible over a period of years. In either case, they represent what *should* govern family members' actions in a particular arena. In actual practice, of course, they are often ignored. For example, although a family has adopted a clear policy that each child is responsible for cleaning up his or her own room and participating in a fair share of the family's general chores, in fact only the mother attempts to enforce the policy, with the father usually absent and typically uninterested in the issue when he is home and the children giving it only the most perfunctory lip service.

Consistent with the argument made in Chapter 3, a better approach is to look for the unacknowledged *emergent* policy that can be observed to be the operative template for family performance in this area. This emergent policy, of course, results from the ongoing psychopolitical struggles around this issue.

Metarules

Metarules are more particular still. They specify the circumstances under which a specific, concrete, first-level rule will be brought into play. The character of the particular metarules employed in any given family is determined by the emergent policies governing that sector of the family's operations and, of course, by the general family paradigm that infuses all of its interactions. For example, in families who operate in the competitive mode, the assumption prevails that each person will be motivated primarily by his or her own interests and therefore the metarules for resolving differences include bargaining and exchange, manipulation, coalition formation, threats, promises, strategic misrepresentation, coercion, and preemptive moves (which operate from the premise that receiving forgiveness is easier than getting permission). In this format, premiums are placed on strength and cunning. Those who are bigger and stronger (generally older and usually male) are prone to rely on the former; those who are smaller and weaker (generally younger and usually female) are prone to rely on the latter.

The policy-governed family also assumes that each member is loyal to the family and its just policies. Differences are resolved by evoking the relevant policy (perhaps debating which policy *is* most relevant) and, in case none seem fully applicable to the case, by negotiating a new policy (following the family's rules for negotiation in the process). Who is biggest and strongest is much less of an issue here. Instead, the key questions concern whose rights are being infringed upon, who has legitimate authority to decide a matter, and what the proper procedure for resolving the difference might be. Age and gender may be as important here as in competitive families if these are the bases for allocating authority and rights. The ultimate appeal, however, is to neither brute strength nor skillful strategy, but to what is proper, right, fair, and agreed-upon.

Principled families begin with the premise that each member is committed to the commonweal and also has an investment in every other member's individual welfare. Given this premise, the metarules would prescribe that differences be resolved by discussions whose goal is to clarify the issues, share each person's perspective with the others, and determine which solutions would be most equitable and sensitive to each member's needs. Apparently, Spiegel's "more effective tactics" of role-reversal, nonderisive humor, and mediation are best categorized as examples of principled approaches to conflict. Thus, his punt up requires families to leap from zero-sum tactics to principled tactics in a single bound. Our hypothesis is that families do not skip a level when they punt up or down. However, only systematic observation of families in natural settings could determine whether family conflict resolution actually is able to progress from competitive to principled approaches only through attempts to invoke family policy as an intermediate step.

Every family has a large repertoire of very particular first-level rules that govern the conduct of members toward one another when differences arise between and among them. Different rules may call for physical confrontation, heated argument, appeals to authority, threats, yielding, defiance, placation, compromise, leaving the scene, changing the subject, or some other set of responses. Which of these will be called into play in a given instance is determined by the family's higher level rules.

Our argument is that virtually all studies of family power to this point have foundered because they ignored differences in the higher level rules of families, treating them as if they were uniformly operating on competitive assumptions. I am not surprised that these studies have found contradictory and inconclusive results. We must acknowledge that it remains an open question as to whether real families are as consistent in their styles of governance as suggested here. Perhaps most families are indeed mixed types, drawing on sets of rules that cut across the three major styles of governance. The matter can be resolved only with actual data. My belief is that a more textured, multilevel, and systemic approach will lead to crisper, more reliable findings.

The Distribution of Family Resources

One axiom holds that just as every family develops hierarchies of rules and policies for resolving conflicts of will, so every family develops hierarchies of rules and policies for allocating its limited resources. The earliest known empirical study of families was an 1855 investigation of the budgets of working-class families in France by Frederick Le Play (1935). Unhappily, this brave start never generated the major research effort that questions of power did. Even though money-related issues cause more family distress than any other concern at every stage of the family life cycle (Olson et al., 1983, p. 123), most family scholars and family therapists seem to have a blind spot in this area.

Happily, the past few years have shown evidence of a renewed scholarly interest in the financial arrangements within families and between families and their kin. The findings of these studies turn out to have significant implications for relational distance management within and between families and for bargaining advantage in the psychopolitical process (see, for example, the work of Blumstein & Schwartz, 1983; Wilson, 1987; Treas, 1988; Goldscheider & Goldscheider, 1988; Rossi & Rossi, 1990; and Millman, 1991). The task of incorporating these new data into a hierarchical, family process format has yet to be done.

I am not aware of comparable research on how other equally important family resources such as space, possessions, attention, and physical care are allocated among competing family members over the life
cycle. We have little empirical evidence concerning the range of typical
or the consequences of atypical patterns of distribution. The theory we
have reviewed, however, suggests certain patterns that future researchers
might wish to investigate. For example, one might hypothesize first
that, in competitive and especially in zero-sum competitive families,
those with more power would also control a greater share of the
family's scarce resources, and second, that this relationship would not
hold in policy-governed or principled families. The logic would be that
those with power in the competitive family would be more likely to
use it to meet their own needs, whereas in the other formats policy or
principle would allocate more resources to the neediest and least
productive members (young children, the handicapped, the aged, and
so on) than to more self-reliant and productive members.

Some information is available on the reciprocal question: How much
impact does differential access to income from external sources have
on a member's influence in family decision making? Several studies
of unemployed fathers have found that they are liable to lose status
and power in their families. Their wives decrease their verbal loyalty
to them as they discuss the families' difficult situation with other wives,
and their children are likely to become less respectful and less compli-
ant (Bakke, 1940; Liker & Elder, 1983; Larson, 1984). Evidence also shows
that when family organizational principles permit husbands and
wives to compete openly for power (as occurs in Western democracies), women are better off if they have independent income; but where
the organizational principles prescribe a rigid patriarchal power structure (as in several traditional societies), an independent income provides her with no advantage (Rodman, 1967, 1972).

The Allocation of Prestige

Like power and property, prestige is not a simple or unitary concept.
Before many conclusions can be drawn about how it is differentially
assigned to family members, both conceptual and operational clarifications probably will be required. Four decades ago, Robert F. Bales
(1950) studied the social processes that occurred in ad-hoc, task-oriented
small groups and found that the individual who emerged as the *task leader*
in a group was often not the same person as the *sociometric star* (or
expressive leader). The task leader first mobilized the group's efforts to

achieve their assigned goals, and the sociometric star took responsibility for maintaining good interpersonal relationships and promoting group morale. The former was viewed with *respect* by group members, while the latter was viewed with *affection*. Talcott Parsons (who had an office on the same floor as Bales in Harvard's Emerson Hall) quickly incorporated Bales's concept into his model of family process, assigning the role of task leader (which he renamed *instrumental leader*) to the father and expressive leader to the mother (Parsons & Bales, 1955). As noted in our discussion of Parsons's work in Chapter 1, this overly glib assignment by gender has drawn the criticism of many scholars over the years, including feminists, and it is scarcely noted today without derision. Independent of its gender connection, however, the idea remains a provocative one by suggesting that more than one prestige hierarchy may operate in a family and that the ranking for respect may be quite different from the ranking for affection.

Given how little is understood about hierarchies of power or of access to the material resources of the family, we may not be surprised that still less is known about the interrelationship of either respect or affection among family members. In their pioneering work *Inside the Family*, Kantor and Lehr (1975, Chapter 4) identify *affect* (along with *meaning* and *power*) as *target dimensions* in their general model of the family system. Their notion was that families and their members seek after these *target dimensions* (read "goals") through patterning their resources of space, time, and energy. Unfortunately, we are aware of no research that followed up by testing this model's utility or by illuminating the relations among these variables.

Coalitions and Alliances

Before turning to the question of family placement in the outside world, one other issue that pertains to internal family hierarchies deserves some attention. At least from the days of German sociologist Georg Simmel, who wrote more than a century ago, theorists have well understood that when analyzing the distribution of power in groups of three or more persons, they must consider *coalitions* (for an English translation of his work, see Simmel, 1950). Gamson, a social psychologist who did research on the subject (1964, p. 85), defined coalitions as "the joint use of resources to determine the outcome of a decision in a mixed motive game situation involving more than two units." Gamson (1961) asserted that coalitions are most likely to form in the following situations:

1. A decision must be made and more than two parties have an interest in the outcome.
2. No single solution is equally satisfactory to all.
3. No single participant has sufficient power to impose his or her will unilaterally.
4. No single participant has effective veto power—that is, the ability to block the decision of any combination of other participants.

Theodore Caplow further developed these ideas in *Two Against One: Coalition in Triads* (1968). He was particularly interested in what he called the *revolutionary coalition*. Both his theory and later confirmatory research (in experimental groups of undergraduates) found the following: When members of a triad have clearly unequal power but the two weaker members perceive that in combination they might prevail over the dominant member, a high probability exists that they will attempt to do so. For example, Caplow predicts that in a family of three in which the father has more influence than the mother and the mother more influence than the child, the probability that the mother and child will join together in a coalition against the father depends on whether the two of them together can overmatch the father standing alone. If they cannot, then forming such a coalition has little point.

Such an application of Caplow's coalition theory appears to be limited to families who operate in the competitive modality. Yet even competitive families have built-in structural features that are lacking in the ad-hoc experimental groups on which Caplan tested his theory. Social norms support an authority structure that features a conservative coalition of parents linked against the counterauthoritative challenges of their children. Common observation, however, clearly shows that parents in real life are not always successful in establishing a unified position; and when the parental common front is breached, the probability is higher that revolutionary, crossgenerational coalitions will form. Our society is known for its "patriarchal skew," and thus we cannot be surprised that the most prevalent form of this revolutionary structuring in competitive families involves the mother and one or more children in coalition against the father.

The family therapy literature is replete with discussions of the dysfunctionality of such crossgenerational coalitions. A careful reading of the use of the term *coalition* by clinical theorists, however, reveals that they impute a substantial surplus of meaning beyond the definition used by social psychologists, which was spelled out in the previous paragraphs. More than competition for power is involved. The family therapists are less concerned with the *instrumentally motivated* joining of weaker members to increase their bargaining leverage and are more concerned with the *affectively motivated* realignment of family allegiances and patterns of interaction. These issues are as relevant to families operating in the policy-driven as in the competitive mode.

Some of the complexities of the clinical uses of *coalition* are discussed in a 1979 survey article that attempted to summarize the topic:

> Another form of paradoxical bonding between a child and his family occurs when the child is caught in a parental power struggle. . . .
>
> Minuchin, . . . in discussing the disengagement of one parent, . . . points out that this is almost always associated with a cross-generational *coalition* between the other parent and the symptomatic child. It is not implied . . . that such "coalitions" are typically warm and supportive relationships. Rather, the lack of culturally approved involvement between husband and wife is compensated for by an inappropriate degree of involvement between parent and child. The emotional tone of the involvement . . . is likely to be paradoxical. [Minuchin, 1974]
>
> We believe that this is closely related to the pattern which Vogel and Bell (1960) described as *scapegoating*. In this conceptualization the symptomatic child is seen as bearing the sins of his parents' split much as the "scapegoat" was ordained to bear the sins of the people in ancient Israel. Ultimately the goat was abandoned as a propitiation. In parallel fashion when a family feels that its basic stability is threatened by a growing rift between the parents, one alternative is to divert attention from the threatening parental split to a relatively safe scapegoat from among the children. Some have argued that the weakest and most vulnerable child is chosen (van der Veen & Novak, 1971; Novak & van der Veen, 1970). Others find it more credible to believe that the child who is most disruptive is chosen (Hill, 1979). In either case, a classic vicious cycle develops in which the attacks on the child evoke worse behavior which in turn warrants further attack and so forth until the child's symptoms are fully developed.
>
> On the face of it, it would seem that Minuchin's *coalition* and Vogel and Bell's *attack* are almost semantic opposites. Yet a careful reading of the clinical examples offered suggests that each is describing the same type of paradoxical relationship. In one case the connectedness and in the other the hostility is focal. (Broderick & Pulliam-Krager, 1979, pp. 608-609; emphases in the original)

The preceding discussion shows that any theory that includes *family coalitions* as a construct must be explicit as to the nature of the relationships among father, mother, and child(ren). I would prefer to reserve the term *coalition* to describe simple two-against-one disputes in competitive families. Using the term in this limited sense, a *cross-generational coalition* simply refers to the situation of a child taking sides in a parental dispute. The quite different and more complicated phenomenon described by Minuchin and others deserves another name. Haley (1971) has called that pattern *the perverse triangle*, because of its dysfunctionality for the child. Perhaps this pattern might be less pejoratively labeled a *paradoxical crossgenerational alliance.*

Still a third pattern is sometimes bracketed with the other two as an example of how the child is *triangled* in a parental conflict. This occurs when the child becomes a mediator, taking it upon him- or herself to defuse the parental conflict. Some writers refer to these as *parentified* children, because they assume the traditional parental responsibility of keeping the family peace, treating their quarreling parents as though *they* were fractious children. This burden is often too heavy for a child and leads to the development of symptoms, just as perverse triangles do. (On the other hand, observers often note that many professional therapists received their earliest training in their own families.) This third form of triangulation need involve neither crossgenerational coalitions nor alliances. It is, rather, one subtype of a larger class of families in which children are moved into the parental role (as, for example, in families with absent or incompetent parents). The generic case may be called *generational inversion.* In all of its variations, this arrangement does introduce important paradoxical elements into the parent-child relationship and deserves to be cataloged with the other dysfunctional intergenerational patterns noted in previous paragraphs.

In reviewing these triangular matters from the perspective of the regulation of vertical space in families, perhaps the following conclusions may be asserted. First, in families with a competitive style of interaction, the decisions of members at the top of the power hierarchies may be challenged when less powerful members join forces in a revolutionary coalition. Although the impact of these crossgenerational coalitions on the family power hierarchy is direct and obvious, the implications for other aspects of family functioning are less clear. The matter needs further study.

Second, in families with parental splits (whether competitive or policy-based paradigms are in force), children tend to be triangled in to bridge the gap either through *paradoxical crossgenerational alliances* or *generational inversions.* Although the implications of these arrangements for family governance have not been fully sorted out, persuasive clinical evidence suggests that they are problematic for children's healthy development.

Family Positioning in a Stratified Society

Few of us would challenge Weber's assertion that all societies are stratified. Few would quarrel with his selection of power, property, and prestige as the limited societal resources whose unequal distribution define that stratification. Beyond that, the matter gets more complicated and the opinions of scholars more diverse. The problem is partly that contemporary urban communities are so diverse and complex.

Model building used to be a little simpler, or at least those who studied the matter in earlier days were able to come up with simpler models of social stratification. Early studies of social rankings were done in small, long-established communities in settled parts of New England (Warner & Lunt, 1941) or the Old South (Davis, Gardner, & Gardner, 1941). In those settings, one might well reach a community consensus on the several social strata that existed and on which families belonged to which strata. In fact, these scholars typically were able to identify and differentiate the following six classes: the *old aristocrats*, the *nouveau riches*, the solid *upper middle class* (entrepreneurs, managers, and professionals), the humbler *lower middle class* (white-collar clerks, office workers, salespeople, and schoolteachers), the respectable blue-collar *working class*, and, at the bottom, the not-so-respectable *underclass*. Movement up and down the class system was possible, both within and between generations, but it was resisted, and few if any families moved more than one level up or down in their own lifetimes. The Old South also had an established *caste system* that separated white strata from parallel black strata. Caste boundaries were not possible to cross (and illegal to marry across).

Undoubtedly, no one could devise such a simple model to describe the social stratification structure of a contemporary urban environment such as Los Angeles or New York (or, for that matter, Portland or Orlando). Consensus might be possible on who belonged in the very top and very bottom strata, but finding a consistent set of criteria for meaningfully ranking all of the families in between would present a real challenge. Yet this is the challenge that real families deal with everyday as they locate themselves vertically in relation to other families in this stratified society.

Various studies of stratification seem to indicate that when families do attempt to locate their own position in the complex social hierarchy, they do so in two steps. First, they identify their own *reference group*; and second, they then identify their own vertical placement within it. Most people have no difficulty identifying other families who are ranked just above or just below their own within that reference group; outside of it, they have a much more difficult task.

Almost half a century ago, Benoit-Smullyan coined the term *situs* to designate that vertical slice of society within which social comparisons could be readily made (1944) (see also Hatt, 1950, and Morris & Murphy, 1959, for pioneering discussions of this concept). By definition, we have difficulty in making accurate comparisons of the social rankings of families positioned in different situses. For example, within the military situs, everyone knows exactly what his or her vertical relationship is to any other person in the military. Within the entertainment industry (a different situs) rankings are also rather precise. So they are within the political, academic, business, space industry, and medical situses, just to name a few. But who can be sure of the exact equivalent within the entertainment industry of a lieutenant colonel in the U.S. Army, or who within the world of business is the precise peer of a tenured full professor at a major university?

Aside from occupationally based situses, any multiethnic city also has cultural and language enclaves with tightly structured social hierarchies of their own that stand independently to some degree from any other general ranking system. Undoubtedly, the vertical dimension is a key axis in the structuring of the larger societal system, but the social fabric is complexly woven, and no simple system of ordering does justice to reality.

An observer would find the discussion interesting if he or she could eavesdrop on a family that is trying to determine whether its son or daughter is marrying up, down, or straight across when the proposed spouse is from an unfamiliar situs. In their effort to estimate the prospective in-law's social ranking and suitability, other family members may require information on the candidate's age, religion, marital history, parental status, education, current occupation, and future prospects. And almost certainly they will want to know about the candidate's family background, the parents' occupations, and the type of home, neighborhood, and life-style they have.

This whole discovery process was vividly enacted recently when one of my daughters became engaged to a young graduate student who was the only son of a successful graphic artist father and an equally successful clothing designer mother. The young man turned out to be the "crown prince" of a tight little colony of artists and literati in a San Francisco suburb. His parents invited us to fly up from Los Angeles with our daughter to meet a few of their close friends. A veteran sociologist was not needed to discern that the central purpose of this event was for the bride-elect and her parents to be interviewed and evaluated by the impressively accomplished attendees. Early in the evening, the assemblage had established that, no, I had never written a novel nor had a show of my work, *but* I had published a dozen books with reputable publishers, some of which were still in print after 10 years (an important bench mark in this group), and I had been translated into German, French, Italian, and Dutch. Yes, we loved Paris and London and could readily agree that we too had found Frankfurt "cold" and Rome "fascinating." Yes, it was true that we had recently returned from an anniversary trip to the Great Barrier Reef (courtesy of an Australia group that had brought me over to lecture). There was more, but I would be embarrassed to record the extent of our shameless self-aggrandizement on that occasion. Eventually, the moment came when everyone seemed to relax and the conversation became more general. An unspoken consensus had been achieved. The prince was, after all, marrying a princess of suitable rank from another kingdom.

The societal placement of families also is a complicated issue in another sense. Not only are families in different situses difficult to compare and rank, but also all members of the family may not share the same reference groups. Indeed, individual members often have meaningful statuses in two or more reference groups. Beyond the status conferred by his occupation, education, and residence, the father of a family may be a Worshipful Pooh Bah in his lodge, a steward in his union, a deacon in his church, the star of his ball team, or the leader of his musical group. Significant status may accrue to him in certain situations because he is Gladys's husband or Julie's father or Tom's son. Similarly, his wife may accrue status beyond that generated by either her own or her husband's (or children's or parents') occupation, education, and residence. She may be a mover and shaker in the local pro-life or pro-choice group, the president of her condo association, the lead soloist in the choir, or a member of the board of education. In her later years, my own mother established a niche for herself as the chief resource of a network of troubled women who spent hours on the phone or visiting with her each day. Her husband called them her "pigeons," but whatever one called them, they honored and looked to her for emotional sustenance and advice.

Children, too, especially as they widen their arenas of operation in the outside world, may garner status from their own achievements and associations, in many cases, quite independently of their parents' standing in the community. The school and the peer group are the most obvious social stratification systems in which young people may find their own place, but for the enterprising (and sometimes for the adequately sponsored) meaningful social rankings also are available in work settings, athletic leagues, competitions and activities outside of school, and friendship groups (not to mention street gangs and drug-distribution networks). As previously noted, some research has linked status in the occupational world to relative influence or respect within the home. I know of none that investigates the influence of these auxiliary sources of personal status for family members on how they fare at home. Neither is a broadly based research literature available on the type of family processes or transactions that facilitate or restrict members' status achievement on the outside. Pending the accumulation of some empirical foundation, attempting to develop theory in this area would seem premature. If this discussion holds a message for future family process researchers and theorists, it is this: More profitable research will focus on the links between family processes and family members' involvements in multiple, situs-specific rankings than on attempting to identify links to some more generic concept of social status. Some of the processes by which families attempt to place their children in a status at least as high as their own are considered in Chapter 8 (The Socialization Process).

Summary: The Vertical Dimension

Despite the enormous volume of research on the vertical dimension of family interactions and transactions, the careful scholar is left with more questions than answers. Partly the problem is that the question has been poorly conceptualized and therefore poorly investigated. As a result, the findings are most often contradictory and nonilluminating. Studies are badly needed that examine family interactions and transactions in natural settings. Such studies should use a mixed methodology, interviews as well as observations, to identify the metarules and policy-level and paradigm-level rules as well as directly observable sequences of exchanges.

In the arena of family placement in the larger social stratification system, a more sophisticated model of social stratification clearly is needed. As a minimum, an adequate model ought to recognize both multiple hierarchies (situses) and also that families and individual family members may be ranked meaningfully in more than one such hierarchy because of the multiplicity of roles that each member assumes. Only such a model of stratification in the external social system is complex enough to permit articulation with the observed complexities of family transactional life. In systems terms, only a system that is at least this complex could have the requisite variety of rules and responses to be meaningfully linked with the equally complex family system in any unified model of articulated social systems. Until more data of the type outlined above are available, further theoretical work in this area seems to me to be premature.

PART III

Socializing Children and Each Other

CHAPTER 7 ▼

Family Meanings and Shared Realities

Through its own development, the family fashions fundamental and enduring assumptions about the world in which it lives. The assumptions are
shared by all family members despite the disagreements, conflicts, and
differences that exist within the family. Indeed, the core of an individual's
membership in his or her own family is the acceptance of, belief in, and
creative elaboration of these abiding assumptions. (Reiss, 1981, p. 1)

The plausibility and stability of the world, as socially defined, is dependent
upon the strength and continuity of significant relationships in which conversation about this world can be continually carried on. (Berger & Kellner,
1985, p. 5)

[U]nderstanding may be important to marital satisfaction primarily when
sharing is an important value. When autonomy and distance are valued,
then maintaining a surface calm may be more important to a couple than
understanding. (Sillars & Scott, 1983, p. 167)

The Semantic Component of Family Process

Virtually every student of family process has come to recognize that some of the most important dimensions of the family experience cannot be directly observed by outsiders. These elusive but crucial dimensions are in the realm of family meanings and include such germane issues as family assumptions, expectations, beliefs, values, world views, and understandings. Yet, in truth, only an individual can have a belief or value or world view or an understanding of something. Therefore, when we speak of *family* beliefs or understandings, we have committed a serious logical error. It is serious because it ignores the crucial fact that any group of individuals has as many realities as people.

In discussing meanings in families, we can never avoid the issue of shared and unshared realities. As soon as the issue is thus stated, a whole list of subordinate issues immediately suggest themselves. How do couples construct joint realities? To what extent are they aware of differences in the way they see the world and each other? When does that matter? How do they socialize their children into their disparate realities and how and to what extent is a joint family world view fashioned? These questions may be beyond our power to answer fully, but they need to be posed as background for any discussion of the semantic component of family process.

As Kantor and Lehr (1975) have pointed out:

> It is almost impossible to overstate the importance of family meaning regulation in a society that is intellectually concerned with the meaning or meaninglessness of existence. A world as complex as ours puts extra strain on both individual and family identities. . . . [S]hared meanings can be so strongly emphasized by a family that they are the only meanings members are permitted to hold or express. . . . Other families, of course, can emphasize unshared meanings to such a degree that a subsystem, an individual or a faction of the family can feel constantly isolated from or opposed to the meanings, values, and ideology of the rest of the family. (p. 52)

In the domain of relational space, we spoke of bonding and buffering, bounding and bridging. In the domain of family meaning, we find equal importance in discussing both the mechanisms by which family members are joined together through shared realities and those by which separate realities are constructed and maintained; both the mechanisms by which family insiders incorporate the beliefs of certain outside groups and identify them as their own and those by which they defend against the beliefs of other groups that are viewed as alien and threatening to the well-being of the family and its members.

In this chapter, we shall look first at a general model of how families establish and maintain their own balances between sponsoring a unified view of the world and accommodating individual perspectives. Then, in somewhat greater detail, we will review the literature on two of the more colorful mechanisms that families have been observed to use in establishing their sense of identity as generation-spanning units with histories and symbolic legacies peculiar to themselves. The first is the construction of a unique folklore complete with family stories, myths and memorabilia. The second is the development within each nuclear and extended family of its own set of valued, recurring rituals.

Although research into these important areas is somewhat skimpy, as it happens, these topics have generated a particularly rich clinical literature. For this reason, I have elected to modify the format of presentation followed in other chapters and will include here subsections on the clinical utilization of family stories and memorabilia and also of family rituals. The history of family process theory began as the distillation of clinical experience. Perhaps this particular topical area will also follow that developmental pattern.

The Construction and Maintenance of Shared Realities

A family relationship can be constructed in two ways: through marriage and through birth (or its functional equivalent of adoption). In marriage, two relatively mature adults, coming from different family experiences, establish a new family system of their own. They bring a great deal with them: certainties and doubts, passions and prejudices, clarities and blindnesses. They bring rules and expectations from their previous family experiences, and sometimes they bring children as well. Yet both of them understand that their mutual task is to construct a workable unity out of their initial separateness. As Berger and Kellner (1985) put it, "Marriage in our society is a *dramatic* act in which two strangers come together and redefine themselves" (emphasis in original).

Even in a process-focused text, I find traces of my early training as a structural functionalist showing through from time to time. As a case in point, I cannot forbear noting that every society provides at least four mechanisms for sponsoring the attainment of a sufficiently common reality for married couples: preselection, establishing a joint identity, commingling separate realities through communication, and experiencing a new shared reality.

Preselection

In every culture, the mate-selection process is designed to discourage the pairing of individuals from backgrounds that are too dissimilar. The most common pattern is for parents or their surrogates to take responsibility for the selection process, but even in our own participant-run system, a remarkable degree of homogamy is achieved. And it is widely understood, fairy tales to the contrary, that Cinderella and her prince were in for a challenging posthoneymoon period of adjustment.

Establishing a Joint Identity

Beginning early in the courtship process, the two individuals come to be identified as a unit. At certain points, this new joint identity is likely to be reinforced with photographs of them as a couple, with mementos, and ultimately with a ring. The wedding ceremony is nothing more or less than the legal and social formalization of this union. In most cases, the couple assumes a common name and a common address. By social fiat, their separate realities have been declared joined. Although the declaration, in and of itself, obviously does not create the actuality, it does serve to promote the process of accommodation.

Commingling Separate Realities Through Communication

Courtship and marriage offer both the opportunity and the cultural mandate for the individuals in the couple to communicate their separate realities to each other. As we shall see in the section on separate realities, some individuals are more skillful at this task than others, and some also define the process as more important to their definition of marital success than do others. But it must be acknowledge that the simple circumstance of living together guarantees at least a minimum exposure to and awareness of each other's distinctive view of the world.

Experiencing a New Shared Reality

Courtship and marriage provide innumerable shared experiences to the once separate individuals who are now a couple. Many of these are unique to the couple and may be viewed as particularly meaningful. Prominent among the more memorable pair events are likely to be certain romantic moments, the engagement, the wedding, the honeymoon, and even particular quarrels and minor disasters. Indeed, if the stories that couples fondly tell about their courtship and wedding are any indication of what they find significant in these experiences, the shared disasters are a major part of their unifying joint reality (Zeitlin, 1980). Living together under a common roof, sleeping in a common bed, operating a common economy and household, eating common meals, and sharing common rituals, crises, and developmental unfoldings tend to build a deep reservoir of common history. This is not to suggest that a multitude of shared experiences automatically increases the bonding in a relationship. Each experience also provides the opportunity to be reminded of how differently each views the world and the relationship. One might argue that disappointment is the main cause of divorce—disappointment that the unity of perspective and identity that was hoped for never materialized.

The alternative avenue to creation of a family is birth or adoption. This may occur within or without the marital bond. In either case, the addition of an infant to the parents' life has a double impact. First, simply by enlarging the size of the family and the number of potential dyadic and triadic relationships within it, the addition creates a new reality. In many families, at least, parents begin to assign a nickname, attribute personality characteristics, and direct conversations toward the child before it is born. Once born, the new baby is a virtually irresistible reorganizer of family routines, rituals, and meanings. Second, a child presents the family with the challenge of introducing a new citizen into its private universe of meanings. Some aspects of that process will be commented on in the next chapter, which deals with the intergenerational transmission of values, beliefs, and meanings.

We note here, however, that the process is bidirectional from the beginning. That is, children challenge and enlarge the realities of their parents as well as receive socialization at their hands. Initially, this may occur through the mechanism of inexperienced parents being forced to seek outside information and support from their own parents, more experienced friends, or professionals. But as children grow, their involvement with people and ideas from outside the immediate family inevitably expands. And equally inevitably, these exposures will cause them to challenge the established world views of their parents and to become agents of continuing resocialization for them. The teenage daughter who persuades her mother to update her wardrobe or to go back to school or the teenage son who persuades his family to buy a VCR or a personal computer are only the most easily perceived examples.

The Construction and Maintenance of Separate Realities

Jesse Bernard (1972) was the theorist who raised our collective consciousness to the fact that always and inevitably two marriages exist: his and hers. The husband could be serenely satisfied with his marriage, and the wife could be miserable with hers; she could be perfectly content and he terminally dissatisfied. The reasons for this are not difficult to discern. People come to marriage with different expectations. If satisfaction is a function of the correspondence between expectations and realizations, then it is clear that the same life-style might well please one and disappoint the other.

But even in the unlikely case that expectations and perceptions of marriage are virtually identical, ample room remains for differences in levels of satisfaction. For example, nothing is more common than for a husband and wife to have quite unequal commitments to pleasing each other. And if one were to look only at those rare couples in which the spouses shared the same expectations and were also equally motivated to please, one would yet expect to find a variety of degrees of sensitivity to the other's actual needs.

As a result of all these factors, studies that have gone to the trouble to ask husbands and wives to evaluate their marriages separately have found only moderate correlations between the ratings of the two spouses. For example, Olson and his colleagues (1983, Table 3.1), in their study of 1,000 mostly conservative, mostly Midwestern families, found that couples' scores on the widely used Locke-Wallace Marital Inventory correlated only .48, and they correlated only .45 on ENRICH, Olson's own instrument for measuring marital satisfaction. As further evidence of the separateness of husbands' and wives' realities, their ratings of their general satisfaction with their family life correlated only .35, as did their ratings of their overall quality of life. Because the best indicator of the actual impact of one factor on another is not the correlation coefficient itself but its square, what these figures mean is that, at best, something less than one-fourth of the statistical variance in the satisfaction of either spouse can be accounted for by the level of his or her partner's satisfaction, while more than three-fourths is independent of that factor.

A quite separate issue from whether a couple shares an opinion (on the quality of the marriage or on some other matter) is whether each partner correctly understands the other's view. Over the past 40 years, a variety of scholars have investigated the question of what leads to greater or lesser accuracy of interspousal perception and what follows from it. In their particularly perceptive review of this literature, Sillars and Scott (1983) conclude that the following principles are credibly supported by research findings:

1. Individuals are most likely to be inaccurate in their perceptions of their partners when:
   a. strong negative or positive emotions (especially those generated by stressful or conflicted interactions) are present;
   b. attitudes or ideological views are dissimilar;
   c. one partner has undergone a substantial change in attitude or ideology;
   d. the perception must be based on very subtle or ambiguous cues (as, for example, when trying to estimate a partner's underlying motivation).
2. Accuracy of perception is related to the length of the relationship:
   a. positively in the case of instrumental issues (because of the acquisition of tacit understandings and specialized codes); and
   b. negatively in the case of expressive issues (because overconfidence in one's intimate knowledge leads to the persistence of false assumptions).
3. The relationship between accuracy of perception and marital satisfaction is generally positive except when:
   a. unconfronted, irreconcilable differences are present;
   b. hurtful secrets or benevolent misconceptions are at risk; and
   c. greater value is placed on emotional buffering and autonomy than on intimacy or understanding.
4. Individuals have a tendency to ascribe more positive motivations to themselves than to their partners.

Less research has been done on the topic of the shared and unshared realities of parents and their children (see Chapter 8 for a more detailed review of that literature). What has been done is equally instructive, however. On strictly theoretical grounds (ignoring one's own experiences with one's own teenagers), one would suppose that the children in a family, having been socialized within that marital union, would more or less faithfully reflect their parents' perceptions and values. Alas, as every parent has suspected, the facts fail to support this supposition (Larson, 1974). Olson and his colleagues, as cited earlier (1983, Table 3.1), found that the correlations between the scores of teenage children and either of their parents on instruments designed to get valid descriptions of joint family living patterns tended to vary around a mean of approximately .30. Thus, only some 10% of the variance in children's scores could be predicted by either of their parents' perceptions of the very same family issues.

This result is not what one might expect from reading the clinical family literature. From the beginning, family therapists have been preoccupied with the tendency they have observed among clinical populations of family members to be overidentified with one another. Bowen (1971b) uses the vivid image of the *undifferentiated family ego mass* to describe the condition he observed. Indeed, we would not exaggerate by saying that many therapists hold this lack of sufficient differentiation to be the chief source of family and individual dysfunction. The fact remains that, at least in Olson's nonclinical sample, this condition does not seem to be a major threat. Despite all of the mechanisms that we have discussed (and have yet to discuss in this chapter) whose function is to build a joint reality for family members, the evidence is compelling that the effort is only fractionally successful. Barring persuasive new evidence to the contrary, we must conclude that the typical pattern is for each family member to construct an individual reality from his or her unique experiences and perspectives. Such modest sharing of beliefs and perceptions that does occur may be assumed to be conducive to successful family functioning. In fact, in this population, Olson and his colleagues found a strong positive linear relationship between the degree of shared reality and satisfaction with both marital and familial relationships (1983, Table 10.2), just the opposite of what clinicians (including Olson himself) would have predicted.

A variety of attempts have been made to account for this discrepancy between the clinical observation and the research finding. Several have suggested that perhaps the instruments used to measure cohesion by Olson and others may not be tapping into the same dimension that concerns family therapists. This suggestion may indeed be the case, but we are prone to support an alternative explanation proffered by Burr and Lowe (1987). The research has conclusively shown that, within the nonclinical population, families typically operate within the low to moderate range of shared family meanings. Burr and Lowe suggest that, within that range, the more cohesive the members are, the happier they tend to be. Only in the relatively rare cases of extreme overconnection are the negative consequences of enmeshment manifested. These are, of course, the very families that clinicians are most likely to see.

The chief mechanisms for limiting the superimposition of family members' realities upon one another are the separate ties each has with the world outside the family, including school, media, informal networks of strong and weak ties, and so on. Paradoxically, these very outside connections also may be utilized by families to facilitate the establishment of shared and coordinated realities.

Connection With and Protection From Outsider Realities

On the first day of kindergarten, my daughter's new teacher said to us, "School will be a whole new world for Jenifer. Things will be done differently here than at home, and she may at first find that uncomfortable. But I will make a pact with you. I promise to believe only half of the unlikely tales Jenifer tells about what happens at home, if you will believe only half of the unlikely tales she tells about what happens at school." If that sounds slightly sinister today—in the light of everyone's heightened awareness of child abuse—it did not when it was said in the early 1960s. Indeed, it sounded like an unusually sound suggestion, and we followed it with good results. Because one of the purposes of sending her out of the home to school was for her to learn the ways of the larger world so that she could one day confidently take her place in it. In pursuit of that same goal, she was taught to read, allowed to watch television, taken to church, sent to girls' camp and eventually to college and to a job. Yet, while she was thus exposed to an ever-widening circle of ideas and experiences, she was also protected from other ideas and experiences that would have been at least as broadening, but which we viewed as potentially harmful or subversive of our core values. Ever since she became a young adult, we and other members of her family have been free with advice on jobs and the men she dates and the way she spends her money and her time.

Under the heading "Establishing Boundaries of the Family's World of Experience," Hess and Handel (1959) wrote:

> A family constitutes its own world, which is not to say that it closes itself off from everything else but that it determines what parts of the external world are admissible and how freely. The family maps its domain of acceptable and desirable experience, its life space. . . . Limits to experience—broad or narrow—are established. . . . How deep or how shallow experience is, . . . how much of the world it is important to know about and be interested in. . . . Families differ . . . in how insistently they will impose their images on their children. (pp. 14-17)

Obviously, then, the two chief *transactional* mechanisms for maintaining the integrity of a family's shared world view are carefully selected bounding and bridging processes. By these means (and by the judicious use of appropriate submechanisms described in Chapter 5 such as possessive tracking and channeling), the family may hope to protect its members, at least to some degree, against the subversive influence of competing outsiders' world views. The internal, *interactional* processes by which families reinforce members' loyalties to their own paradigm of reality are less studied. Two important mechanisms have received considerable attention, however: the construction of *family folklore* and the institution of *family rituals*.

Family Folklore: Stories, Myths, and Memorabilia

One of the standard plots in grade B adventure stories involves the kidnapping (or murder) of a key personage who is then replaced by a twin or look-alike impostor. Frequently, the impersonator has made a detailed study of the person he or she is replacing—idiosyncrasies of posture, habit, and taste. Except for a few tense moments when a minor slip makes an intimate friend or family member pause in temporary confusion (which is quickly shaken off), the substitution is a complete success. For days or weeks, this impersonator fools everyone, until at the very end of the story he or she is unmasked by some clever observer who was not fooled for long!

Even as a child, I had a hard time suspending my disbelief in this premise long enough to enjoy the story. It seemed absurd to me then, as it does now, to think that anyone could believe that a person could be counterfeited like a $20 bill. I do not believe that anyone could fool the intimates of any person on earth for as long as five minutes of ordinary interaction. At least part of the reason is that each of us is embedded in what Bellah and his associates (1985) have called *communities of memory*. Every group that is more than an ad-hoc collection of strangers has a history and a culture of its own. Each of us has experienced being the outsider who doesn't quite understand the allusions, who isn't in on the jokes, who doesn't know quite what is expected of us, which are the taboo or tender subjects, what are the unchallenged assumptions or the traditional quarrels, or the informal pecking order or coalitional structure. In short, each of us knows first-hand how many opportunities present themselves for a stranger to blunder into the subtle web of rules that defines the acceptable paths of interaction within any ongoing system. Nor could any briefing process prepare one adequately to become an instant initiate. The only repository of these rules is the participants' collective memory.

In families, as in other continuing systems, this corpus of shared direct memories is always augmented by frequently repeated stories and valued photographs and mementos. This interwoven collection of tales and treasures constitute what Zeitlin and his associates (1982) have called *family folklore*.

A family's folklore is different from its history. . . . For an individual family, folklore is its creative expression of a common past. As raw experiences are transformed into family stories, expressions, and photos, they are codified in forms which can be easily recalled, retold, and enjoyed. Their drama and beauty are heightened, and the family's past becomes accessible as it is re-shaped according to its needs and desires. (Zeitlin, Kotkin, & Baker, 1982, p. 2)

Family Stories

As Walter Benjamin once wrote, "Every real story . . . contains, openly or covertly, something useful" (1969, p. 86). We have already hinted that one of those uses is to reassure the family that it is indeed a unique and significant unit. "Almost always," wrote Elizabeth Stone, " there are family stories to fasten the identity in place and keep it from floating off, slithering away, or losing its shape" (1988, p. 34). She then suggests four ways in which this *fastening* is effected.

First, these stories spotlight certain personal qualities that are viewed as being archetypal of family members: the Murphy temper, the Belcher sense of humor, or the Bartholomew hardheadedness. Yet, taken as a set, these oft-told tales will always include enough variety to accommodate nearly any real, complex, flesh-and-blood member. For example, the Broderick clan views itself not only as unusually bookish, but also as uncommonly good at interpersonal relationships—as well as being religiously committed, resistant to arbitrary authority, appre-ciative of fantasy, and loyal to family traditions. That list (and every similar list) has enough flex and paradox to include us all.

Second, whatever an outsider might think of this particular collec-tion of traits, to the members they define the family as "special" and in some ways superior to other families. Third, these stories of what it means to be a Broderick (or a Murphy, a Belcher, or a Bartholomew) are also intended to be instructional by reminding family members what they are supposed to be like as well as what they have been and are. Finally, Stone contends that the stories that a family tells identify the wellspring of its identity, the people living or dead who are seen as the founders of this unique kin group. Whether a member of the present family or someone several generations removed, this "origi-nal" member's story is the cornerstone of what we might call the *core family story*.

Presumably, most core story cycles celebrate continuities and the links between the generations, but often enough these interconnecting retold tales celebrate a crucial discontinuity with the past. My own family is an example of the latter tradition. The theme of the *transitional character*—that is, the person who determines not to be a transmitter of the pathologies of former generations (see Chapter 8)—has permeated my own professional lecturing and writing for over a decade, but not until I was preparing this chapter did it occur to me that this also was the central theme of the family stories that I have told my children since they were tots. Any one of the eight of them could recite verbatim the story of how my mother, finding herself in an unpleasant situation at home, married my father on a dare, but divorced him a year and a half later because he was unstable and could not keep a job; married an older, economically successful man who became my wicked stepfather; and after he died, married the mailman (which, incidentally, turned out to have been a good choice; I never tell the story without adding that I am grateful that my mother kept marrying until she got it right).

My children also know that both of my grandfathers were saloon-keepers. One was prayed into bankruptcy by his pious Mormon wife, who had despaired of getting him into some more respectable profession any other way; as a result, he became a traveling salesman, still a bit too marginal an occupation, although infinitely more acceptable than a bartender). The other grandfather was deserted by his wife and left with eight young children whom he promptly turned over to a Catholic orphanage to raise, before he died a year later of cirrhosis of the liver. My father grew up uncertain of his own exact age, not knowing his maternal grandmother's name, and believing that two of his brothers were twins, when, in fact, their baptismal records (which, apparently, only I have ever bothered to look up) show them born a year and a few days apart. My children know that my "Aunt Fern," the chief corrector of my table manners and one of the most present and puissant of my female kin, was, to be genealogically precise, my mother's brother's first wife's second husband's father's third, fourth, and fifth wife (she married seven times, including three times to "Uncle Lew"). Almost no one in my parents' generation was married happily—or married fewer than three times.

By contrast, my children have also heard a hundred times that their father and mother met in church at the age of 3, were in the same kindergarten class (he is the tallest one in the back row and she the shortest one in the front row in the class picture), that they starred together in the third-grade play about William Tell (he was William Tell, and she played his son), and that although the script called for him to aim the toy arrow high and for her to pull the apple off her head by the string attached to it, instead (to her mother's consternation) he cleanly knocked the apple off with a bulls-eye shot—a pretty impressive feat considering he had never shot an arrow before. They have heard how he finally got up his nerve to invite her to a football game in 10th grade and how, their friendship surviving a love-crossed period in high school, they got back together on senior ditch day (on an afterdate date), and how three years later, over objections from her mother (who thought he was too much like her unreliable first husband) married when they were 20 and had eight bright, stable children and lived happily ever after.

I was embarrassed to discover after so many years that I was not just passing on a rich family lore and giving my children a sense of their roots (as I would have insisted, if asked about my motives), but also was (albeit unwittingly) establishing as our family theme the striking and significant discontinuities between previous generations and this one.

Family Themes and Family Myths

Some theorists have asserted that all families are possessed of some small number of core themes, around which they structure their meaningful interactions. Perhaps the fullest statement of this principle was made by Hess and Handel in their 1959 volume, *Family Worlds*:

> A family theme is a pattern of feelings, motives, fantasies, and conventionalized understandings grouped about some locus of concern. . . . The pattern comprises some fundamental view of reality and some way or ways of dealing with it. . . . Thus a family's feelings about most of its activities can be construed as particular manifestations of a more inclusive organizing principle. . . . The theme is an implicit point of departure and point of orientation for this family's behavior. (pp. 11-12)

A variation on the idea of a family theme is the clinically derived notion of the *family myth* (Ferreira, 1963, 1966; Byng-Hall, 1973, 1988), which has been defined as

> a number of well-systematized beliefs, shared by all family members about their mutual roles in the family, and the nature of their relationship. . . . Although to an outsider they may appear as blatant misstatements of the facts in the family, these organized beliefs—in the name of which the family initiates, maintains and justifies many interactional patterns—are beliefs shared and supported by all family members as if they were some sort of ultimate truths beyond challenge or inquiry. (Ferreira, 1966, p. 2)

As we may deduce from this definition, a family myth is a family theme that is particularly rigid and toxic in its content and therefore likely to be of special interest to therapists. A typical family myth might be the often-encountered scapegoat myths that hold a child's chronic misbehavior to be the root cause of a couple's marital difficulties (Vogel & Bell, 1960).

Family stories are by no means the only mechanisms for identifying family themes and myths. For example, these stories may be expressed spatially through family sculpture (Duhl, Kantor, & Duhl, 1973), through projective techniques administered jointly to families (Hess & Handel, 1959), or through communication patterns exhibited in carefully controlled experiments (Straus & Tallman, 1971; Reiss, 1981). But in the natural family environment, a more revealing medium of the core themes than the standard repertoire of family stories is hard to imagine.

Family Photos and Memorabilia

Augmenting and documenting the collection of family narratives is a more-or-less extensive collection of family photographs and other memorabilia (old graduation tassels, athletic and debate trophies, newspaper clippings, pressed flowers, family heirlooms, and on and on). Our dresser drawers, basements, attics, garages, and spare bedrooms are veritable archeological repositories of the family's past, especially if a family has not had to move too often. Even the house itself may constitute a monument to memories.

In earlier chapters we discussed the material milieu of the family and indicated that the meanings attached to particular objects may give them a significance that far transcends their obvious function. Igor Kopytoff (1986) argues that, over time, articles tend to change status from exchangeable *commodities* to irreplaceable *singularities*. He writes, "There is clearly a yearning for singularization in complex societies. . . . [T]he longevity of the relationship [between familiar objects and their owners] assimilates them in some sense to the person and makes parting from them unthinkable" (1986, p. 80).

What may be true for familiar objects in general would appear to be doubly true for that most meaningful of all memorabilia, the family photo album. In their discussion of the place of family photography in family folklore, Zeitlin and his associates (1982) make three provocative observations. First, although they note that "Photos serve as mnemonic devices, helping families to recall stories and preserve knowledge of past experiences" (p. 188), they further observe that photos also play a more active role in shaping family lore:

> Never a passive observer, the camera records selectively and often seems to direct the performance on which it intrudes. Bridal couples hold their embrace at the altar to afford the photographer ample time to record the "moment."

> Families pause at their annual reunions to hug and smile, creating a portrait of unity and affection for posterity. (p. 188)

Second, Zeitlin and company point out that picture taking not only records and directs certain significant family events, but also may itself become an intrinsic element in the event. For example, at many weddings, the role of the photographer is almost sacerdotal; and in certain circles, a baby is not counted as born if its entry into the world is not recorded in living color on videotape. As one of Zeitlin's interviewee's said, "On Christmas mornings my father was a photographer. My sister and I, called to attention, stared ferociously at those awful bulbs, not understanding that even as we sat there, blooming from the ribbons and wrapping paper, we were part of a ceremony; that we were, in fact its motive" (p. 188).

Third and finally, Zeitlin and associates note that photographs may serve as both aids to collective memory and as the more formal representations of the significant events they document. The more intriguing, behind-the-scenes, juicy details are still the province of the irreverent story teller.

Certain events are more centrally featured in a family's folklore than others, but perhaps the most fully documented is the founding event: the wedding and associated events such as the honeymoon. Nearly every family has both oft-told tales and an extensive photographic record of these events, as well as other memorabilia such as the wedding dress, the veil, or at least a couple of "Dan and Sue" embossed napkins. Having the founding events in a family's history called to mind seems to be a particularly trusted mechanism for fixing the family's sense of identity.

Beverly Farb, a doctoral candidate at the University of Southern California, is currently investigating the question of what becomes of these multiple memorabilia when divorce and remarriage would appear to render them subversive rather than supportive of the new unit. Are some or all of the photos and mementos destroyed? Are they secreted away for disloyal private viewing? Or deposited with one's parents or grown children for their own history-refreshing use at a safe distance from the tender new relationship? I am aware of one woman who convened a ceremonial gathering of all of her female friends and gleefully pasted animal-head stickers over each and every likeness of her ex-spouse in the family photo collection. We hope that Farb's findings will shed new light on such events and, more generally, on the functions of wedding folklore in families with discontinuous histories.

Using Stories, Photos, and Memorabilia in Family Therapy

We have noted already that the family therapist is in a particularly advantageous position to observe and to manipulate family process. Not surprisingly, many of the insights at the heart of family process theory grew out of therapeutic experience. Therefore, we may note that, although most of the research on family folklore has been done by social anthropologists and English majors, many therapists still use these elements in their work with families. All of the intergenerationally oriented therapists use the *genogram* or some equivalent device to get families to tell their core story cycle. Many have family members bring scrapbooks and picture albums to the therapy session. Probably no better portals are available into the systems of meanings that constitute the family's psychosocial interior.

Just as there is always his marriage and her marriage, so there is also his story and her story of the marriage. Much of marital counseling involves dealing with the disparate views of connubial reality that the couple bring to therapy. In some cases, we have difficulty in believing that both sets of stories could have come from the same set of shared experiences. I have had clients who flatly contradicted each other's stories in matters so concrete (such as whether the last time they had sexual intercourse with each other was last Tuesday or two years ago) that it was a real challenge simply to establish a common baseline for further joint discussion. If we remember, however, that stories are *never* merely historical accounts, but are *always* (whether mutually confirming or contradictory) important statements of feelings about the relationship, of the *meaning* of the relationship to the narrator, then the therapist can use the material constructively without the necessity of establishing exactly where the truth lies.

In my own practice, I often have the couple tell its courtship story in the first session. The "Let's get acquainted" task is viewed by the couple as sensible and benign, for the most part, and yet it can be exceptionally informative and is frequently a therapeutic experience. Both the story's thematic content and the way they share (or fail to share) the telling of it are richly reveling of the couple's dynamics. Beyond that, however, in most cases the process of recounting the story reconnects both parties with the positive emotions and perspectives of an earlier more hopeful and more appreciative period in their relationship. It reminds them once again of the soft, committed core of their union rather than the prickly exterior that has been their more recent focus of attention.

Storytelling by the therapist can also be an effective device for helping family members reframe their views of their own relationships. There is a long history of both lay counselors and professionals helping conflicted families see their situation differently with an intervention that begins "You know, that reminds me of the time. . . " The story that follows such an introduction, although clearly understood to be instructive and remedial in its intent, is easier to listen to than direct advice because it is one step removed. Each combatant is free to hear what he or she is ready to hear and to make the applications that fit. It also elevates the family's problems from the level of unique personal conflict to the level of a more universal human dilemma. The general principles that apply to the solution of all such conflicts may be easier to see and appreciate than the particular requirements of the immediate situation in which one is passionately involved.

The clinical case literature provides many examples of the therapeutic uses of stories, both the family's own and those provided by the therapist. A wide variety of techniques and rationales may be observed. So far as we know, the task of systematically sorting through these materials and developing a metaperspective on the topic, remains unattempted.

Family Rituals

The concept of family rituals was introduced into social science literature by James H. S. Bossard and Eleanor S. Boll with their 1950 publication of *Ritual in Family Living*. The book was undertaken in the belief that one "phase of family study [that is] relatively neglected, is that of its internal life. . . . How does the family operate? How does it work and how does it do its work? What are the means it uses to accomplish its purposes? What are families like on the inside?" (p. 8). Having posed the question, Bossard and Boll then proceeded to collect information from students and others on the most meaningful of their family experiences. Early on they discovered the central importance of "certain forms of family behavior so recurrent as to suggest the term 'habit,' and yet having about them aspects of conscious rigidity and a sense of rightness and inevitability not generally associated with mere habits. . . . We came ultimately to think of these as family rituals" (p. 9).

It was a bold intellectual stroke to appropriate the term *rituals*, which had come to be associated with rather formal religious ceremonies, to describe the richly meaningful but often informal and often secular patterned activities of ordinary family living. Recent years have seen a renewed interest in the phenomenon, among both mainline social scientists (e.g., Dreyer & Dreyer, 1973; Stinnett & DeFrain, 1981; Reiss, 1981; Caplow, 1982; Stinnett, Sanders, DeFrain, & Parkhurst, 1982) and family therapists (e.g., Wolin & Bennett, 1984; Imber-Black, Roberts, & Whiting, 1988).

Bossard and Boll's original definition of family ritual identified it as "a form or pattern of social interaction, which has three unvarying characteristics. First, it is definitely prescribed. . . . Second, there is the element of rigidity. . . . And finally, there is a sense of rightness which emerges from the past history of the process" (1950, p. 16). More contemporary authors have instead described this phenomenon "as a symbolic form of communication that, owing to the satisfaction that family members experience through its repetition, is acted out in a systematic fashion over time" (Wolin & Bennett, 1984, p. 401). In combination, the two definitions begin to give the reader a feel for the sort of practice that might qualify as a ritual.

Following Wolin and Bennett (1984), recent convention has divided family rituals into three more-or-less-distinct categories: family celebrations, family traditions, and patterned family interactions.

Family Celebrations

According to Wolin and Bennett, family celebrations

> are those holidays and occasions that are widely practiced throughout the culture and are special in the minds of the family. In this category are rites of passage such as weddings, funerals, baptisms, and bar mitzvahs; annual religious celebrations such as Christmas, Easter, the Passover seder; and secular holiday observances such as Thanksgiving, New Year's, or the Fourth of July. (1984, p. 404)

Duality distinguishes all family celebrations. On the one hand, they underscore the family's connectedness to its larger community by incorporating its symbols and traditions into the celebration and usually assigning representatives of that larger world key roles in the ritual itself. On the other hand, each family expresses its own individuality in its choice of which traditional element to include or exclude, as well as in the unique symbols and formatting that it elects to use in its own customized version of the celebration. As we have already noted, the camera's special assignment often is to record the more traditional elements.

For example, at a traditional wedding the photographer is virtually required to get shots of the couple alone, the couple with his parents, the couple with her parents, the couple cutting the wedding cake, the tossing of the bridal bouquet, the hands displaying the wedding rings, the couple leaving the reception, and so on. Similarly, at Christmas, the family photographer must catch everyone sleepy-eyed in their pajamas, the tree, the stuffed stockings, and the opening of presents. The idiosyncratic variations, however, especially the unplanned ones, are more likely to be the subject of family stories: how Daddy had too much to drink and had to be supported and led down the aisle by his daughter, how the groom was late for the ceremony, how the bride had a temperature of 103° and had to leave the reception line repeatedly to run to the bathroom, how the car broke down 30 minutes into the honeymoon, how the hotel maid walked in on them on their first morning, and so forth.

Rituals have been described as the means of educating the participants in the values they share, of regulating their behavior, and of celebrating their common identity (Moore & Meyerhoff, 1977; Wolin & Bennett, 1984). The function of publicly reaffirming the family's ethnic roots probably is nowhere more evident than in those ceremonies that are designed to introduce newborn infants into their religious and ethnic communities. Rituals such as christening or bris (the public, ritual circumcision of Jewish male infants) or the Mormon practice of fathers joining with a circle of close male friends and relatives to give their infants a name and a father's blessing in front of the congregation are specifically designed to obligate the parents to bring up the child in a particular religious tradition and to bind them to a particular religious community. The dynamics are circular. The very values and sense of religious identity that leads the family to participate in such a ceremony are then reinforced by it.

We find value in noting that, within the category of family rituals that they call family celebrations, Wolin and Bennett have included two quite different classes of events: rites of passage and annual holiday observances (whether religious or secular in origin). Although they share certain important elements, each also has important and unique characteristics.

Rites of Passage

One of families' most important characteristics is that they are developing systems. They have beginnings and endings, and in between they have significant points of transition from one stage of family life to another. Rites of passage are the mechanisms through which the family and the community coordinate their perceptions and definitions of the developmental status of the family and its members. These rituals mark and, to some degree, actually effect major shifts in the policies and metarules of the family as it moves inexorably through its life cycle. The family has an investment in these rituals because, in the nature of things, transitions are intrinsically stressful, requiring the family to cross over into unfamiliar territory, to assume new obligations or to sustain significant losses. To the extent that all rites of passage are public to some degree, they put the family in touch with its social and religious resources to help it through the challenges of the shift in metarules.

The society also has a stake in the family's successful navigation of these crucial transition points. Families who, for whatever reason, fail to successfully negotiate these prescribed shifts are perceived as defective and dysfunctional to that degree. The failure challenges core values of the larger community. For example, the wedding ceremony is explicitly designed to effect the transition of the new couple as it (1) establishes a common residence, (2) disengages from the partners' intimate involvement with their families of origin, and (3) draws boundaries of romantic and sexual exclusivity around the partners. Partners who continued to live separately with their respective parents or with former lovers after the wedding ceremony would be certain to receive a great deal of negative reaction to their failure to make the prescribed transition. We commonly and explicitly recognize that if all couples failed to make the approved shift in status, then the established social structure would be threatened.

Evidence shows some correspondence between how conforming a family is to the values of the society to which it belongs and the degree to which it incorporates traditional symbols and practices in its celebrations. For example, research shows that couples whose partners have been living together or are in second marriages tend to have less traditional wedding ceremonies (e.g., Risman, Hill, Rubin, & Peplace, 1981).

Cultural anthropologists such as Turner (1969, 1974) have observed a sequence of stages through which participants in certain rites of transition pass as part of that process. First, a period of segregation and preparation serves to underscore the termination of the old status. Then comes a *liminal* or transitional stage in which the magic of the change occurs. Often a new name is given to signify the new status. Finally comes the stage of rejoining and reintegration into the larger community in the new capacity.

In our own culture, these elements can be most fully observed in the naming ceremony by which infants are inducted into their religious or ethnic group, graduation ceremonies, the secret rites of fraternal organizations, the assumption of clerical vows, and, most centrally to our concern, traditional wedding ceremonies. In the last ceremony, the bride is sequestered beforehand, and the liminal portion of the ritual requires her to partially obscure her former identity with a veil. And at the end of the ceremony, custom calls for the announcement of her new name: "Ladies and gentlemen, I give you Mr. and Mrs. John Quincy Jones." The transition clearly is mostly seen to be hers: His part in the ritual is less central, and his name is not changed. Feminists are correct in their observation that the traditional wedding ceremony perpetuates the family's traditional patriarchal structure.

Some contemporary commentators on family ritual (e.g., Wolin & Bennett, 1984; Roberts, 1988) have attempted to apply this anthropologically derived model to all family celebrations, examining, for example, the stages of preparation, liminality, and reaggregation in the annual Thanksgiving ritual. This clearly seems an inappropriate application of the model, however. Annual holiday observances have many significant functions, but effecting a transition from one status to another is not one of them.

Annual Holiday Observances

Like rites of passage, annual holiday observances function to renew the family's sense of unity with the larger community, which shares the event's symbols and significance. Feelings of solidarity are increased among Jews when they participate in the seder feast, and Christians are united by their joint participation in the religious music and pageantry associated with Christmas and Easter. The patriotism of the French is bolstered by Bastille Day, and that of Americans by the Fourth of July and Thanksgiving. But whereas rites of passage celebrate transitions, annual holiday observances celebrate the immutability of valued traditions and connections. Studies of rituals have consistently found that respondents commonly identify these recurring celebrations as the very heart of the family's sense of itself as a continuing entity. Indeed, in some ways they are the very antithesis of rites of passage, constituting a kind of inertial force that resists even developmental changes. Continuity, not discontinuity, is celebrated.

I am not saying that the shape of annual celebrations does not change as developmental events inexorably change the shape of the family. They must evolve to accommodate to changing reality and they do,

but these changes are not built into the scripts of the celebrations themselves. In fact, a family's flexibility and creativity may be measured by
its success in adapting change-resisting rituals to its ever-changing
circumstances.

In his intriguing analysis of the rules governing Christmas gift
giving in Middletown, U.S.A., Caplow (1982, 1984) shows that ritual
observances may reflect rather precisely (and reinforce) certain structural features of the family and its kin network. For example, he
observed the following four virtually universal rules of Christmas gift
giving in this community:

1. An individual is expected to give a gift every year to grandparents, parents,
   spouses, children, and all siblings and siblings' spouses with whom one
   has maintained an ongoing face-to-face relationship. This rule is broken
   only under the most compelling and unusual circumstances. To ignore a
   relative at Christmas signals a family rift of very serious proportions.
2. Unless a couple is estranged, a spouse's relatives are to be treated exactly
   as if they were one's own relatives.
3. Practically all gifts to kin are ritually wrapped, displayed, and distrib-
   uted in family gatherings according to an almost invariable ritual. Gifts
   given to nonkin do not require the full ritual presentation.
4. In general, the cost of a gift is roughly proportional to the closeness of
   the relationship. (Caplow, 1982, p. 389)

The gift-giving pattern apparently not only reinforces the kin group
structure, but also may have the power to define relationships within
the kin-friend network. Actual kin may be virtually excommunicated
by the simple (but emotionally weighty) process of eliminating them
from the Christmas gift list. On the other hand, the special status of
fictive kin may be strongly signaled by including them in the family
gift-opening ceremony. Subtler shifts in closeness may be reflected or
even affected by scaling the gifts exchanged up or down.

Caplow also found four additional Christmas gifting rules that
supported the immediate family's internal structure, its bonding patterns, and its hierarchical layering:

5. Parents are supposed to give multiple gifts to young children and to each
   other. Multiple gifts may be given in other relationships, but the probability of this diminishes rapidly as the degree of kinship becomes more
   distant.
6. Men give more expensive gifts than women, and parents give much more
   expensive gifts to children than they receive in return.

7. Women do all but a small portion of the gift buying and wrapping, reflecting their traditional role as relationship specialists in the family.

8. Money is an acceptable gift down the status hierarchy, but not up. Parents and grandparents may give money to children, but for children to give money to parents or grandparents is to signal a major reversal in role. Similarly, husbands in traditional marriages may give gifts of money to their wives, but the reverse is not acceptable. (Caplow, 1982, 1984)

We are not aware of any research that has compared the gift-giving patterns in traditional and less traditional families, but we would expect the ritual form to be adapted to reflect the family's life-style and values. Whether one would observe some *cultural lag*—that is, a time lag between changes in a family's actual current life-style and the life-style celebrated in its rituals—is another issue awaiting investigation.

Family Traditions

Family traditions "as a group, are less culture-specific and more idiosyncratic for each family . . . commonly including summer vacations, visits to and from extended family members, birthday and anniversary customs, [and so on]" (Wolin & Bennet, 1984, p. 405).

Although family traditions differ from annual holiday observances in that they are more particular to the family itself and less tied to religious or national loyalties, they also may draw on widely shared cultural symbols. In this society, birthday celebrations, especially when a child is being honored, virtually always include such standard culture-wide symbols as a birthday greeting card; birthday party complete with a cake, candle-blowing ceremony, and traditional singing of "Happy Birthday to You"; and the ritual preparation and presentation of gifts to the person who is now officially one year older. Of course, as with all other rituals celebrated by families, significant idiosyncrasies always attend the birthday celebration as it manifests *this* family's special status.

Wedding anniversaries are typically more individualized rituals than birthday celebrations, but here, too, couples frequently draw on traditional symbols such as sentimental (or, for those uncomfortable with sentiment, humorous) greeting cards, flowers, dining out alone, and exchanging gifts. On certain special anniversaries such as the 25th and the 50th, a wider circle of kin and friends are commonly invited to join in the celebration and to give gifts to the couple. Couples who fail to observe birthdays and anniversaries altogether are not so much negatively sanctioned as pitied.

Fewer culture-wide societal symbols are to be drawn from in constructing a family vacation, except that the event requires the whole family or some significant subset to leave home as a group for at least several days of activities that are different from the customary family routine and that generally may be loosely labeled "recreational." From that point on, scripts may differ widely, and many families do not take vacations together (or do so at such irregular intervals that ritual elements scarcely have the opportunity to develop).

On one hand, perhaps the very uniqueness of family vacation rituals, when they do develop, make them more valued and memorable to the participants. Certainly that is the impression given by those who are asked in a classroom setting to share descriptions of these rituals with others. On the other hand, in one of the few scholarly discussions of family process on family vacations, Rosenblatt and Russell (1975) found that the challenge of establishing territoriality and interpersonal buffers in the restricted space of the family camper or cabin often resulted in more tension than enjoyment. Apparently, family vacations, involving as they do the uprooting of the family from its ordinary setting, offer a natural laboratory for studying family adaptation to stress. What are the factors that determine the difference between fond memories and forgettable disasters? We suspect that one crucial element may be the family's ability to discover or design effective vacation rituals to buffer the stress points.

Patterned Family Interactions

According to Wolin and Bennett, patterned family interactions

are the ones most frequently enacted but least consciously planned by the participants. Included in this category belong rituals such as regular dinnertime, bedtime routines for children, the customary treatment of guests in the home, or leisure activities on weekends or evenings. (1984, p. 406)

This category of family rituals also includes regular patterned pair rituals such as weekly date nights or sexual protocols and weekend rituals such as church attendance, visiting relatives, going to the movies, or passing out the various sections of the Sunday paper in a prescribed fashion. Many contemporary family rituals revolve around television and televised events such as sports contests or game shows. As with rites of passage, many of these rituals serve to smooth a potentially difficult transition, such as getting the children to bed, gathering the family for dinner, or making the sometimes tricky transition from mundane to sexual pair interaction. As with other categories of ritual, the system's values are celebrated and transmitted through their observance. Prayers at meals or at bedtime convey a religious world view; or serious talk about world affairs at the dinner table may teach not only a cosmopolitan perspective, but also a particular political philosophy. Deference to father or mother on ritual occasions conveys the family's sense of status hierarchy.

As with other rituals, these daily or weekly experiences also reinforce the loyalty and morale of those who participate in them. In fact, if one knows the pattern of participation in these regular ritual events, then one has a key to the family's internal structure. Some families do many things together in which the attendance of every member is required; in other families, virtually no such occasions may occur. In some families, the ritual life excludes the father; in others, he is the chief ritual master. In some families, the marital pair has a full repertoire of its own rituals; in others, ritual is absent from marital life. In each case, the best guess would be that the sense of identity and oneness is strongest in those units where it is supported with ritual, and weakest in those where it is not.

A Typology of Families as Observers of Ritual

Some years ago, David Olson and his colleagues (1979, 1983) developed a general model for characterizing family styles of interaction that they called the circumplex model of family interaction. The model used two dimensions to categorize families: *cohesiveness* and *adaptability*. All families could be described in terms of their scores on both of these dimensions and their location plotted on the model's circular grid.

Wolin and Bennett adapted this format in proposing a useful typology of families with respect to the way they incorporate rituals into their experience. In the Wolin and Bennett model, the two dimensions are *commitment to ritual* (which is virtually identical to cohesiveness as described by Olson and his colleagues) and *adaptability*. By dividing families into those who are high and low on each dimension, Wolin and Bennett generated the following fourfold typology:

1. Families that are highly committed to family ritual and highly inflexible in their administration of it. These families run the risk of being insufficiently adaptive to both developmental changes and individual needs.
2. Families that are highly committed to family ritual but highly flexible in their administration of it. These families have those members who report the greatest satisfaction with their patterns of family living.

3. Families that have little commitment to family ritual but a highly rigid authority structure. These families run the risk of suffering from arbitrary and abusive patterns of interaction.

4. Families that have little commitment to family ritual and a highly flexible and permissive authority structure. These families run the risk of being chaotic.

The reader will recognize some correspondence between this typology and those developed by Constantine (in press) and Reiss (1981) as discussed in earlier chapters. As with all attempts to categorize families into some small number of groupings, the described categories represent "ideal types." Real families are more complex and more difficult to characterize.

Using Family Ritual in Family Therapy

The first therapists to write about the use of rituals in family therapy were those who constituted the Milan Group (Selvini-Palazzoli, 1974; Selvini-Palazzoli, Bosco, Cecchici, & Prata, 1977). These therapists described the rituals they assigned as consisting of "a series of actions, accompanied by verbal formulae and involving the whole family" (p. 238). But by all odds, the therapists who have done most to develop and popularize the use of family rituals in this country are Imber-Black, Roberts, and Whiting, whose book, *Rituals in Families and Family Therapy* (1988), explores the subject in depth. In a fashion exactly parallel to the clinical uses of family stories, they find that getting families to describe their rituals provides a great deal of information on their internal structure and functioning and is usually a positive experience for family members. They also prescribe rituals or modifications in already established rituals that are intended to help the family to operate more effectively. Imber-Black and associates specify the following five functions that these therapeutic ritual assignments are designed to accomplish:

1. *membership* (that is, changing or clarifying family boundaries through, for example, arranging for all members in a newly reconstituted family to sit down together every evening at supper rather than eating separately as each found convenient),

2. *healing* (for example, finding an effective series of symbolic actions for mourning an unresolved loss),

3. *identity* (that is, reinforcing a challenged identity or helping make the transition to a new identity through carefully designed celebrations),

4. *belief expressions and negotiation* (that is, resolving painful conflicts or ambivalences in family members' beliefs), and

5. *celebration* (that is, affirming family loyalty and building family morale by successfully designing and executing one of the major annual holiday celebrations or family traditional occasions).

Summary of Family Meanings and Shared Realities

In this chapter we have focused on the semantic component of communication within family systems. We have defined this component as including beliefs, values, world views, and understandings and have noted that only individuals are capable of these. Family systems and subsystems may appropriately be described, however, in terms of the balance between shared and individual perceptions of reality. They also may be characterized as to how they manage this aspect of their functioning. Some families focus their energies primarily on generating common understandings through such mechanisms as clear-channel communication among the members, the sponsoring of joint activities, the sharing of family folklore and rituals, and by being vigilant in monitoring the boundaries of the family and vigorous in channeling members into extrafamilial associations and experiences that reinforce rather than challenge family beliefs. Other families seem less invested in such activities and are more willing to permit and even to encourage members in their individual pursuits, associations, and opinions.

In consideration of this subject, we have only touched on the important issue of the socialization of children and the principles and mechanisms of intergenerational transmission. This topic has attracted so much attention from such a wide variety of scholars that it deserves a chapter of its own.

CHAPTER 8

The Socialization Process

Perhaps no subject we have considered so far in this book has as extensive a research base as has the topic of socialization. It not only has been a core concern of family process researchers and theorists from the beginning, but also has generated literally thousands of studies by scholars in other branches of the social sciences. For this reason, it serves well as the subject of analysis in this final chapter. It provides a summary opportunity to compare and contrast the process approach with more traditional approaches. Before proceeding with that task, however, we must first acknowledge certain difficult problems within the family process literature itself.

Thorny Issues

Over the history of the family process movement, no premise has been more central and no preoccupation more durable than the doctrine that individual behavior, personality, and pathology are products and reflections of family processes. To me, the explanations of the socialization process as put forth by family process researchers and theorists have at least three important weaknesses:

1. The explanations are *linear!* By insisting adamantly that children's behaviors, personalities, and pathologies are the product of the styles of interaction in their families (and may trace their origins back for several generations, according to many of the theory's founders, such as Murray Bowen [1978] and Ivan Boszormenyi-Nagy and Geraldine Sparks [1973/1984]), they fall into the trap of linear explanation that systemic perspective was invented to avoid.

2. As Don Jackson once wrote, family process research is blighted by "an embarrassing simultaneity of observation" (1965, p. 5). Almost without exception, process-oriented studies of socialization have observed the supposedly prior, causal patterns of family interaction concurrently with the supposedly subsequent, resultant child outcome. Obviously, children's qualities are shaped not only by current patterns of family interaction but also by their whole experience as participants in the evolving family dance from their birth forward.

3. Family process explanations for child outcome have been *too narrowly based*. Like other researchers, family process researchers have frequently fallen prey to the naive assumption that their observed samples of family and child behavior are unbiased reflections of stable, enduring patterns of parent-child interaction as they occur in the natural environment. In fact, the evidence is persuasive that the frontstage family behavior observed in the laboratory or therapy office is *not* representative of backstage behavior at home and that, in any case, patterns of interaction are likely to have changed over time in response to both benign, developmentally scripted events and disruptive, unscripted events. One would also be naive to assume that socialization is a process largely contained within the boundaries of the coresident family, one that excluded the impact of peers, neighbors, teachers, noncustodial parents, other relatives, and so on.

These are not readily solved problems. Fortunately, we have seen a shift toward a more interactive, nonlinear modeling of the socialization process (although, ironically, the leadership for this new approach has come from scholars who, although influenced by systems theory, operate entirely outside of the process movement).

The second problem is not so easily remedied. Longitudinal research into the parent-child relationship has a long and honored place in the socialization literature, but the data collection methods have seldom been observational past the earliest years of development, and we know that people are not very good observers or reporters of their own interactive behavior. The fact is, we may never be able to get adequate samples of these long-term, developmental processes, many of which occur within the bounds of protected family space and time and involve very extended, complex chains of actions and reactions. As for the third set of problems, by their nature they will always resist being fully resolved. As we shall see in the body of the chapter, however, a variety of creative efforts has obtained more inclusive sets of data on familial and extrafamilial social processes and developed theoretical models that reflect these closer approximations of real life experience.

In a later section of the chapter, we will review the unique contributions of the systems perspective to the understanding of the socialization process. Before doing so, however, we will attempt to summarize the very substantial contributions of the large body of social scientists who have studied the subject without the benefit of that perspective. I do not intend to set up a straw man, but rather to glean what may be gleaned from this rich literature, despite whatever conceptual limitations it may suffer by virtue of its blindness to systemic principles. I think of this highly distilled set of linear causal propositions as the legacy of linear models bequeathed to family process scholars by those who have preceded them.

For more detailed and therefore more fully accurate descriptions of the vast socialization literature, examine some of the excellent integrative and evaluative summaries of various segments of the field such as those by Bronfenbrenner (1979), Rollins and Thomas (1979), Gecas (1979), Steinmetz (1979), Troll and Bengtson (1979), Belsky and Vondra (1985), Doan (1985), and Peterson and Rollins (1987).

The Legacy of Linear Models

Theorists in the linear mode are prone to divide variables into four groups, depending on the function assigned to them in a particular model (Burr, Hill, Nye, & Reiss, 1979b). They may be assigned the functions of *independent, dependent, intervening,* or *contingency variables.*

In a linear causal model, an independent variable (x) is chosen as the causal force in the model, and a dependent variable (y) is identified as the ultimate result of the influence of the independent variable:

$$x \longrightarrow y$$

The model also may include one or more intervening variables (i), which are seen as part of a causal chain of variables that links the independent to the dependent variables:

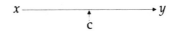

Finally, the model may include contingency variables (*c*), which are seen as influencing the strength or direction of the relationship between the independent and dependent variables.

$$x \longrightarrow y$$
$$c$$

Two complementary but different sets of explanations for how children turn out the way they do may be identified: Those that rely on variables internal to the family, and those that introduce external variables into the explanatory model. We call the first set *interactional* models and the other, *transactional*. Next we will attempt to construct a summary linear model that explains children's characters as resulting from the various styles of parenting to which they are subjected. Then we will expand the model to include the impact of extrafamilial influences.

A Model Based on the Quality of Family Interaction

The Independent Variables: Styles of Parenting

The Warmth or Support Factor

Of all of the different aspects of parental behavior that have been found to influence the way children grow up, their emotional warmth is consistently found to be the most important. Rollins and Thomas (1979) suggested that the degree of warmth in the relationship is best conceptualized and operationalized as the balance of supportive versus nonsupportive behaviors toward the child. Supportive behaviors would include "praising, approving, encouraging, helping, cooperating, expressing terms of endearment, and physical affection" (p. 320). Nonsupportive behaviors would include blaming, criticizing, punishing, threatening, ignoring the child, and expressing anger and negative evaluations of him or her. In the language of family process theory, all of these behaviors would be categorized as either *positive* or *negative metamessages*, because each defines the relationship in either affirming or disaffirming ways. This variable is continuous, ranging from a heavy preponderance of positive metamessages to a heavy preponderance of negative metamessages over some determined period of interaction. Over the years, the variable has been measured in every imaginable way, including by observation, parental self-report, child report, and third-party global evaluation. The variable is robust: It emerges as a crucial factor no matter how it is measured.

Style of Control Attempts and Frequency of Control Attempts

Another universally acknowledged causal factor has been labeled *style* of control attempts (Rollins & Thomas, 1979). As a factor, it is more complex than support. We must first differentiate it from a related variable with which it is often confounded, namely, *frequency* of control attempts. Parents high on the latter variable would be those with many rules and a narrow calibration; they constantly find occasions to intervene in their children's ongoing activities with control attempts. Those parents who score low on this variable, by contrast, would be viewed as permissive or, in the extreme case, negligent; they have few rules and broad calibration.

The variable style of control attempts, however, is logically independent of frequency. It is concerned with the type of intervention attempted and is conceived of as ranging from *coercion*, the unilateral imposition of the parental will at one end of the continuum, to *induction*, the most egalitarian, reason-based attempts to induce voluntary compliance, at the other end (Rollins & Thomas, 1979).

The problem with this definition of the style dimension is that, although it may be logically independent of the frequency dimension, it is not at all logically independent of the support dimension. In fact, as defined by Rollins and Thomas, the indicators of nonsupport have a great deal in common with the indicators of coercion, and the descriptors of supportive parenting overlap considerably with the descriptors of the inductive style of parenting. The two dimensions are by no means identical, however. When the overlapping content is removed, what is left in the style variable is a familiar "vertical" continuum along which metamessages from parent to child may vary. Such messages may range from *one-up complementary* (which assert the right to evaluate and direct the other) to *symmetrical* (which conveys the quality of respect due an equal) and then *one-down complementary* (which acknowledges the other's right to evaluate and direct the speaker).

The advantage of using this "cleaner" version of the parental style variable is twofold. First, it is truly independent of the support-nonsupport dimension. The full range of support and nonsupport logically can and empirically does occur at each level of the style scale (that is, we can find many examples of nurturant, supportive, one-up meta-messages as well as demeaning, nonsupportive, one-up messages, and many examples of warm, egalitarian symmetrical messages as well as hostile, competitive symmetrical messages). Second, this revised, vertical version of the style scale makes explicit the possibility that the power relationship between parent and child can be reversed—that is, with the child in the one-up position. This phenomenon is virtually ignored in the research and theoretical literature on socialization because it is at odds with societal norms. Yet every observer of families would agree that it occurs often enough in the real world to need attention.

Coherence and Consistency Factors

The degree of coherence and consistency in the various components of the messages exchanged among family members has been well recognized as an important factor in the socialization process. In the deviance literature, for example, consistency of discipline and parental consensus on family values and expectations are viewed as key explanatory variables (Bahr, 1979). Family therapists, from the beginning, have emphasized the mischief done to children if the messages they receive from parents are systematically *paradoxical* (that is, characterized by contradictions between the message and the metamessage) or *conflicting* (that is, characterized by contradictory demands within the messages or within the metamessages) (Broderick & Pulliam-Krager, 1979). However it is labeled or measured by various scholars, the root concept holds that the degree of internal consistency in the parental demands and evaluations of the child are an important issue in the child's performance.

The Dependent Variable:
The Child's Socioemotional Competence

The most frequently used dependent variables may be grouped under the heading of socioemotional competence and include such elements as conformity to the significant norms of society and the absence of the symptoms of emotional illness (including excessive hostility or passivity). Such competence implies an array of social skills, a degree of independence, and a level of moral development that is appropriate to the child's developmental level. Each factor has been studied separately and has its own unique correlates, but for the purposes of this analysis, they may be lumped together because they all relate in the same way to the four independent variables we have listed. We thus exclude certain other child outcomes such as *creativity*, which relate to the independent variables in a more complicated way (Rollins & Thomas, 1979).

Intervening Variables: Self-Esteem and Parental Identification

Self-esteem. One of the clusters of linking mechanisms by which particular types of parenting patterns become translated into particular child outcomes may be labeled *self-esteem*. Included under the umbrella of this construct is not only positive self-regard, but also its corollary of internalized locus of control. Implied also are certain personal coping mechanisms that are appropriate to the child's level of development. To say that this is an intervening variable is to assert that the immediate consequence of parents' behavior is to affect the child's self-esteem and that the level of self-esteem in turn determines the child's level of socioemotional competence (rather than positing a direct, unmediated effect). It also suggests that if a child were able to maintain a positive self-esteem despite parental abuse (presumably through the influence of some interpersonal or intrapsychic factor not specified in the model), that he or she could still attain high levels of socioemotional competence; conversely, any child who, despite positive parenting, failed to achieve self-esteem, could be expected to exhibit deficits in his or her level of functioning. Neil Smelser (1989) has argued that the construct should be used with care, because it has not always performed well in empirical studies where it was used to predict child outcomes. He considers several possible explanations, including the fact that the concept is often measured poorly. However, I am persuaded by the overall burden of evidence and by clinical observation that it belongs in the model.

Parental identification. A second intervening factor of comparable importance is the cluster of variables that we have labeled *parent identification*. It includes what has been called *parent attachment* and implies its corollary, the internalization of parental values and world views. It is closely related to the concept of *cohesion* as discussed by Olson (1989) and to several of the dimensions of *solidarity* as discussed by Bengtson and Schrader (1981), except that both of those concepts refer to properties of the relationship while parent identification is explicitly an attitude of the child. Placing this attitude as an intervening variable in the model identifies it as one of the two key mechanisms (together with self-esteem) that mediates between parenting patterns and child outcomes.

Contingency Variables

In attempting to study the circumstances that influence the effects of these various independent and intervening variables on how children turn out, scholars have found it necessary to take several factors into account. In a linear model, contingency variables are defined as those variables that determine the conditions under which other variables have their effect. In a nonlinear, systemic model, system constraints have a parallel function. Thus we might reasonably use the same three headings for grouping contingency variables that were used in Chapter 2 for listing constraints on the family systems model: (1) individual constitutional factors, (2) family structural factors, and (3) historic and cultural factors.

Individual constitutional factors. Relationships among humans are always mediated by symbols and the meanings imputed to them. In that sense, no variable that involves human interaction is entirely biological. Every biological drive or structural feature is inextricably intertwined with its associated social and personal significances. Certainly this is the case with the three most frequently cited variables in this category: gender, developmental level, and genetic factors.

Gender effects. As Pollack and Grossman (1985) wrote, "Virtually all of the studies that have data to examine parent and child gender interactions find them" (p. 614). In other words, the impact of parental behavior on children depends partly on the sex of the parent and the sex of the child. We may not assume, for example, that because the use of corporal punishment by fathers has a particular effect on their sons that it necessarily has the same effect on their daughters. Nor may we assume that the effects would be the same if it were a mother administering the punishment. Steinmetz (1979) reviews a substantial number of studies that examined this effect, as did Pollack and Grossman (1985).

Similarly, studies by sociologists on patterns of intergenerational transmission have found that not all values and life-style components flow as freely through cross-sex as through same-sex intergenerational linkages. Some things are passed on primarily from mothers to daughter and from fathers to sons. Other things are more likely to be transmitted through cross-sex linkages. For a summary of some of these effects, see Troll and Bengtson (1979).

Developmental level effects. A second biologically constraining factor that affects socialization and intergenerational transmission might be called the *developmental level effect*. What one can successfully teach a child clearly depends on the child's level of physical and cognitive development. A child-rearing strategy that is very effective at one age may become quite ineffective at another. The same result is found in the intergenerational transmission literature. One may not expect parents' interest in liberal or conservative politics or their penchant for abusing alcohol to manifest themselves in the lives of their children while they are still young. If these patterns are to show up in the next generation at all, they are likely to appear in the late adolescent or young adult stage of their lives (Schuman & Scott, 1989). Similarly, research has shown that any tendency to replicate the religious commitments or sexual conservatism of one's parents is far more likely to be manifested after one becomes a parent oneself than at some earlier developmental stage (Cohen & Tenenbaum, 1988; D'Antonio, 1988).

But even though most researchers and therapists who incorporate a developmental dimension into their work restrict their discussion to the developmental level of children, others have also noted the importance of this as a parental variable, at least at the extremes of the developmental range. Several scholars have examined the impact of a parent's extreme youth on the effectiveness of his or her parenting strategies (see, for example, Roosa, Fitzgerald, & Crawford, 1985; or the special issue of *Family Perspectives*, Vol. 22, No. 3, 1988). On the other end of the spectrum, gerontologists have studied whether the same factors predict the closeness of the parent-child bond (i.e., parent identification) at various points in the aging parents' developmental life cycle. For example, different factors seem to operate when the parents may be classified as merely old rather than as very old (Treas & Bengtson, 1987).

Genetic factors. In addition to gender and developmental level, genetic factors have frequently been cited as moderating the effect of various independent variables. They may manifest themselves in a variety of ways, such as *native ability, constitutional components of temperament, genetic vulnerabilities and predispositions, body build,* and *health.* Among the large number of studies that document the interaction between social and genetic factors in the process of socialization, we cite only one by way of example. In their Danish study of the factors that contribute to a child becoming a criminal, Hutchings and Mednick (1977) found that 12% of adopted men became criminals when neither their natural nor adoptive fathers had criminal records, approximately 20% became criminals when either their natural or their adoptive fathers had criminal records, and 36% did so when both sets of fathers had criminal records.

Family structural factors. A variety of structural issues have been evaluated as contingency factors that affect the way these independent and dependent variables relate to one another. Among these are birth-order effects, family size, age and gender composition (including the presence of one or two parents and one, two, or three generations), kin composition (including stepparent, half-parent, adoptive-parent, and foster parent relationships), coalitional structure, and location of the family in the adaptability-cohesiveness grid that we know as the circumplex model (Olson, 1989).

Of all the family-level contingency variables that we might have made a case for including, we have chosen only two: (1) the *perceived power of the parent* vis-à-vis the child, and (2) the social deviance or normalcy of the parents' values and life-style, or, in other words, the *parents' own socioemotional competence.*

Historic and cultural factors. The only way to study the impact of the larger historical and cultural forces on socialization or intergenerational transmission is to do comparative studies of these processes across times and cultures. A small but growing literature does just that, but we will not take the space to review it here. Two issues that deserve mention at this point because they play such pivotal roles in the research on socialization and intergenerational transmission are *ethnic prescriptions* and *cohort effects.*

Ethnic prescriptions. Studies that have compared the disciplinary techniques of various ethnic groups have found that the same behavior (for instance, corporal punishment) has different meanings in different groups. For example, one study of San Diego fathers found that children responded quite differently to beatings that were seen as normative than they did to beatings that were seen as arbitrary inflictions of a father's wrath. Where both the father and the child saw the punishment as a legitimate, traditional response to the breaking of universally understood rules, even quite severe punishment was likely to be accepted philosophically by everyone, including the child and his or her peers. By contrast, when the father was viewed as arbitrarily making up the rule and the punishment ad hoc, then the response of the child was likely to be resentment and rebellion (Broderick, 1977).

Cohort effects. A cohort is a group of people born at about the same time. Thus, cohort effects are those that grow out of the reality that each generation begins its life at a unique point in the history of humankind and experiences the unfolding of world and local events over its life course from that unique perspective. The extent to which a child absorbs and imitates the life view and values of his or her parents depends at least partly on how similar or different their life experiences have been. Actually, older and younger children in the same family may sometimes be thought of as belonging to different cohorts. Some researchers have suggested that in this rapidly changing world, any two people born more than five years apart probably experience history in substantially different ways (see, for example, Glenn, 1977; Troll & Bengtson, 1979; Schuman & Scott, 1989).

Linear Propositions in the Interactional Model

Proposition 1. The greater the preponderance of positive metamessages in parents' communications with their children, the greater the children's self-esteem.

This is a simple linear relationship that is stable across a wide range of contingencies.

Proposition 2. The greater the preponderance of positive metamessages in parents' communications with their children, the greater the children's identification with their parents and the more imitative of their values and life-styles.

This is a simple linear relationship that is stable across many conditions and yet interactive with some, such as child's developmental level and parents' perceived power.

In one form or another, these two propositions are central to every linear model of socialization or intergenerational transmission in the literature. Of course, in this model both the variable *self-esteem* and the variable *parent identification* are compound, "umbrella" variables standing respectively as surrogates for a cluster of related attitudes toward the self and a cluster of related attitudes toward the parental "other."

The evidence is compelling that several contingency variables influence the logical linkage between parents' warmth and the children's identification with them and their values. As noted earlier, the child's level of development is one important factor. Many components of one's parents' value system or life-style are not possible to express until one reaches maturity or even parental status oneself. Also, both theory and research have indicated the importance of the perceived power of the parent as a factor that interacts with parental warmth in influencing identification with parental values.

Proposition 3. Parental control attempts may vary in style from highly dominating demands through egalitarian requests and negotiations to submissive pleas. A *curvilinear* relationship is seen between this variable and children's self-esteem such that the latter is most effectively promoted by control attempts in the egalitarian range.

The exact point of optimal effect varies with the child's developmental level, moving from moderately dominating at the earliest ages toward frank equality as the child achieves adulthood. Gender and ethnic effects may also affect the relationship between the variables.

Proposition 4. The relationship between style of parental control attempts and parent identification is curvilinear.

The developmental effects on this relationship exactly parallel those described in Proposition 3 above. Likewise, it also shares complex gender effects and interactions with cultural prescriptions for parental styles of discipline.

Proposition 5. The relationship between frequency of control attempts by parents and children's self-esteem is curvilinear, with moderate frequencies having the most positive effects.

Proposition 6. The relationship between frequency of control attempts by parents and parent identification is curvilinear, with moderate frequencies having the most positive effects.

All four of these propositions enjoy substantial support. As a single example, Miller, McCoy, Olson, and Wallace (1986) found that among teenagers living with their parents, the highest levels of sexual activity occurred among those whose parents were most permissive (that is, at the lower end of both the style and frequency continua). The next most active group consisted of those whose parents were the strictest (that is, at the upper end of both continua). The least active were those whose parents were moderately strict (that is, they tended toward the strict end of the scale but were substantially more moderate than those in the most extreme category).

Systematic research is scarce on the impact of various contingency variables on these propositions. All indications are, however, that at least three—gender, developmental level, and ethnic prescriptions—have important effects.

Proposition 7. The greater the degree of coherence and consistency in parents' demands and evaluations of the child, the greater the child's self-esteem.

This is a simple linear relationship that is stable across many conditions but interactive with the degree of positiveness of the metamessages as well as with the family structural feature of boundary permeability.

Proposition 8. The greater the degree of coherence and consistency in parents' demands and evaluation of the child, the greater the children's identification with their parents and the more imitative of their values and life-styles.

This is a simple linear relationship.

The importance of consistency and coherence as determinants of children's attitudes toward themselves and others is well established. However, clinical experience and common sense affirm that if the messages received are consistently negative, then the net impact on self-esteem will be negative rather than positive. This contingency variable does not appear to operate in the same manner in the case of parent identification. The clinical evidence is that children with consistent parenting identify with their parents' view of them whether it be positive or negative. (For the most comprehensive exposition of this point, see Boszormenyi-Nagy & Spark, 1973).

The clinical literature also has established that the degree to which the family boundaries are open may modify the impact of the parent's coherence or incoherence on the child. In effect, an open boundary permits the child to check parents' opinions against an external criterion and may therefore dilute the potential negative consequences of confusing messages from within the family (Broderick & Pulliam-Krager, 1979). Again, this effect is clear in the case of self-esteem but less clear in the case of parent identification.

Proposition 9. The greater children's self-esteem, the greater their socioemotional competence.

This is a simple linear relationship.

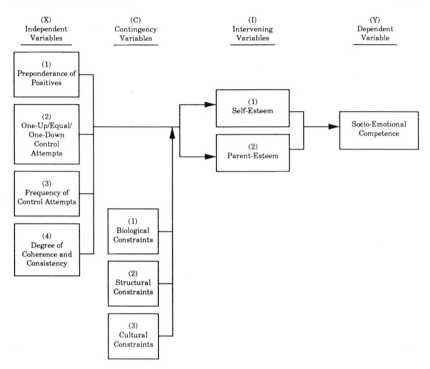

Figure 8.1. Linear Model of Socialization Process: Interactional Variables

Proposition 10. The greater children's identification with their parents and the more imitative of their life-styles, the greater their socio-emotional competence.

This is a linear relationship, but it interacts with the parents' level of socioemotional competence.

Despite Smelser's reservations (1989), these two clusters of variables do appear to be the immediate explanations of why some children turn out one way and some another. Self-esteem in all of its manifestations seems to be a logical precondition to the achievement of a wide variety of positive child outcomes. In the case of identification with parents' values and life-styles, however, how children turn out clearly depends not only on the degree to which that identification occurs, but also on the particular values and life-styles modeled by their parents (Bahr, 1979).

Figure 8.1 is a schematic representation of the whole interactional model.

The Expanded (Transactional/Interactional) Model

The addition of transactional variables to the model permits the identification of factors that are external to the immediate family that contribute to the explanation of how children turn out. Specifically, two new sets of issues are addressed. The first comprises those factors outside the immediate parent-child relationship that influence parents' child-rearing styles. Researchers have identified two such factors as of particular significance: (1) the styles of child rearing to which the parents themselves were exposed in their own families of origin and (2) the indirect effects of the parents' current socioeconomic placement in the larger society. In this expanded model, the ways parents behave toward children (the independent variables in the preceding model) are reduced to the status of intervening variables in the chain of effects that lead to the ultimate child outcome.

The second elaboration of the original model introduces the factor of the greater or lesser use of parental *channeling* in determining the child's outcome. This term refers to the practice of augmenting direct parental efforts to socialize children by channeling them into associations and settings that will reinforce the parents' values.

Independent Variables: Parents' Placement in the External World

Styles of parent-child communication in the parents' families of origin. One of the most important external connections that influences parents' behavior is their historic experience as children in another family. We might reasonably suppose that parents model their own styles of child rearing after those used by their own parents (Bowen, 1978; Boszormenyi-Nagy & Sparks, 1973). All of the mediating influences have not been established. For example, we may be tempted to assume that the replication would be most complete if the relationship between the generations were positive; however, we know that negative, abusive parenting styles are as faithfully passed down the generations as any. I am not aware of any studies of the differential dynamics of positive versus negative identification.

Independent of that issue, one contingency variable has been reliably found to affect the degree to which children imitate their parents' child-rearing styles. I refer to the well-established modifying influence of *cohort effects* (Peterson & Rollins, 1987). (See Box A.) When our parents' philosophy is consistent with the most widely accepted theories and practices of our own day, we are more likely to imitate them than when they are out of synch with current trends. This principle has been found to hold true for many other issues beyond child-rearing philosophies, such as political and religious beliefs (Troll & Bengtson, 1979).

BOX A   COHORT EFFECTS

A *cohort* is a group of people who are born in the same set period of time. Members of successive cohorts are known as *sequential generations*, and they influence the degree to which a succeeding generation is willing to adopt the practices and belief systems of those that went before. Thus, cohort effects on intergenerational transmission are those that grow out of the reality that each generation begins its life at a unique point in human history and experiences the unfolding of world and local events over its life course from that unique perspective.

For example, my mother was born in 1910, experienced World War I as a child, was a teenager in the "flapper" period of the 1920s, raised her children in the Great Depression and in World War II, and saw her grandchildren grow up in the period of the Viet Nam War and the revolutionary challenges to her values that accompanied that national experience. By contrast, my generation grew up in the Great Depression and World War II; went to college during the period of Joseph McCarthy's anticommunist witch hunts; entered the job market at a point of unparalleled prosperity; experienced the movements for civil rights, women's rights, zero population, and peace (not to mention the sexual revolution, the drug culture, and the environmental crisis) as thirtysomething adults; and are watching our grandchildren grow up in the relatively placid 1980s and 1990s. No one should be surprised if my mother and I have seen events and trends quite differently, even though I was raised by her in a shared historic period.

One good illustration of the interplay between intergenerational transmission and unique cohort experience can be seen when we compare certain features of our respective parenting styles. Both the way I treated my children when they were sick and also the policy we had for our children about whether they had to finish what was on their plates at dinner are clearly compounds from two generations of overlapping but separate experiences. When I was sick as a child, I could count on being entertained by my mother. A centerpiece of the show would be a rousing performance of the Charleston and the cancan, dances she learned as a teenager during the Roaring '20s. As for dinner plate policies, times were hard when I was growing up. In the first few years of my life, we struggled with the pervasive poverty of the Depression, and after the war came we had to cope with recurring food shortages and rationing. In our and in many other families, leaving food on one's plate was considered a grave sin. I vividly remember being embarrassed in a restaurant as a young adult when my mother insisted on eating the food I left rather than see it go to waste.

Neither practice was simply incorporated without change into my own child-rearing patterns. My experience of the world differed dramatically from my mother's, and this fact was reflected in my parenting as well as in every other aspect of my life. On the other hand, it would not take a Ph.D. researcher to identify the intergenerational influences at work as I sing and tell stories to my children when they are ill (no Charleston or cancan, but we each must live with our limitations). Nor do we tax the intellect when we seek to find the lineal roots of our fully rationalized policy that requires our children to eat what is on their plates at home (they put the food on their plate themselves and thereby accrue the obligation not to waste it) but are explicitly exempt from finishing what is served in restaurants (they did not choose the portions; besides, we are there to enjoy ourselves, not to acquire admirable character traits). Clearly, both intergenerational transmission *and* cohort effects are required to explain these patterns. ▲

Social placement of parents in the socioeconomically stratified external world. As we discussed in some detail in Chapter 6, a family's socioeconomic placement is not a unitary variable. We noted Weber's widely accepted definition of class as being determined by power, property, and prestige. In practice, sociological researchers most often use income, occupation, education, and consumer patterns as empirical indicators. In the socialization literature, the aspects of socioeconomic placement that are deemed most relevant have been the parents' education and the degree to which their daily occupational activities were self-directed. Each of these have been seen as contributing to certain values and communication styles that were in turn predictive of parenting styles.

Intervening Variables: Set I (Parents' Parents' Socialization Style)

Values favoring self-direction over conformity. Evidence shows that the more education one gets and the higher up the socioeconomic ladder that one climbs, the more likely one is to have a job that requires self-direction. The more one's daily work life rewards self-direction, the more likely one is to foster it in one's children, even at the expense of their challenging one's authority. Therefore, one is likely to use more reasoning and less coercion with them (Kohn, 1977; Gecas, 1979).

We also can reasonably assume that the more these values are modeled in one's home, the more likely one is to adopt them as a basis for one's own parenting style.

Using elaborated codes in communication. Basil Bernstein (1960, 1964, 1970, 1971-1973), a British social scientist, introduced the concepts of restricted and elaborated linguistic codes into the sociological literature in the early 1960s to help explain how social class perpetuated itself across generations. The notion, echoing the opinion of Shaw's famous Professor Higgins, was that it was the way a Britisher spoke that determined his placement in society. Bernstein wrote of the restricted code, "Such a communication code will emphasize verbally the communal rather than the individual, the concrete rather than the abstract, the substance rather than the elaboration of process, the here and now rather than explorations of motives and intentions" (1970, p. 29).

By contrast, Bernstein's concept of the elaborated code (as summarized by Gecas, 1979) was as follows:

> [It] is characterized by language which is more complex (i.e., larger vocabulary, greater frequency of modifiers, greater use of subordinate clauses, greater grammatical accuracy and sentence complexity); meanings are elaborated and explicit rather than assumed, and they are relatively context-free. The speaker using an elaborated code is more aware of and more likely to take into account the perspective of the listener. . . . It is a more analytic mode, compared to the restricted code which is more subjective. (p. 368)

The strong relationship between social-class placement and linguistic code that Bernstein found in Great Britain has not been replicated in U.S. samples, but we have no reason to doubt the importance of the language style that children grow up with in shaping their thinking and performance.

Intervening Variables: Set II
(Parents' Direct and Indirect Control Attempts)

Direct control attempts: Styles of parent-child communication. This, of course, is the same cluster of variables that served as the independent variables in the interactional model. In the expanded transactional interactional model, the set is seen as only one of two parallel parental efforts that influence the values and behaviors of children.

Indirect control attempts: Channeling. One of the most important mechanisms that families use for shaping their children's values, behaviors, and world views is channeling. We have encountered the concept in several earlier chapters (see also Box B). The term is borrowed from the sociology of religion (e.g., Cornwall, 1988) and refers to the strategy used by parents of various religious persuasions to channel their children into friendship networks, youth organizations, schools, camps, colleges, and causes that reinforce loyalty to the parents' religious affiliation and beliefs. For purposes of this discussion, we expand the definition to include the intentional reinforcement of any important family values (not just religious) through the manipulation of children's external connections. This variable has its most direct effect on the child's identification with his or her parents' values and life-style.

BOX B CHANNELING: SHAPING FAMILY VALUES THROUGH SELECTIVE INTERCONNECTIONS WITH THE EXTERNAL SYSTEM

We may define *channeling* as the intentional reinforcement of important family values by manipulating family members' external connections.

Preserving the Faith

This concept was first developed to describe one of the more successful strategies that parents use to increase the probability that their children will follow in their religious footsteps (Cornwall, 1988). Researchers noted long ago that the impact of channeling is enhanced by what might be called "natural snowballing." In other words, children who are enrolled in a parochial school (or in Hebrew class or in the early morning religious classes that Mormons provide for their youth) are also more likely to choose their friends and dates from within their own religious group, to attend religiously sponsored social events, and so forth. Ultimately, they are more likely than others to marry within their faith and to raise their own children in that tradition (Cornwall, 1988).

Among certain groups such as the Amish, whose life-style is sufficiently at odds with the surrounding culture to warrant them, protective measures go beyond channeling to what might be called *flooding*. This strategy requires insulating the young as much as possible from all outside influences by providing every aspect of living and learning within the community. The Amish, for example, maintain a distinctive and separatist life-style, dress, and even language, preserving a dialect of German as their primary medium of communication. Under no circumstances would they permit one of their children to attend a public school. They have negotiated with state boards of education to meet the requirements of the minimum education laws by providing their own teachers through eighth grade and then removing their young from the educational system altogether (Hostetler, 1980; Kephart, 1982).

Clearly, these denominationally segregated experiences owe their effectiveness to at least two factors. First, they expose children to multiple reinforcements of their parents' belief system while simultaneously protecting them from challenges to it. Second, they restrict the opportunities for behavior that is contrary to their parents' values. These same factors are equally operative in the passing on of parents' secular values.

Preserving Secular Values and Perpetuating Life-Styles

Not all families are religious, but we take it as an axiom that all families are committed to pass on their core values to their children. We can identify at least four major types of extrafamilial experiences that parents regularly channel their children into in their efforts to achieve this task: basic education, enrichment activities, employment opportunities, and approved informal networks.

Basic Education

The goal of many poor and middle-class families is simply to see that their children "get an education." This goal may have different meanings in different social strata. For some, the achievement of basic literacy or fluency in English might be considered success. For others, graduation from high school or admission to college might be required. Among the affluent citizens, the object is not merely an education, but also an education in a "good" school—that is, in a school that caters to those of higher social status and is dedicated to perpetuating their class values.

Enrichment Activities

In the service of promoting a wider range of social values than mere academics could provide, schools offer a variety of activities such as athletics, cheerleading, debate, musical performance groups, drama, and student government, as well as interest clubs and social fraternities and sororities. Of course, the schools are by no means the only vehicles that families use in sponsoring their secular values through enrichment activities. A well-developed network of extracurricular athletic groups also exist through which children can be channeled, including Little League baseball, Pop Warner football, and youth soccer leagues, not to mention more elite swimming, gymnastics, and martial arts programs. Beyond these programs are a variety of opportunities for training in dance, music, and the arts. Millions of children participate regularly in Boys Clubs, YMCAs and YWCAs, Boy Scouts, Girl Scouts, 4-H Clubs, and Future Farmers and Future Homemakers of America, all of which have as their explicit goal the shaping of their young members' character through uplifting activities and programs.

Employment Opportunities

Historically, the main instrument that parents used to shape their children's character (in other words, embedding the family's values in a child) was providing the opportunity to work. Young boys and girls were apprenticed out to learn a trade or were taught by their own parents how to run a household, farm, or family business. In recent years, this mechanism has been gradually replaced by education and by enriching activities. In many contemporary families, the children's main responsibility is to do their homework and practice the piano (or their batting). Even today, however, many families expect children to perform work around the house and to seek paid employment as soon as the local customs permit. Many children still baby-sit, have paper routes, do yardwork for neighbors, or work for minimum wage at a fast-food place or the local supermarket because their families think the experience is important. Still others put in long hours at the family business. The money earned is welcome and sometimes an essential component of a family's financial welfare. But even where the contribution is considered trivial, the work experience itself is judged to be valuable to the young person. It teaches him or her "responsibility," "that money doesn't grow on trees."

Approved Informal Networks

From the dawn of time, humans have understood that "birds of a feather flock together" and that "a man is judged by the company he keeps." Thus, part of the motivation for channeling one's children (and oneself) into relationships with "good" companions is a matter of maintaining and possibly improving one's reputation and status in the larger community. To the extent that "good" implies "having values like our own," such mixing also is a means of reassuring ourselves that we and our values are unimpeachable. Stating an obvious truth and having everyone around us nod in affirmation is a great comfort, more so than having others ignore it or dispute it, which is profoundly unsettling.

One of the best methods for ensuring the former and avoiding the latter is to construct a protective circle of like-minded folk as our buffer against the unappreciative outside world. Assuming that each of these buffering families is equally selective in its choice of friends and that this third layer follows a similar pattern, the resulting network resembles an onion; every family is surrounded by layers of insulation from conflicting values and beliefs. Depending on how selective and protective the member families in each succeeding layer actually are, a child will experience the socially meaningful world as more or less univocal in its support of his or her own cherished views of reality. Views that differ radically from one's own would be found only at some remove—among strangers and outlanders.

Although they may not be aware of the confirming research, most parents are familiar with the principle that the probability of their children getting involved with drugs, sex, delinquency, or, for that matter, some other religion or philosophy of life is a direct function of the proportion of their associates who are so involved. In selecting a new home, parents routinely evaluate the neighborhood and school from this point of view. If their means permit, they attempt to shape their children's choice of companions by choosing a home in a "good" neighborhood in which their own pre-ferred life-style and value system predominates. Evidence has shown that one of the most serious losses that divorcing mothers must confront in their efforts to raise their children successfully is losing the financial ability to maintain their children's residence in such a neighborhood (Fleisher, 1966; Willie, 1967). ▲

Intervening Variables: Set III

This set includes the child's self-esteem and identification with his or her parents.

Dependent Variable: Child's Socioemotional Competence

The addition of transactional variables requires us to add the follow-ing linear propositions to complete the model.

Proposition 11. The more effective the style of parent-child commu-nication in the parents' families of origin, the more effective their own direct control attempts. This is a simple linear relationship, but it does interact with cohort effects.

Proposition 12. The more effective the style of parent-child communica-tion in the parents' families of origin, the more that parents will sponsor self-direction rather than conformity in their own children. This is a simple linear relationship.

Proposition 13. The more effective the style of parent-child communica-tion in the parents' families of origin, the more such parents will use elaborated codes in their own parent-to-child communication. This is a simple linear relationship.

Proposition 14. The greater the parents' socioeconomic status (as measured by level of education and degree of self-direction in their occupation), the more energy they will invest in channeling their children into external systems that support parental values. This is a simple linear relationship.

Proposition 15. The greater the parents' socioeconomic status (as measured by level of education and degree of self-direction in their occupation), the more they will sponsor self-direction rather than conformity in their own children.
This is a simple linear relationship.

Proposition 16. The greater the parents' socioeconomic status (as measured by level of education and degree of self-direction in their occupation), the more they will use elaborated codes in their own parent-to-child communication.
This is a simple linear relationship.

Proposition 17. The more parents sponsor self-direction rather than conformity, the more effective their direct control attempts will be.
This is a simple linear relationship.

Proposition 18. The more parents use elaborated codes in their parent-to-child communication, the more effective their direct control attempts will be.
This is a simple linear relationship.

Proposition 19. The more energy parents invest in channeling their children into external systems that support parental values, the more the children will identify with their parents' values and life-styles.
This is a simple linear relationship.

The final expanded linear model is represented in Figure 8.2. (Contingency variables have been omitted to reduce clutter in the table.)

We have taken a considerable amount of space and energy to summarize the contributions of the myriad laborers in the socialization vineyard who do not use systems approaches. We have done this for two reasons. First, this body of insights is, of necessity, the foundation upon which systems approaches build. Second, the contributions of the systems approach are only evident against the background of the alternative approach.

The Unique Contributions of the Systemic Approach

The first step in shifting from a linear to a systems perspective is to recast the socialization process into systems terminology. This is not a

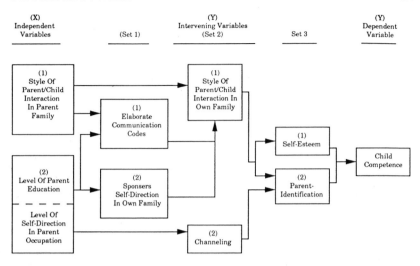

Figure 8.2. Expanded Linear Model of Socialization Process: With Transactional Variables Added

trivial exercise; it immediately focuses our attention on several systemic issues that were not pivotal in the linear perspective. For example, the most minimal linear definition of socialization—that parent behaviors and attitudes help shape children's personalities—might be restated in systemic terms as repeated, patterned interactions between parents and children that have a cumulative effect on the internal patterning of the child as a personality subsystem (and on both the parents as personality subsystems and the relationships between them).

This systemic reframing of the definition provides a more provocative formulation of the topic. As soon as the matter is stated in these terms, certain important aspects of the process become immediately obvious: Socialization is a circular, cumulative process; the influences between the generations are reciprocal; and the qualities of the ongoing relationships among family members both shape and are shaped by the spiraling process. Other questions, although not resolved by the definition, are provoked by it. For example, is the reciprocal interchange between parents and children symmetrical? If not, why not? According to this definition of the process, what operations must be assumed to occur within the personality subsystems of the parent and child? And when it becomes necessary to expand the definition to include inputs from outside of the family system (as we were required in the development of our linear model), how may these external inputs be accommodated?

Based on the consideration of such issues, several sets of systemic principles may be identified.

1. The Principles of the Transcybernetic Process

All of the principles of the transcybernetic model spelled out in Chapter 3 apply to the processes of socialization, just as they apply to any other sector of family interactions. Still, certain principles touched on in that chapter deserve more particular development in this context.

2. The Principle of Reciprocal Effects

Principle 2A. Socialization is an ongoing, circular (or spiral) interactive process that is cumulative in its effects. A substantial and growing body of research documents the impact that children have on parents. We will not review this literature in detail here because conscientious reviews are readily available in other places such as Maccoby and Martin (1983), Belsky and Vondra (1985), and Peterson and Rollins (1987). In some ways, the effects of children on their parents may be thought of as generic; that is, they depend not so much on the particular characteristics of the particular child as on the mere introduction of child into the family system. By definition, children are immature, dependent, and demanding. But other effects depend precisely on the differential qualities of the child such as gender, temperament, and developmental level.

The effects of children on parents and of parents on children are viewed not only as reciprocal, but also as interactive and incremental. In other words, through their constant interaction, the parent and the child are creating the rules that pattern their relationship.

This principle also underlines the cumulative nature of these reciprocal effects. The family has a history and with rare, traumatic exceptions, the child's personality (and the parents') are not shaped by single incidents but by layer on layer of joint experiences that accumulate over years of daily interactions. Also true is that the meaning of each separate incident is mediated by an awareness of that history. If a mother strikes her 10-year-old for talking back to her, the incident is likely to have a different meaning in a chronically abusive parent-child relationship than in a relationship in which neither mother nor child had participated in such an event before.

If socialization is an ongoing, interactive process, then it is not best characterized as a fully intentional activity of parents. As noted in an earlier chapter, people can be shown to be very poor observers of the rules that govern their own normal interpersonal behavior and cannot be assumed to be at all sophisticated about the unintended consequences of these unexamined behavior patterns. Thus, the second subprinciple that differentiates systemic from linear thinking on this topic is the following:

Principle 2B. Socialization consists largely of unintended, unnoticed, and unanalyzed reciprocal effects. One of the chief strategies of family therapists who attempt to reshape parent-child patterns of interaction is to raise everyone's consciousness to the currently practiced "dance" and its unintended consequences and to induce new patterns that have more positive outcomes. To put this point in clear perspective, we must note two things that are *not* implied. First, parents are readily acknowledged as sometimes taking thoughtful action and developing fully intentional policies for directing their children's development. Only in the most chaotic families would one fail to find such committed efforts. This principle reminds us, however, that such efforts at best constitute a small minority of the interactions that cumulatively shape the child's (and the parents') personality. Second, to say that reactions most often are unintended, uncataloged, and unanalyzed on the conscious level is not to suggest that they are not determined by rules. Quite the contrary. As we have seen, family process theory is centrally concerned with the complex processes by which a particular instigation generates a particular response. The dancers, for the most part, need not focus their attention on the intricate patterns of the family minuet. Their feet know the steps.

Principle 2C. Although they are reciprocal, socialization processes are not symmetrical. The impact of parents' actions on children will be greater than the impact of children's actions on parents to the extent that the following results are seen:

1. Children's influence vis-à-vis their parents is constrained by biological and family structural and cultural factors; and
2. In the cumulative process of development, children's personalities have acquired less content than their parents' so that the relative impact of each new input is greater with them.

Among the operational biological constraints, developmental factors that impinge on a growing child's capacities seem particularly pertinent. Among family structural constraints, we are especially mindful of the greater access to family resources and the greater control of family assets that parents have over children. Among cultural constraints, the powerful norms of filial subordination that permeate all cultures, some more than others, seem particularly important.

3. The Principle of Multiple Significant Others

The previous principles have presumed that the primary unit of the socialization process is the reciprocating parent-child dyad. One must recognize at this point that the matter is not so simple. Only a pathologically isolated child is socialized in a single dyadic relationship. Not only mothers, but also fathers, siblings, baby-sitters, grandparents, stepparents, foster parents, teachers, pastors, scout leaders, gang leaders, and friends are likely to play significant roles in the process. Every child does not draw from the same list, but a every child does have such a list of role influences. Indeed, in recognizing such a principle, George Herbert Mead (1934), one of the founders of socialization theory, coined the term *significant other*. Every time the term *parent* appears in the earlier principles, reality would be better reflected by substituting *significant other*. Moreover, clearly the child must—more or less simultaneously—order, evaluate, and respond to inputs from many significant others.

Principle 3A. From the child's viewpoint, the socialization process involves the evaluation and selective incorporation of inputs from many significant others. Urie Bronfenbrenner (1979, 1986) is the scholar who has done more than any other to conceptualize this aspect of the socialization process. He calls the immediate caretakers and companions of a child its *microsystem*, and he calls the extended network of significant others who also affect a child's development directly its *mesosystem*. As an example of the influence of the latter, Bronfenbrenner (1986, p. 725) cites research that shows the correlation of IQs of twins raised in separate households but in the same community was .83, but only .66 among twins raised in different communities. This finding strongly implies that the first group had overlapping and interchangeable mesosystems (including schools, neighbors, and playmates), while the second did not and that the difference made a difference. A further analysis showed that twins raised in similar communities (i.e., similar in size, economics, culture, and so on) showed a correlation of .86 compared to only .26

for those raised in substantially different communities. Clearly, these findings show that each significant other represents a community of values and perspectives and that a whole network of interrelated and reinforcing significant others have a very significant impact.

The systems theory perspective prompts us to look past the direct effects of individual significant others to the effects of the relationships among them as a factor in the socialization process.

Principle 3B. Relationships among significant others have a direct effect on the socialization process beyond the net effect of individual inputs. Are one's parents perceived as adversarial to each other (or to the school or toward one's friends) or in accord on relevant matters? Is a single parent structurally unsupported or is strong network reinforcement available for her interventions? Does child care have continuity from hour to hour and day to day or is it a poorly mediated, disjointed bumping about from setting to setting and from caretaker to caretaker? Each issue has been addressed by researchers and found to be of great importance in projecting child outcomes. To my knowledge, the processes by which children deal with these issues have not been researched, although family process-oriented scholars have conducted a few provocative studies.

For example, Bronfenbrenner cites Dornbusch and colleagues (1985), who found that, holding socioeconomic status constant, the children of single parents were less conforming to adult standards than were children from two-parent families. Furthermore, the difference was mitigated when another adult was in the household, except when the adult was a stepparent. Similarly, Buhr (1974) and Broderick (1977) found that abuse by a stepfather had less negative effects on a child than did abuse by a natural father, because in the former case the mother intervened as a buffer more than in the latter. All of this is to say that the nature of the relationships among those in the child's microsystems or mesosystems (to use Bronfenbrenner's nomenclature) are important components of the socialization process.

4. The Principle of Indirect Effects (via External Systems)

As we noted in the discussion of the linear model, one of the most effective strategies for influencing children's development involves manipulation of the external system that we have called *channeling*. In the language we have used in this section, we might define channeling as an attempt to provide children with a parent-designed mesosystem.

Principle 4A. Significant others may augment their direct influence on children's development by controlling their immediate social environment. A different category of indirect influences on children are those that act directly on significant others and affect their behavior toward their children. From the children's point of view, these interactions take place out of their presence and are thus part of what Bronfenbrenner calls their exosystem, but they are part of the involved significant other's microsystem or mesosystem. The parents' work, school, or support network may often have a great deal to do with how the parents interact with their children. Probably the largest body of research on this topic has examined the effects of a mother's involvement in outside employment. As noted in a previous section, the effects of the father's daily work environment on his socialization practices have also attracted considerable research attention.

Other issues also have been investigated. For example, Bronfenbrenner (1986, p. 730) cites a series of studies that show the initial mother-child bonding process to be shaped by the support she experiences from her husband, friends, and others, and that such support buffers her from the negative effects of biologically or environmentally induced stress. Unmarried mothers are even more susceptible to stress, but whether their support systems buffer or subvert the mother-child bonding process depends on its nature (i.e., was it perceived as more of a drain or a support?). This point may be summarized in the following subprinciple:

Principle 4B. The microsystems and mesosystems of significant others may influence children's development indirectly by shaping the interaction between the other and the child. The final principles that differentiate systemic from linear models of the socialization process might be called the principles of multifinality and equifinality.

5. The Principles of Multifinality and Equifinality

The principal of multifinality posits that any complex interactive system may have many different outcomes for any given input. The principle of equifinality posits that many different inputs may have the same outcome. These do not suggest that the rules governing systems have no lawfulness. With the librettist of *Sound of Music*, we are confident that "Nothing comes of nothing; nothing ever could."

Rather, the point is that complex systems have no simple, linear causal effects. Even such massively destructive inputs as ongoing child abuse may sometimes be associated with the outcome of child competence. We might say that the healthy outcome occurs despite rather than in any way because of the abuse, but evidence suggests that this is too simple a claim.

Instead, facts seem to show that the abuse interacts directly with other features of the system in producing the well-tempered result. Elsewhere I have distinguished between *untested normal* and *achieved normal* (Broderick & Pulliam-Krager, 1979). This seems to me to be a better terminology for describing unexpected positive outcomes than the more popular conceptualization of *vulnerable* versus *invulnerable* children. As Fisher and his associates (1987) (among others) have persuasively argued, "no living object is truly invulnerable" (p. 223), and the term evokes an image up to which no real child could or should have to be held.

Principle 5A. Some children will achieve social competence even in the face of highly negative models and adverse family experience. In recent years, a spate of studies have been made of children who somehow manage to escape destructive home environments reasonably intact. Various factors have been identified as contributing to the unlikely positive outcome, but by all odds the most consistent have been a secure maternal attachment in the earliest months of life and an open rather than a closed family environment that provides alternative models, perspectives, and resources to the child. For a comprehensive review of this literature, see *The Invulnerable Child* (1987), Anthony and Cohler, editors; for a compelling recent study of this phenomenon, see Quinton and Rutter, *Parenting Breakdown: The Making and Breaking of Intergenerational Links* (1988).

Having said this, a reading of the case studies in which this literature abounds may leave a residual conviction that an as-yet-unidentified quality of the individual self exists that interacts with these and other elements in the environment to produce what I have called the *transitional character* (Broderick, 1992, pp. 18-19) (see Box C). This is the person who not only survives a toxic family environment but also consciously vows to filter the poison out and *not* pass it on to succeeding generations (see also Spanier, 1989, for a somewhat different view of this phenomenon).

BOX C TRANSITIONAL CHARACTERS

A transitional character

> is one who, in the course of a single generation, changes the course of a
> lineage, . . . who grows up in an abusive, emotionally destructive environ-
> ment, [but] somehow finds a way to metabolize the poison and refuses to
> pass it on to [the next generation]. [Such persons] break the mold. They refute
> the observation that abused children become abusive parents, that the
> children of alcoholics become alcoholic adults, that "the sins of the fathers
> are visited upon the heads of the children to the third and forth generation."
> Their contribution to humanity is to filter the destructiveness out of their
> own lineage so that generations downstream will have a supportive foun-
> dation upon which to build productive lives. (Broderick, 1992, p. 18) ▲

Less research has been done on and less clinical interest shown in
the reciprocal case of the child from the well-functioning, supportive
family who turns out badly. Ours is a society that extols the individual
and is deeply suspicious of the group or institution. We should not be
surprised when social scientists, who are a product of this society, tend
to attribute the pervasive ills of life to social institutions and the intermittent triumph of good to the indomitable individual spirit. Apparently,
few of us are comfortable with casting the institution in the role of con-
servator of good and the individual as the source of evil. We seem to
be content to let theologians and novelists deal with the issue. In any
case, we face an inescapable fact: Just as bad families sometimes produce
good kids, so good families sometimes produce bad kids.

*Principle 5B. Some children will fail to achieve social competence despite
positive family models and supportive experiences.*
     The role of biochemical influences on this pattern is currently attract-
ing some research attention, but in all probability, systematic socio-
psychological investigation could identify some of the life circumstances
and developmental experiences that commonly contribute to these
unexpected negative outcomes. Also possible is that certain qualities of

innate individual character, which are more difficult to discern, may make a difference.

Summary: The Socialization Process

In this chapter, we first constructed a linear model of the socialization process that summarized the main conclusions of many decades of research within that framework. A preliminary version was restricted to variables that reflected interactions among family members. The model was then expanded to include influences that are external to the immediate family. The final model specified the relationships among eight sets of independent and intervening variables and the dependent set of variables, which represent child outcome. Also included were contingency variables that represent biological, structural, and cultural factors that act to modify the relationships among the other variables in the model.

Despite the complexities of this model, the assumptions of linear causality on which it rests limit its capacity to represent adequately an ongoing social process. In the second section of the chapter, we considered those systemic principles that transcend any combination of linear propositions and that would have to be incorporated into any viable attempt to model actual social process.

Afterword:
A Few Concluding Observations

In this "exposition and critique," I have attempted to indicate my own view of some of the strengths and weaknesses of family process theory. Some criticisms have been explicit, such as my conviction that the cybernetic model has been applied too glibly to family systems without sufficient attention to the ways in which families differ from very focused, goal-seeking systems; such as my observation that family process theorists have seldom moved beyond linear models of socialization, leaving that critically important task to others; such as noting that the theoretically crucial linkages between real-time processes and outcomes and developmental-time processes and outcomes have never been systematically worked out; such as the theory's blindness to the impact of opportunity structures inherent in families' natural settings (although absent in the laboratory or therapy setting); such as the disinterest in the financial component of family processes.

Other criticisms have been implicit. Readers familiar with the family process literature will surely have noted that I have nowhere acknowledged (let alone joined) the extensive philosophical debates on epistemology that have absorbed the attention of many family process theorists in recent years. This omission is not an oversight; it reflects my own prejudicial view that the understanding of how families actually operate is not much advanced by these debates.

In the same vein, I have attempted to be frugal with my introduction of special vocabulary. Over the history of the movement, each major contributor has developed his or her own unique conceptual schemata and terminology. As a result, the family process literature has not always been very "reader-friendly." I am aware that my attempt to make it so has costs attached for myself as well as for the reader. For myself, I run the risk of not being taken seriously by the true initiates, of being viewed as a nonmember of the inner circle of genuine process theorists (it is true, of course; I write from the perspective of a friendly margin dweller). For my readers, the risk is that they might read this entire volume on process theory and still find themselves lacking in that mastery of the local patois that would make them confident venturers into that literature on their own.

Finally, it is implicit in my treatment of the subject that I consider the family process movement too insular, too parochial. Not only can they provide vibrant insights into the dynamics of family life that are enriching to every branch of family scholarship, but also the reciprocal is true: Every branch of family scholarship has something significant to contribute to family process theory. This volume is an attempt to document both points.

On the plus side, clearly I am fully persuaded that families can never be understood in any important degree without investigating their ongoing processes in real time and, through repeated observations, over the span of developmental time. Very substantial progress has already been made in setting up both the methodology for such research and the guiding theoretical models. But it is clear to me that the greatest contributions are yet to be made by the rising generation of family scholars. In several places in the text I have suggested fruitful areas of inquiry. Doubtless I have altogether overlooked some of the most generative questions that need to be addressed.

We are in a period of explosive growth of knowledge and understanding in almost every field. A friend of mine who is an expert in neurophysiology told me recently that he would not hesitate to mortgage his soul for a few hours with a neuropsychiatric textbook from the year 2020. I am, perhaps, more protective of my soul, but I cannot doubt that the family textbooks of that year would be equally dazzling to my 20th-century eyes. And I do not doubt that work on unraveling the matrices of family process will be at the core of those new insights.

References

Adams, B. N. (1964). Structural factors affecting parental aid to married children. *Journal of Marriage and the Family, 26*, 327-331.

Adams, B. N. (1968). *Kinship in an urban setting*. Chicago: Marklean.

Ahrons, C. R., & Rogers, R. H. (1987). *Divorced families: A multidisciplinary developmental view*. New York: Norton.

Ainsworth, M. D. (1979). *Attachment: Retrospect and prospect*. Address to the Society for Research in Child Development, San Francisco, March.

Ainsworth, M. D., Blehar, M., Waters, R., & Wall, S. (1978). *Patterns of attachment*. Hillsdale, NJ: Lawrence Erlbaum.

Altman, I. (1975). *Environment and social behavior: Privacy, personal space, territory and crowding*. Belmont, CA: Brooks/Cole. (Reprinted by Irvington Press, NY, 1981)

Altman, I., & Gauvain, M. (1981). A cross-cultural and dialectic analysis of homes. In L. S. Liben, A. H. Patterson, & N. Newcombe (Eds.), *Spatial representation across the life span* (pp. 283-320). New York: Academic Press.

Ammons, P., & Stinnett, N. (1980). The vital marriage: A closer look. *Family Relations, 29*, 37-42.

Andreason, M. S. (1990). Evolution on the family's use of television: Normative data from industry and academe. In J. Bryant (Ed.), *Television and the American family* (pp. 3-58). Hillsdale, NJ: Lawrence Erlbaum.

Anthony, E. J., & Cohler, B. J. (Eds.) (1987). *The invulnerable child*. New York: Guilford.

Auerswald, E. H. (1968). Interdisciplinary vs. ecological approach. *Family Process, 7*, 202-215.

Auerswald, E. H. (1971). Family change and the ecological perspective. *Family Process, 10*, 263-280.

Bach, G. R., & Wyden, P. (1969). *The intimate enemy.* New York: Avon.

Bahr, S. J. (1979). Family determinants and effects of deviance. In W. R. Burr, R. Hill, F. I. Nye, & I. L. Reiss (Eds.), *Contemporary theories about the family* (Vol. 1, pp. 615-644). New York: Free Press.

Bakke, E. W. (1940). *The unemployed worker.* New Haven, CT: Yale University Press.

Bales, R. F. (1950). *Interaction process analysis: A method for the study of small groups.* Reading, MA: Addison-Wesley.

Bank, S. P., & Kahn, M. D. (1982). *The sibling bond.* New York: Basic Books.

Barker, R., & Wright, H. (1951). *One boy's day.* New York: Harper & Row.

Barker, R., & Wright, H. (1955). *Midwest and its children.* New York: Harper & Row.

Bateson, G. (1972). *Steps to an ecology of the mind.* New York: Ballantine.

Bateson, G., Jackson, D. D., Haley, J., & Weakland, J. H. (1956). Toward a theory of schizophrenia. *Behavioral Science, 1,* 251-264.

Beck, R. W., & Beck, S. H. (1989). The incidence of extended households among middle-aged black and white women: Estimates from a 15 year panel study. *Journal of Family Issues, 10,* 147-168.

Becker, H. S. (1960). Notes on the concept of commitment. *American Journal of Sociology, 66* (July), 32-40.

Bellah, R. N., Madson, R., Sullivan, W. M., Swidler, A., & Tipton, S. M. (1985). *Habits of the heart: Individualism and commitment in American life.* Berkeley: University of California Press. (Reprinted by Harper & Row, NY, 1986)

Belsky, J., & Vondra, J. (1985). Characteristics, consequences, and determinants of parenting. In L. L'Abate (Ed.), *The handbook of family psychology and therapy* (Vol. 1, pp. 523-556). Homewood, IL: Dorsey.

Benjamin, W. (1969). The story teller. In W. Benjamin (Ed.), *Illuminations.* Bloomington: Indiana University Press.

Bengtson, V. L., & Schrader, S. (1981). Parent-child relations. In D. Mangen & W. Peterson (Eds.), *Handbook of research instruments in social gerontology* (Vol. 2, pp. 119-185). Minneapolis: University of Minnesota Press.

Benoit-Smullyan, E. (1944). Status, status types, and status of stratification. *American Sociological Review, 9,* 154-161.

Berger, P., & Kellner, H. (1985). Marriage and the construction of reality: An exercise in the microsociology of knowledge. *Diogenes, 46,* 1-24.

Berk, S. F. (1985). *The gender factory: The apportionment of work in American households.* New York: Plenum.

Bernard, J. (1964). The adjustments of married mates. In H. T. Christensen (Ed.), *Handbook of marriage and the family.* Chicago: Rand McNally.

Bernard, J. (1972). *The future of marriage.* New York: World.

Bernard, L. L. (1908). The teaching of sociology in the United States. *American Journal of Sociology, 15,* 164-213.

Bernstein, B. (1960). Language and social class. *British Journal of Sociology, 11,* 271-276.

Bernstein, B. (1964). Elaborated and restricted codes: Their social origins and some consequences. In J. J. Gumperz & D. Hymes (Eds.), *The ethnography of communication.* Special Publication of the *American Anthropologist, 66.*

Bernstein, B. (1970). A sociolinguistic approach to socialization with some reference to educability. In F. Williams (Ed.), *Language and poverty* (pp. 25-61). Chicago: Markham.

Bernstein, B. (1971-1973). Class, codes and control. *Theoretical studies toward sociology of language* (Vols. 1-2). London: Routledge & Kegan Paul.

Bertalanffy, L. von (1934). *Modern theories of development* (J. H. Woodger, Trans.). Oxford, UK: Oxford University Press. (Original work published in 1928)

Bertalanffy, L. von (1950). The theory of open systems in physics and biology. *Science, 3*, 23-29.

Bertalanffy, L. von (1951). Problems of general systems theory. *Human Biology, 23*, 302-312.

Bertalanffy, L. von (1952). Theoretical models in biology and psychology. In D. Krech & G. S. Klein (Eds.), *Theoretical models and personality theory* (pp. 24-38). Durham, NC: Duke University Press.

Bertalanffy, L. von (1955). General systems theory. *Main Currents in Modern Thought, 11* (4), 75-83.

Bertalanffy, L. von (1959). Human values in a changing world. In A. H. Maslow (Ed.), *New knowledge in human values* (pp. 65-74). New York: Harper & Row.

Bertalanffy, L. von (1968). *General systems theory: Foundations, development, applications.* New York: George Braziller.

Bertalanffy, L. von (1972). The history and status of general systems theory. In G. J. Klir (Ed.), *Trends in general systems theory* (pp. 21-41). New York: Wiley-Interscience.

Blumstein, P., & Schwartz, P. (1983). *American couples.* New York: William Morrow.

Bolger, N., DeLongis, A., Kessler, R. C., & Wethington, E. (1989). The cartogram of stress across multiple roles. *Journal of Marriage and the Family, 51*, 175-183.

Bossard, J. H. S., & Boll, E. S. (1950). *Ritual in family living.* Philadelphia: University of Pennsylvania Press.

Boszormenyi-Nagy, I., & Sparks, G. (1973). *Invisible loyalties: Reciprocity in intergenerational family therapy.* New York: Harper & Row. (2nd ed. published by Brunner/Mazel, New York, 1984)

Bott, E. (1955). Urban roles: Conjugal roles and social networks. *Human Relations, 8*, 345-383.

Bott, E. (1971). *Family and social network* (2nd ed.). New York: Free Press.

Bowen, M. (1960). A family concept of schizophrenia. In D. D. Jackson (Ed.), *Etiology of schizophrenia* (Chap. 12). New York: Basic Books.

Bowen, M. (1965a). Family psychotherapy with schizophrenia in the hospital and in private practice. In I. Boszormenyi-Nagy & J. Framo (Eds.), *Intensive family therapy* (pp. 214-244). New York: Harper & Row.

Bowen, M. (1965b). Intrafamily dynamics in emotional illness. In A. D'Agostino (Ed.), *Family, church and community.* New York: P. J. Kennedy.

Bowen, M. (1971a). Family therapy and family group therapy. In H. Kaplan & B. Sadock (Eds.), *Comprehensive group psychotherapy* (pp. 384-421). Baltimore: Williams and Wilkins.

Bowen, M. (1971b). The use of family theory in clinical practice. In J. Haley (Ed.), *Changing families.* New York: Grune & Stratton.

Bowen, M. (1973). Toward the differentiation of self in one's own family. In J. L. Framo (Ed.), *Family interaction: A dialogue between family researchers and family therapists.* New York: Springer Verlag.

Bowen, M. (1974). Toward the differentiation of self in one's family of origin. In F. Andres & J. Lorio (Eds.), *Georgetown Family Symposia* (Vol. 1). Washington, DC: Georgetown University Medical Center.

Bowen, M. (1978). *Family therapy in clinical practice.* New York: Jason Aronson.

Bowlby, J. (1969-1973). *Attachment and loss* (12 vols.). New York: Basic Books.

Brazelton, T. B., Koslowski, B., & Main, M. (1974). The origins of reciprocity: The early mother-infant interactions. In M. Lewis & L. A. Rosenbloom (Eds.), *The effect of the infant on its caregiver* (pp. 49-76). New York: John Wiley.

Brazelton, T. B., Yogman, M. W., Als, H., & Tronick, E. (1979). The infant as a focus for family reciprocity. In M. Lewis & L. A. Rosenbloom (Eds.), *The child and its family: The genesis of behavior* (Vol. 2, pp. 29-44). New York: Plenum.

Brickman, P. (1987). *Commitment, conflict and caring*. Englewood Cliffs, NJ: Prentice-Hall.

Broderick, C. B. (1971). Beyond the five conceptual frameworks: A decade of development in family theory. *Journal of Marriage and the Family, 33*, 139-159.

Broderick, C. B. (1975). Power in the governance of families. In R. E. Cromwell & D. H. Olson (Eds.), *Power in families* (pp. 117-130). New York: John Wiley.

Broderick, C. B. (1977). Fathers. *Family Coordinator, 26*, 269-275.

Broderick, C. B. (1979). *Couples*. New York: Simon & Schuster.

Broderick, C. B. (1983). *The therapeutic triangle*. Beverly Hills, CA: Sage.

Broderick, C. B. (1988). To arrive where we started: The field of family studies in the 1930s. *Journal of Marriage and the Family, 50*, 569-584.

Broderick, C. B. (1990). Family process theory. In J. Sprey (Ed.), *Fashioning family theory: New approaches* (pp. 171-206). Newbury Park, CA: Sage.

Broderick, C. B. (1992). *Marriage and the family* (4th ed.). Englewood, NJ: Prentice-Hall.

Broderick, C. B. (in press). A family process approach to elder abuse. In K. Johnson (Ed.), *Elder abuse*. Bethesda, MD: National Institute of Aging.

Broderick, C. B., & Hicks, M. W. (1970). Toward a typology of behavior patterns in courtship in the United States of America. In G. Leuschen (Ed.), *Soziologie der familie* (pp. 473-489). Opladen, West Germany: Westdeutcher Verlag.

Broderick, C. B., & Pulliam-Krager, H. (1979). Family process and child outcome. In W. R. Burr, R. Hill, F. I. Nye, & I. L. Reiss (Eds.), *Contemporary theories about the family* (Vol. 1, pp. 604-614). New York: Free Press.

Broderick, C. B., & Schrader, S. (1991). The history of professional marriage and family therapy. In A. S. Gurman & D. P. Kniskern (Eds.), *Handbook of family therapy II* (pp. 3-40). New York: Brunner/Mazel.

Broderick, C. B., & Smith, J. (1979). The general systems approach to the family. In W. R. Burr, R. Hill, F. I. Nye, & I. L. Reiss (Eds.), *Contemporary theories about the family* (Vol. 2, pp. 112-129). New York: Free Press.

Bronfenbrenner, U. (1979). *The ecology of human development*. Cambridge, MA: Harvard University Press.

Bronfenbrenner, U. (1986). Ecology of the family as a context for human development research perspectives. *Developmental Psychology, 22*, 723-742.

Bryant, J. (Ed.). (1990). *Television and the American family*. Hillsdale, NJ: Lawrence Erlbaum.

Buckley, W. (1967). *Sociology and modern systems theory*. Englewood Cliffs, NJ: Prentice-Hall.

Buhr, K. (1974). *Stress, marital interaction and personal competence in natural parent and step-father families*. Unpublished doctoral dissertation, University of Southern California.

Burgess, E. W. (1926). The family as a unit of interacting personalities. *Family, 7*, 3-9.

Burgess, E. W., & Locke, H. J. (1945). *The family from institution to companionship*. New York: American Book.

Burgess, E. W., & Wallin, P. (1953). *Engagement and marriage*. Philadelphia: J. B. Lippincott.

Burr, W. R., Hill, R., Nye, F. I., & Reiss, I. L. (Eds.) (1979a). *Contemporary theories about the family* (2 vols.). New York: Free Press.

Burr, W. R., Hill, R., Nye, F. I., & Reiss, I. L. (1979b). Meta theory and diagraming conventions. In W. R. Burr, R. Hill, F. I. Nye, & I. L. Reiss (Eds.), *Contemporary theories about the family* (Vol. 1, pp. 17-26). New York: Free Press.

Burr, W. R., & Lowe, R. A. (1987). Olson's circumplex model: A review and extension. *Family Science Review, 1*, 5-22.

Buunk, B. (1982). Strategies of jealousy: Styles of coping with extramarital involvement of the spouse. *Family Relations, 31*, 13-18.

Byng-Hall, J. J. (1973). Family myths used as defense in conjoint family therapy. *British Journal of Medical Psychology, 46*, 239-250.

Byng-Hall, J. J. (1980). Symptom bearer as marital distance regulator: Clinical implications. *Family Process, 19*, 355-365.

Byng-Hall, J. J. (1988). Scripts and legends in families and family therapy. *Family Process, 27*, 167-179.

Caplow, T. (1968). *Two against one: Coalition in triads.* Englewood Cliffs, NJ: Prentice-Hall.

Caplow, T. (1982). Christmas gifts of kin networks. *American Sociological Review, 47*, 383-392.

Caplow, T. (1984). Role enforcement without visible means: Christmas gift giving in Middletown. *American Journal of Sociology, 89*, 1306-1323.

Cervantes, L. F. (1965). *The drop outs: Causes and cures.* Ann Arbor: University of Michigan Press.

Chapple, E. (1970). *Culture and biological man.* New York: Holt, Rinehart & Winston.

Cheal, D. J. (1983). Intergenerational family transfers. *Journal of Marriage and the Family, 45*, 827-839.

Cicirelli, V. G. (1984). Marital disruption and adult children's perceptions of their elderly parents. *Family Relations, 33*, 613-621.

Cicirelli, V. G. (1985). Sibling relationships throughout the life cycle. In L. L'Abate (Ed.), *The handbook of family psychology and therapy* (pp. 177-214). Homewood, IL: Dorsey.

Clemens, A. W., & Axelson, L. J. (1985). The not-so-empty nest: The returning of the fledgling adult. *Family Relations, 34*, 259-265.

Coburn, D., & Edwards, V. L. (1976). Job control and child rearing values. *Canadian Review of Sociology and Anthropology, 13*, 337-344.

Cohen, L. E., & Felson, M. K. (1979). Social change and crime prevention: A routine activity approach. *American Sociological Review, 44*, 588-608.

Cohen, S. M., & Tenenbaum, S. (1988). Age cohort and life cycle: The impact of marriage and parenthood. In S. M. Cohen (Ed.), *American assimilation or Jewish revival?* (pp. 58-70). Bloomington: Indiana University Press.

Constantine, L. L. (in press). The structure of family paradigms: An analytical model of family variations. *Journal of Marriage and Family Therapy.*

Cooley, C. H. (1909). *Social organization.* New York: Scribner.

Cornwall, M. (1988). The influence of three agents of religious socialization: Family, church, and peers. In D. L. Thomas (Ed.), *The religion and family connection* (pp. 207-231). Provo, UT: Brigham Young University.

Cowan, C. P., Cowan, P. A., Cole, I., & Cole, J. D. (1978). Becoming a family: The impact of the first child on a couple's relationship. In W. B. Miller & L. F. Newman (Eds.), *The first child and family formation* (pp. 296-324). Chapel Hill: University of North Carolina.

Cowan, C. P., Cowan, P. A., Heming, G., Garrett, E., Coysh, W., Curtis-Boles, H., & Boles, A. J., III. (1985). Transition to parenthood: His, hers and theirs. *Journal of Family Issues, 6*, 451-481.

Cox, E. (1982). *Family structure and external openness: A two-dimensional model.* Unpublished doctoral dissertation, University of Southern California.

Crouter, A. C. (1984). Participative work as an influence on human development. *Journal of Applied Developmental Psychology, 5,* 71-90.

D'Andrade, R. (1986). Three scientific world views and the covering law model. In D. W. Fiske & R. S. Shweder (Eds.), *Metatheory in social science* (pp. 19-41). Chicago: University of Chicago Press.

D'Antonio, W. V. (1988). The American Catholic family: Signs of cohesion and polarization. In D. L. Thomas (Ed.), *The religion and family connection* (pp. 88-106). Provo, UT: Brigham Young University.

Davis, A., Gardner, B. B., & Gardner, M. R. (1941). *Deep South.* Chicago: University of Chicago Press.

Davis, K. (1937). The sociology of prostitution. *American Sociological Review, 2* (October).

Dizard, J. (1968). *Social change and the family.* Chicago: University of Chicago, Family and Community Study Center.

Doan, J. A. (1985). Parental communication deviance and offspring. In L. L'Abate (Ed.), *Handbook of family psychology and therapy* (Vol. 2, pp. 937-960). Homewood, IL: Dorsey.

Dornbusch, S. M., Carlsmith, J. M., Bushwall, P. L., Ritter, P. L., Leiderman, H., Hasdorf, A. H., & Gross, R. T. (1985). Single parents, extended households, and the control of adolescents. *Child Development, 56,* 326-341.

Dreyer, A. S., & Dreyer, C. A. (1973). Family dinner time as a unique behavior habitat. *Family Process, 12,* 291-301.

Duhl, F. S., Kantor, D., & Duhl, B. S. (1973). Learning, space and action in family therapy. In D. Block (Ed.), *Techniques of family psychotherapy.* New York: Grune & Stratton.

Duvall, E. M. (1957). *Family development.* Philadelphia: J. B. Lippincott.

Duvall, E. M., & Hill, R. (1948). *Report of the committee on the dynamics of family interaction.* Washington, DC: National Conference on Family Life.

Eccles, J., Timmen, S. G., & O'Brian, K. (1986). *Psychology Today, 20,* 16-17.

Edwards, N. N., & Booth, A. (1976). Sexual behavior in and out of marriage: An assessment of correlates. *Journal of Marriage and the Family, 38,* 75-81.

Entwisle, D., & Doering, S. (1981). *The first birth: A family turning point.* Baltimore, MD: Johns Hopkins University Press.

Farley, J. (1979). Family separation-individuation tolerance: A developmental conceptualization of the nuclear family. *Journal of Marital and Family Therapy, 5,* 61-67.

Feldman, H., & Rogoff, M. (1968). *Correlates of change in marital satisfaction with the birth of the first child.* Paper presented at the American Psychological Association, San Francisco.

Felson, M. (1986). Linking criminal choices, routine activities, informal controls and criminal outcomes. In D. B. Cornish & R. V. Clark (Eds.), *The reasoning criminal.* New York: Springer Verlag.

Felson, M. (1987). Routine activities and crime prevention in the developing metropolis. *Criminology, 25,* 911-932.

Ferree, M. M. (1990). Beyond separate spheres: Feminism and family research. *Journal of Marriage and the Family, 52,* 866-884.

Ferree, M. M. (1991). The gender division of labor in two-earner marriages. *Journal of Family Issues, 12,* 158-180.

Ferreira, A. J. (1963). Family myths and homeostasis. *Archives of General Psychiatry, 8,* 68-73.

Ferreira, A. J. (1966). Family myths. *Psychiatric Research Reports of the American Psychiatric Association, 20,* 85-90.

Festinger, L., Schachter, S., & Back, K. (1950). *Social pressures and informal process: A study of human factors in housing.* New York: Harper & Row.

Finklehor, D. (1980a). Sex among siblings: a survey on prevalence, society and effects. *Archives of Sexual Behaviors, 9,* 171-194.

Finklehor, D. (1980b). Risk factors in the sexual victimization of children. *Child Abuse and Neglect, 4,* 265-273.

Fisher, L., Kokes, R. F., Cole, R. E., Parkins, P. M., & Wynne, L. C. (1987). Competent children at risk: A study of well-functioning offspring of disturbed parents. In E. J. Anthony & B. J. Cohler (Eds.), *The invulnerable child* (pp. 211-228). New York: Guilford.

Fivaz-Depeursinge, E. (1991). Documenting a time-bound circular view of hierarchies: A micro-analysis of parent-infant dyadic interaction. *Family Process, 30,* 101-120.

Fleisher, B. M. (1966). The effects of income on delinquency. *American Economic Review, 56,* 118-137.

Ford, D. H. (1987). *Humans as self-constructing living systems: A developmental perspective on behavior and personality.* Hillsdale, NJ: Lawrence Erlbaum.

Freud, S. (1912). *Recommendations for physicians in the psychoanalytic method of treatment* (J. Riviere, Trans.). Zentralblatt, Bd. II. Reprinted in Sammlung, Viente Folge.

Freud, S. (1915). *General introduction to psychoanalysis.* New York: Liverright.

Fromm, E. (1941). *Escape from freedom.* New York: Farrar & Rinehart.

Fromm, E. (1947). *Man for himself.* New York: Rinehart.

Gamson, W. A. (1961). A theory of coalition formation. *American Sociological Review, 26,* 373-382.

Gamson, W. A. (1964). Experimental studies of coalition formation. In L. Berkowitz (Ed.), *Advances in Experimental Social Psychology* (Vol. 1, pp. 82-110). New York: Academic Press.

Ganong, L. H., & Coleman, M. (1984). The effects of remarriage on children: A review of the empirical literature. *Family Relations, 33,* 389-406.

Gecas, V. (1979). The influence of social class in socialization. In W. R. Burr, R. Hill, F. I. Nye, & I. L. Reiss (Eds.), *Contemporary theories about the family* (pp. 365-404). New York: Free Press.

Gilbert, R., & Christensen, A. (1985). Observational assessment of marital and family interaction. In L. L'Abate (Ed.), *The handbook of family psychology* (pp. 961-988). Homewood, IL: Dorsey.

Gilligan, C. (1982). *In a different voice: Psychological theory and women's development.* Cambridge, MA: Harvard University Press.

Glenn, N. D. (1977). *Cohort analysis.* Beverly Hills, CA: Sage.

Glick, P. (1947). The family cycle. *American Sociological Review, 12,* 164-174.

Glick, P. (1988). Fifty years of family demography: A record of social change. *Journal of Marriage and the Family, 50,* 861-873.

Glick, P., & Lin, S.-L. (1986). More young adults are living with their parents: Who are they? *Journal of Marriage and the Family, 48,* 107-112.

Goffman, E. (1973). *The presentation of self in everyday life.* Woodstock, NY: One Look Press.

Goldscheider, F., & Goldscheider, C. (1988). *Intergenerational financial flaws, parental investment and children's contribution.* Unpublished paper presented at University of Southern California.

Goodman, I. F. (1983). Television's role in family interaction: A family system perspective. *Journal of Family Issues, 4,* 405-424.

Gordon, M., & Downing, H. (1978). A multivariate test of the Bott hypothesis in an urban Irish setting. *Journal of Marriage and the Family, 40,* 585-594.

Gottman, J. M. (1989). Predicting the longitudinal course of marriage. In K. A. Tilley (Ed.), *Building bridges, creating balance: 1989 AAMFT conference monograph* (pp. 39-46). Washington, DC: American Association for Marriage and Family Therapy.

Gottman, J. M., Markman, H., & Notarius, C. (1977). The topography of marital conflict: A sequential analysis of verbal and non-verbal behavior. *Journal of Marriage and the Family, 39,* 461-478.

Gottman, J. M., Notarius, C., Markman, H., Yoppi, B., & Rubin, M. E. (1976). Behavioral exchange theory and marital decision making. *Journal of Personality and Social Psychology, 34,* 14-23.

Granovetter, M. S. (1983). The strength of weak ties. In R. Collins (Ed.), *Sociological theory* (pp. 201-233). San Francisco: Jossey-Bass.

Green, J. T. (1985). Ernest R. Groves: Explorer and pioneer in marriage and family life education and marriage counseling. In P. Dial & R. Jewson (Eds.), *In praise of fifty years: The Groves Conference on the conservation of marriage and the family* (pp. 116-121). Lake Mills, IA: Graphics.

Green, R. G., Harris, R. N., Jr., Forte, J. A., & Robinson, M. (1991). Evaluating FACES III and the circumplex model: 2440 families. *Family Process, 30,* 55-73.

Greenhaus, J. H., & Beutell, N. J. (1985). Sources of conflict between work and family roles. *Academy of Management Review,* January, p. 10.

Greenstein, T. N. (1990). Marital disruption and the employment of married women. *Journal of Marriage and the Family, 52,* 657-676.

Groves, E. R. (1931). *Social problems of the family.* Philadelphia: J.B. Lippincott.

Guerney, B., Jr. (1977). *Relationship enhancement.* San Francisco: Jossey-Bass.

Haley, J. (1963). *Strategies of psychotherapy.* New York: Basic Books.

Haley, J. (1971). Toward a theory of pathological systems. In G. Zuk & I. Boszormenyi-Nagy (Eds.), *Family theory and disturbed families.* Palo Alto, CA: Science & Behavior Books.

Haley, J. (1973). *Uncommon therapy: The psychiatric techniques of Milton Erickson, M.D.* New York: Norton.

Haley, J. (1976a). Development of a theory: A history of a research project. In C. E. Sluzki & D. C. Ransom (Eds.), *Double bind: The foundation of a communicational approach to the family* (pp. 59-104). New York: Grune & Stratten.

Haley, J. (1976b). *Problem solving therapy.* San Francisco: Jossey-Bass.

Haley, J. (1980). *Leaving home: The therapy of disturbed young people.* New York: McGraw-Hill.

Hall, A. D., & Fagan, R. E. (1956). Definition of systems. *General Systems, 1,* 18-28.

Handel, G. (Ed.). (1967). *The psychosocial interior of the family.* Hawthorne, NY: Aldine.

Hare-Mussen, R. T. (1978). A feminist approach to family therapy. *Family Process, 17,* 181-194.

Hareven, T. K. & Langenbach, R. (1978). *Amoskeag: Life and work in an American city.* New York: Pantheon.

Hatt, P. (1950). Occupation and social stratification. *American Journal of Sociology, 55,* 533-543.

Havighurst, R. J. (1948). *Developmental tasks and education.* Chicago: University of Chicago Press.

Hess, R. S., & Handel, G. (1959). *Family worlds: A psychosocial approach to family life.* Chicago: University of Chicago Press.

Hill, R. (1971). Modern systems theory and the family: A confrontation. *Social Science Information 10* (October), 7-26.

Hill, R. (1979). Personal correspondence with the author.

Hill, R., & Hansen, D. A. (1960). The identification of conceptual frameworks utilized in family study. *Marriage and Family Living, 22,* 299-311.

Hill, R., & Rogers, R. (1964). The developmental approach. In H. T. Christensen (Ed.), *Handbook of marriage and the family* (pp. 171-214). Chicago: Rand McNally.

Hoffman, L. *Foundations of family therapy.* New York: Basic Books.

Homans, G. (1950). *The human group.* Orlando, FL: Harcourt Brace Jovanovich.

Hostetler, J. A. (1980). *Amish society.* Baltimore, MD: Johns Hopkins University Press.

Houseknecht, S. K. (1979). Childlessness and marital adjustment. *Journal of Marriage and the Family, 41,* 259-265.

Houseknecht, S. K. (1987). Voluntary childlessness. In M. B. Sussman & S. K. Steinmetz (Eds.), *Handbook of marriage and the family* (pp. 369-395). New York: Plenum.

Huston, A. C., Donnerstein, E., Fairchild, H., Feshbach, N. B., Katz, P. A., Murray, J. P., Rubinstein, E. A., Wilcot, B. L., & Zuckerman, D. (1992). *Big world, small screen: The role of television in American society.* Lincoln: University of Nebraska Press.

Hutchings, B., & Mednick, S. A. (1977). Criminality in adoptees and their adoptive and biological parents: A pilot study. In S. A. Mednick & K. O. Christinesen (Eds.), *Biological bases of criminal behavior* (pp. 122-164). New York: Gardner.

Imber-Black, E., Roberts, J., & Whiting, R. (Eds.). (1988). *Rituals in families and family therapy.* New York: Norton.

Jackson, D. D. (1959). Family interactions, family homeostasis and some implication for conjoint family therapy. In J. Wasserman (Ed.), *Individual and family dynamics.* New York: Grune & Stratton.

Jackson, D. D. (1965). The study of the family. *Family Process, 4,* 1-20.

Jacobson, N. S., & Margolin, G. (1979). *Marital therapy: Strategies based on social learning and behavioral exchange privileges.* New York: Brunner/Mazel.

Kanter, R. M. (1977). Some effects of proportions on group life: Skewed sex ratios and responses to token women. *American Journal of Sociology, 5,* 965-990.

Kantor, D., & Lehr, W. (1975). *Inside the family.* San Francisco: Jossey-Bass.

Karlsson, G. (1951). *Adaptability and communication in marriage: A Swedish predictive study of marital satisfaction.* Uppsala: Alquist & Wiksells Babtrycheri.

Keith, P. M., & Schafer, R. B. (1980). Role strain and depression in two subfamilies. *Family Relations, 29,* 483-494.

Kephart, W. M. (1982). *Extraordinary groups* (2nd ed.). New York: St. Martin's.

Kibria, N. (1987). *New images of immigrant women: A study of women's social groups among Vietnamese refugees.* Working Paper Series. Wellesley, MA: Wellesley College, Center for Research on Women.

Kibria, N. (1989). Patterns of Vietnamese women's wage work in the United States. *Ethnic Groups: An International Periodical of Ethnic Studies, 7,* 297-323.

Killworth, P. D., Bernard, H. R., & McCarty, C. (1984). Measuring patterns of acquaintanceship. *Current Anthropology, 25,* 391-397.

Klein, D. M., & Hill, R. (1979). Determinants of family problem-solving effectiveness. In W. R. Burr, R. Hill, F. I. Nye, & I. L. Reiss (Eds.), *Contemporary themes about the family* (Vol. 1, pp. 493-548). New York: Free Press.

Klein, J., Calvert, G., Garland, N., & Polomo, M. (1968). Pilgrims' Progress I: Recent developments in family theory. *Journal of Marriage and the Family, 31,* 677-687.

Kohlberg, L. (1969). Stage and sequence: The cognitive-developmental approach to socialization. In D. A. Goslin (Ed.), *Handbook of socialization* (pp. 347-480). Chicago: Rand McNally.

Kohlberg, L., & Turiel, E. (1973). Overview: Cultural universals in morality. In L. Kohlberg & E. Turiel (Eds.), *Recent research in moral development*. New York: Holt, Rinehart & Winston.

Kohn, M. L. (1977). *Class and conformity: A study in values* (2nd ed.). Chicago: University of Chicago Press.

Kopytoff, I. (1986). The cultural biography of things: Commoditization as a process. In A. Appadurai (Ed.), *The social life of things*. Cambridge: Cambridge University Press.

L'Abate, L. (1985). Descriptive and exploratory levels in family therapy: Distance, defeats and dependence. In L. L'Abate (Ed.), *The handbook of family psychology and therapy* (Vol. 2, pp. 1218-1245). Homewood, IL: Dorsey.

Lang, A. M., & Brody, E. M. (1983). Characteristics of middle-aged daughters and help to their elderly mothers. *Journal of Marriage and the Family, 45,* 193-202.

La Rossa, R., & La Rossa, M. M. (1981). *Transition to parenthood*. Beverly Hills, CA: Sage.

Larson, J. H. (1984). The effects of husband's unemployment on marital and family relationships in blue-collar families. *Family Relations, 33,* 503-510.

Larson, R. W., & Bradney, N. (1988). Precious moments with family members and friends. In R. M. Milardo (Ed.), *Families and Social Networks* (pp. 107-126). Newbury Park, CA: Sage.

Laslett, B. (1973). The family as a public and private institution: A historical perspective. *Journal of Marriage and the Family, 35,* 480-494.

Lee, G. (1979). Effects of social network on the family. In W. R. Burr, R. Hill, F. I. Nye, & I. L. Reiss (Eds.), *Contemporary theories about the family* (Vol 1, pp. 27-56). New York: Free Press.

Le Play, P. G. F. (1935) Working-class families of Europe. In C. C. Zimmerman & M. E. Frampton (Eds.), *Family and society: A study of the sociology of reconstruction*. New York: Van Nostrum. (Originally published in Paris, 1855)

Lever, J. (1976). Sex differences in the games children play. *Social Problems, 23,* 478-487.

Levinger, G. (1965). Marital cohesiveness and dissolution: An integrative review. *Journal of Marriage and the Family, 27,* 19-28.

Levy, D. M. (1934). Rivalry between children in the same family. *Child Study, 11,* 235-237.

Levy, D. M. (1936). Hostility patterns in sibling rivalry experiments. *American Journal of Orthopsychiatry, 6,* 183-257.

Levy, D. M. (1937). Studies in sibling rivalry. *Research monographs of the American Orthopsychiatric Association* (No. 2). New York: American Orthopsychiatric Association.

Lewin, K. (1951). *Field theory in social science*. Westport, CT: Greenwood.

Lewis, R. A., & Spanier, G. B. (1979). Theorizing about the quality and stability of marriage. In W. R. Burr, R. Hill, F. I. Nye, & I. L. Reiss (Eds.), *Contemporary theories about the family* (Vol. 1, pp. 268-294). New York: Free Press.

Libow, J. A., Raskin, P. A., & Caust, B. L. (1982). Feminism and family systems therapy: Are they irreconcilable? *American Journal of Family Therapy, 10,* 3-12.

Lidz, T., Cornelison, A. R., Fleck, S., & Terry, D. (1957). The intrafamilial environment of schizophrenic patients, II: Marital schism and marital skew. *American Journal of Psychiatry, 114,* 241-248.

Liker, J. K., & Elder, G. H., Jr. (1983). Economic hardship and marital relations in the 1930's. *American Sociological Review, 48,* 343-359.

Lopata, H. Z. (1971). *Occupation housewife*. New York: Oxford University Press.

Maccoby, E. E., & Martin, J. A. (1983). Socialization in the context of the family: Parent-child interaction. In E. M. Hetherington (Ed.), *Handbook of child psychology: Vol. 4. Socialization, personality, and social development*. New York: John Wiley.

MacDermid, S., Huston, T. L., & McHale, S. M. (1990). Chances in marriage associated with transition to parenthood. *Journal of Marriage and the Family, 52,* 475-486.

Malinowski, B. (1922). *Argonauts of the western Pacific.* New York: E. P. Dutton.

Marks, S. R. (1986). *Three corners: Exploring marriage and the self.* Lexington, MA: Lexington Books.

Marks, S. R. (1989). Toward a systems theory of marital quality. *Journal of Marriage and the Family, 51,* 15-26.

Maslow, A. H. (1970). *Motivation and personality* (2nd ed.). New York: Harper & Row.

Mattessich, P., & Hill, R. (1987). Life cycle and family development. In M. B. Sussman & S. K. Steinmetz (Eds.), *Handbook of marriage and the family* (pp. 437-469). New York: Plenum.

McAllister, R. J., Butler, E. W., & Kaiser, E. J. (1973). The adaptation of women to residential mobility. *Journal of Marriage and the Family, 35,* 197-204.

McChesney, K. Y. (1987). *Women without: Homeless mothers and their children.* Unpublished doctoral dissertation, University of Southern California.

McGoldrick, M., & Carter, B. (1989). *The changing family life cycle: A framework for family therapy* (2nd ed.). Boston: Allyn & Bacon.

McGoldrick, M., & Carter, B. (1989). Forming a remarried family. In M. McGoldrick & B. Carter (Eds.), *The changing family life cycle: A framework for family therapy* (2nd ed.), (pp. 402-432). Boston: Allyn & Bacon.

McGoldrick, M., Pearce, J. K., & Giordano, J. (Eds.). (1982). *Ethnicity and family therapy.* New York: Guilford.

McLeod, J. M., Atkin, C. K., & Chaffee, S. H. (1972). Adolescents, parents and television use. In G. A. Comstock & E. A. Rubinstein (Eds.), *Television and social behavior* (Vol. 3). Washington, DC: Government Printing Office.

Mead, G. H. (1934). *Mind, self and society.* Chicago: University of Chicago Press.

Meetham, A. A. (1969). *Encyclopedia of linguistics, information, and control.* New York: Pergamon.

Merton, R. K. (1945). Sociological theory. *American Journal of Sociology, 50,* 462-473.

Merton, R. K. (1949). *Social theory and social structure* (2nd ed.). New York: Free Press.

Mesarovic, M. D. (1970). *Theory of hierarchical multi-level systems.* New York: Academic Press.

Milardo, R. M. (Ed.). (1988). *Families and social networks.* Newbury Park, CA: Sage.

Miller, B. C., McCoy, J. K., Olson, T. D., & Wallace, C. M. (1986). Parental discipline and control attempts in relation to adolescent sexual attitude and behavior. *Journal of Marriage and the Family, 48,* 503-512.

Miller, S., Nunnally, E. M., & Wackman, D. B. (1975). *Alive and aware: Improving communication in relationships.* Minneapolis, MN: Interpersonal Communications Programs.

Millman, M. (1991). *Warm hearts and cold cash: The intimate dynamics of families and money.* New York: Free Press.

Minuchin, S., Auerswald, E. H., King, C., & Rabkin, R. (1964). The study of treatment of families that produce multiple acting-out boys. *American Journal of Orthopsychiatry, 34,* 125-133.

Minuchin, S. (1974). *Families and family therapy.* Cambridge, MA: Harvard University Press.

Minuchin, S., Baker, L., Roseman, B. L., Liebman, R., Milman, L., & Todd, T. C. (1975). A conceptual model of psychosomatic illness in children. *Archives of General Psychiatry, 32,* 1031-1038.

Minuchin, S., Martalvo, B., Guerney, B., Rosman, B., & Schumer, F. (1967). *Families of the slums.* New York: Basic Books.

Minuchin, S., Rosman, B., & Baker, L. (1978). *Psychosomatic families*. Cambridge, MA: Harvard University Press.

Moore, S. F., & Meyerhoff, B. G. (1977). *Secular ritual*. Amsterdam: Van Gorcum.

Morgan, W. R., Alwin, D. F., & Griffin, L. J. (1979). Social origins, parental values and the transmission of inequality. *American Journal of Sociology, 85*, pp. 156-166.

Morris, L. (1985). Local social networks and domestic organizations: A study of redundant steel workers and their wives. *The Sociological Review, 33*, 327-342.

Morris, R. T., & Murphy, R. J. (1959). The situs dimension in occupational structure. *American Sociological Review, 24*, 231-239.

Mudd, E. H. (951). *The practice of marriage counseling*. New York: Association Press.

Murdock, G. P. (1949). *Social structure*. New York: Macmillan.

Novak, A. L., & Van der Veen, F. (1970). Family concepts and emotional disturbance in the families of disturbed adolescents with normal siblings. *Family Process, 9*, 157-172.

Nye, F. I., & Berardo, F. (1966). *Emerging conceptual frameworks in family analysis*. New York: Macmillan.

Ogburn, W. F., & Nimkoff, M. F. (1955). *Technology and the changing family*. Boston: Houghton Mifflin.

Olson, D. H. (1989). Circumplex model of family systems VIII: Family assessment and intervention. In D. H. Olson, C. S. Russell, & D. H. Sprenkle (Eds.), *Circumplex model: Systematic assessment and treatment of families* (pp. 7-50). New York: Haworth.

Olson, D. H., McCubbin, H. I., Barnes, H., Larsen, A., Muxen, M., & Wilson, M. (1983). *Families: What makes them work*. Beverly Hills, CA: Sage.

Olson, D. H., Russell, C. S., & Sprenkle, D. H. (Eds.). (1989). *Circumplex model: Systematic assessment and treatment of families*. New York: Haworth.

Olson, D. H., Sprenkle, D. H., & Russell, C. S. (1979). Circumplex model of marital and family systems I: Cohesion and adaptability dimensions, family types and clinical applications. *Family Process, 18*, 3-28.

Orden, S. R., & Bradburn, N. M. (1968). Dimensions of marital happiness. *American Journal of Sociology, 73*, 715-721.

Parsons, T. (1951a). *The social system*. New York: Free Press.

Parsons, T. (1951b). Class notes from lectures at Harvard University, Cambridge, MA.

Parsons, T., & Bales, R. (1955). *Family, socialization and interaction processes*. New York: Free Press.

Parsons, T., Bales, R., & Shils, E. A. (1953). *Working papers in the theory of action*. New York: Free Press.

Pearlin, L. I., & Schooler, C. (1978). The structure of coping. *Journal of Health and Social Behavior, 19*, 2-21.

Peterson, G. W., & Rollins, B. C. (1987). Parent-child socialization. In M. B. Sussman & S. K. Steinmetz (Eds.), *Handbook of marriage and the family* (pp. 471-508). New York: Plenum.

Pillemer, K., & Suitor, J. J. (1988). Elder abuse. In V. Van Hasselt, P. L. Morrison, A. S. Bellack, & M. Hersen (Eds.), *Handbook of family violence*. New York: Plenum.

Pineo, P. C. (1961). Disenchantment in the later years of marriage. *Marriage and Family Living, 23*, 3-11.

Piotrkowski, C. S., & Katz, M. H. (1982). Indirect socialization of children: The effects of mothers' jobs on academic behavior. *Child Development, 53*, 409-415.

Piotrkowski, C. S., Rapoport, R. N., & Rapoport, R. (1987). Families and work. In M. B. Sussman & S. K. Steinmetz (Eds.), *Handbook of marriage and the family* (pp. 251-284). New York: Plenum.

Pollack, W. S., & Grossman, F. K. (1985). Parent-child interaction. In L. L'Abate (Ed.), *Handbook of family psychology and therapy* (Vol. 1, pp. 586-622). Homewood, IL: Dorsey.

Preto, N. G. (1989). Transformation of the family system in adolescence. In B. Carter & M. McGoldrick (Eds.), *The changing family life cycle* (2nd ed., pp. 255-284). Boston: Allyn & Bacon.

Quinton, D., & Rutter, M. (1988). *Parenting breakdown: The making and breaking of intergenerational links.* Brookfield, VT: Avebury.

Radcliffe-Brown, A. R. (1922). *The Andaman Islanders.* Cambridge, UK: Cambridge University Press.

Radcliffe-Brown, A. R. (1952). *Structure and function in primitive society.* London: Cohen & West.

Rapoport, A. (1960). *Fights, games, and debates.* Ann Arbor: University of Michigan Press.

Rapoport, A. (1972). The uses of mathematical isomorphism in general systems theory. In G. J. Klir (Ed.), *Trends in general systems theory* (pp. 42-77). New York: Wiley-Interscience.

Raush, H. L., Greif, A. C., & Nugent, J. (1979). Communication in couples and families. In W. R. Burr, R. Hill, F. I. Nye, & I. L. Reiss (Eds.), *Contemporary theories about the family* (Vol. 1, pp. 468-492). New York: Free Press.

Reiss, D. (1981). *The family's construction of reality.* Cambridge, MA: Harvard University Press.

Reiss, D., & Costell, R. (1976). Multiple family group as a small society: Family regulation of interaction with non-members. *American Journal of Psychiatry, 134,* 21-24.

Reiss, I. L., & Miller, B. C. (1979). Heterosexual permissiveness: A theoretical analysis. In W. R. Burr, R. Hill, F. I. Nye, & I. L. Reiss (Eds.), *Contemporary theories about the family* (Vol. 1, pp. 57-100). New York: Free Press.

Richards, E. F. (1980). Network ties, kin ties and marital role organization: Bott's hypothesis reconsidered. *Journal of Comparative Family Studies, 11,* 139-151.

Risman, B. J., Hill, C. F., Rubin, Z., & Peplace, L. A. (1981). Living together in college: Implications for courtship. *Journal of Marriage and the Family, 43,* 77-84.

Roberts, J. (1988). Setting the frame: Definitions, functions, and typology of rituals. In E. Imber-Black, J. Roberts, & R. Whiting (Eds.), *Rituals in families and family therapy* (pp. 3-46). New York: Norton.

Rodman, H. (1967). Marital power in France, Greece, Yugoslavia and the USA: A cross-national discussion. *Journal of Marriage and the Family, 29,* 320-324.

Rodman, H. (1972). Marital power and the theory of resources in cultural context. *Journal of Comparative Family Studies, 3,* 50-69.

Rogler, L. H., & Procidano, M. E. (1986). The effect of social networks on marital roles: A test of the Bott hypothesis in an intergenerational context. *Journal of Marriage and the Family, 48,* 693-701.

Rollins, B. C., & Thomas, D. L. (1979). Parental support, power and control techniques in the socialization of children. In W. R. Burr, R. Hill, F. I. Nye, & I. L. Reiss (Eds.), *Contemporary theories about the family* (Vol. 1, pp. 317-364). New York: Free Press.

Roosa, M. W., Fitzgerald, H. E., & Crawford, M. (1985). Teenage parenting, delayed parenting and childlessness. In L. L'Abate (Ed.), *Handbook of family psychology and therapy* (Vol. 1, pp. 623-659). Homewood, IL: Dorsey.

Rosenblatt, P. C., De Mik, L., Anderson, R. M., & Johnson, P. A. (1985). *The family in business.* San Francisco, CA: Jossey-Bass.

Rosenblatt, P. C., & Russell, M. G. (1975). The social psychology of potential problems in family vacation travel. *Family Coordinator, 24,* 209-215.

Ross, L., & Nisbett, R. (1991). *The person and the situation: Perspectives of social psychology.* Philadelphia: Temple University Press.

Rossi, A. S. (1984). Gender and parenthood. *American Sociological Review, 49,* 1-18.

Rossi, A. S., & Rossi, P. H. (1990). *Of human bonding.* Hawthorne, NY: Aldine.

Ruesch, J., & Bateson, G. (1951). *Communication: The social matrix of society.* New York: Norton.

Ryder, R. G. (1973). Longitudinal data relating marriage satisfaction and having a child. *Journal of Marriage and the Family, 35,* 604-608.

Scanzoni, J., Polonko, K., Teachman, J., & Thompson, L. (1989). *The sexual bond: Rethinking families and close relationships.* Newburg Park, CA: Sage.

Schachter, F. F. (1982). Sibling identification and split-parent identification: A family tetrad. In M. E. Lamb & B. Sutton-Smith (Eds.), *Sibling relationships: Their nature and significance across the life span* (pp. 123-151). Hillsdale, NJ: Lawrence Erlbaum.

Schachter, F. F., Gilatz, G., Shore, E., & Adler, M. (1978). Sibling identification judged by mothers: Cross validation and development studies. *Child Development, 49,* 543-546.

Schachter, F. F., Shore, F., Feldman-Rotman, S., Marquis, R. E., & Campbell, S. (1976). Sibling de-identification. *Developmental Psychology, 12,* 418-427.

Schulz, B., Bohrnstedt, G. W., Borgatta, E. F., & Evans, R. R. (1977). Explaining premarital sexual intercourse among college students: A causal model. *Social Forces, 56,* 148-165.

Schuman, H., & Scott, J. (1989). Generations and collective memories. *American Sociological Review, 54,* 359-381.

Selvini-Palazzoli, M. (1974). *Self-starvation: From the intra-psychic to the transpersonal approach to anorexia nervosa.* London: Chaucer.

Selvini-Palazzoli, M., Bosco, L., Cecchici, G. F., & Prata, G. (1977). A powerful tool in family therapy. *Family Process, 16,* 445-453.

Sillars, A. L., & Scott, M. D. (1983). Interpersonal perceptions between intimates. *Human Communication Research, 10,* 153-176.

Simmel, G. (1950). *The sociology of Georg Simmel* (K. H. Wolff, Ed.). New York: Free Press.

Smelser, N. J. (1989). Self-esteem and social problems: An introduction. In A. M. Mecca, N. J. Smelser, & J. Vasconcellos (Eds.), *Social importance of self-esteem* (pp. 1-23). Berkley: University of California Press.

Smith, D. E. (1987). *The everyday world as problematic: A feminist sociology.* Boston: Northeastern University Press.

Solomon, M. (1973). A developmental conceptual premise for family therapy. *Family Process, 12,* 179-188.

Spanier, G. B. (1989). Bequeathing family continuity. *Journal of Marriage and the Family, 51,* 3-13.

Spiegel, J. P. (1960). The resolution of role conflict within the family. In N. W. Bell & E. L. Vogel (Eds.), *A modern introduction to the family* (pp. 361-381). New York: Free Press.

Sprey, J. (1979). Conflict theory and the study of marriage and the family. In W. R. Burr, R. Hill, F. I. Nye, & I. L. Reiss (Eds.), *Contemporary theories about the family* (Vol. 2, pp. 130-159). New York: Free Press.

Stack, C. B. (1974). *All our kin: Strategies for survival in an urban black community.* New York: Harper & Row.

Steinmetz, S. K. (1979). Disciplinary techniques and their relationship to aggressiveness, dependency and conscience. In W. R. Burr, R. Hill, F. I. Nye, & I. L. Reiss (Eds.), *Contemporary theories about the family* (Vol. 1, pp. 405-438). New York: Free Press.

Stern, P. N. (1978). Stepfather families: Integration around child discipline. *Issues in mental health nursing.*

Stinnett, N., & DeFrain, J. (1981). Strong families: A national study. In N. Stinnett & J. DeFrain (Eds.), *Family strengths 3: Roots of well-being.* Lincoln: University of Nebraska Press.

Stinnett, N., Sanders, G., DeFrain, J., & Parkhurst, A. (1982). A nationwide study of families who perceive themselves as strong. *Family Perspective, 16,* 1.

Stocker, C. M., & McHale, S. M. (1992). The nature and family correlates of preadolescents' perceptions of their sibling relationships. *Journal of Social and Personal Relationships, 9,* 179-195.

Stoller, E. P. (1983). Parental care giving by adult children. *Journal of Marriage and the Family, 45,* 851-858.

Stone, I. (1971). *The passions of the mind.* New York: Doubleday.

Stone, E. (1988). *Black sheep and kissing cousins: How our family stories shape us.* New York: Times Books.

Stouffer, S. A. (1940). Intervening opportunities: A theory relating mobility and distance. *American Sociological Review, 5,* 845-867.

Stouffer, S. A. (1949-1950). *The American soldier* (4 vols.). Princeton, NJ: Princeton University Press.

Straus, M. A., Gelles, R. J., & Steinmetz, S. K. (1980). Behind closed doors: Violence in the American family. Garden City, NY: Doubleday.

Straus, M. A., & Tallman, I. (1971). SIMFAM: A technique for observational measurement and experimental study of families. In J. Aldous, T. Condon, R. Hill, M. Straus, & I. Tallman (Eds.), *Family problem solving* (pp. 379-440). Hinsdale, IL: Dryden.

Suitor, J. J., & Pillemer, K. (1988). Exploring intergenerational conflict when adult children and elderly parents live together. *Journal of Marriage and the Family, 50,* 1037-1047.

Sullivan, H. S. (1947). *Conceptions of modern psychiatry.* Washington, DC: William Alanson White Psychiatric Foundation.

Sullivan, H. S. (1953). *Interpersonal theory of psychiatry.* New York: Norton.

Sussman, M. B. (1953). The help pattern of the middle-class family. *American Sociological Review, 18,* 22-28.

Sussman, M. B., & Burchinal, L. (1962a). Unheralded structure in current conceptualizations of the family. *Marriage and Family Living, 24,* 231-240.

Sussman, M. B., & Burchinal, L. (1962b). Parental aid to married children: Implications for family functioning. *Marriage and Family Living, 24,* 320-332.

Szinovacz, M. E. (1987). Family power. In M. B. Sussman & S. K. Steinmetz (Eds.), *Handbook of marriage and the family* (pp. 651-694). New York: Plenum.

Terkelsen, K. G. (1983). Schizophrenia and the family. II: Adverse effects of family therapy. *Family Process, 22,* 191-200.

Terkelsen, K. G. (1984). Response to Greenbaum. *Family Process, 23,* 425-428.

Thomas, E. J. (1977). *Marital communication and decision making: Analysis, assessment, and change.* New York: Free Press.

Thorne, B. (1992). *Boys and girls, together and apart, in school.* Rutgers, NJ: Rutgers University Press.

Ting-Toomy, S. (1983). An analysis of verbal communication patterns in high and low marital adjustment groups. *Human Communication Research, 9,* 306-319.

Tognoli, J. (1980). Male friendship and intimacy across the life span. *Family Relations, 29,* 273-279.

Tornstam, L. (1992). Loneliness in marriage. *Journal of Social and Personal Relationships, 9*, 197-217.

Treas, J. (1988). Money in the bank: Transaction costs and privatized marriage. Unpublished paper, University of Southern California.

Treas, J., & Bengtson, V. L. (1987). The family in later years. In M. B. Sussman & S. K. Steinmetz (Ed.), *Handbook of marriage and the family* (pp. 625-648). New York: Plenum.

Troll, L., & Bengtson, V. L. (1979). Generations in the family. In W. R. Burr, R. Hill, F. I. Nye, & I. L. Reiss (Eds.), *Contemporary theories about the family* (Vol 1, pp. 127-161). New York: Free Press.

Turner, V. W. (1969). *The ritual process: Structure and anti-structure.* Hawthorne, NY: Aldine.

Turner, V. W. (1974). *Drama, fields, and metaphors: Symbolic action in human society.* Ithaca, NY: Cornell University Press.

Udry, J. R. (1988). Biological predispositions and social control in adolescent sexual behavior. *American Sociological Review, 53,* 709-722.

Ulrich, D. N., & Dunne, H. P., Jr. (1986). *To love and work: A systematic interlocking of family, workplace and career.* New York: Brunner/Mazel.

Van der Veen, F., & Novak, A. L. (1971). Perceived parental attitudes and family concepts of disturbed adolescents, normal siblings, and normal controls. *Family Process, 10,* 53-75.

Visher, E. B., & Visher, J. (1979). *Stepfamilies: A guide to working with stepparents and stepchildren.* New York: Brunner/Mazel.

Visher, E. B., & Visher, J. (1982). *How to win in a stepfamily.* New York: Dembner.

Visher, E. B., & Visher, J. (1987). *Old loyalties, new ties: Therapeutic strategies with stepfamilies.* New York: Brunner/Mazel.

Vogel, E. F., & Bell, N. W. (1960). The emotionally disturbed child as the family scapegoat. In N. W. Bell & E. F. Vogel (Eds.), *A modern introduction to the family* (pp. 382-397) New York: Free Press.

Vuchinich, S. (1985). Arguments, family style. *Psychology Today, 19,* 40-46.

Ward, J. L. (1987). *Keeping the family business healthy.* San Francisco, CA: Jossey-Bass.

Warner, W. L., & Lunt, P. S. (1941). *The social life of a modern community.* New Haven, CT: Yale University Press.

Watzlawick, P., Beavin, J. H., & Jackson, D. D. (1967). *Pragmatics of human communication.* New York: Norton.

Weber, M. (1946). Class, status, party. In H. H. Gerth & C. W. Mills (Eds.), *Essays in sociology* (pp. 180-195). New York: Oxford University Press.

Wellman, B. (1979). The community question: The intimate networks of East Yorkers. *American Journal of Sociology, 84,* 1201-1231.

Werner, C. M., Altman, I., & Brown, B. (1992). A transactional approach to interpersonal relations: Physical environment, social context and temporal qualities. *Journal of Social and Personal Relationships, 9,* 297-323.

Werner, C. M., Altman, I., & Oxley, D. (1985). Temporal aspects of homes: A transactional perspective. In I. Altman & C. M. Werner (Eds.), *Home environments: Human behavior and environment* (Vol. 8). New York: Plenum.

Werner, C. M., Altman, I., Oxley, D., & Haggard, L. (1987). People, place and time: A transactional analysis of neighborhood. In W. H. Jones & D. Perlman (Eds.), *Advances in personal relationships* (pp. 243-276). Greenwich, CT: JAI.

White, L. K., & Booth, A. (1985). The quality and stability of remarriages: The role of stepchildren. *American Sociological Review, 50,* 689-698.

Whyte, M. K. (1990). *Dating, mating and marriage.* Hawthorne, NY: Aldine.

Wiener, N. (1948). *Cybernetics: On control and communication in the animal and the machine.* Cambridge: Technology Press.

Willie, C. V. (1967). The relative contributions of family status and economic status in juvenile delinquency. *Social Problems, 14,* 326-334.

Wilson, G. (1987). *Money in the family: Financial organization and women's responsibility.* Brookfield, VT: Aveburg.

Wolin, S. J., & Bennett, L. A. (1984). Family rituals. *Family Process, 23,* 401-420.

Wynne, L. C. (1984). The epigenesis of relational systems: A model for understanding family development. *Family Process, 23,* 297-318.

Wynne, L. C., Rychoff, L., Day, J., & Hirsch, S. (1958). Pseudomutuality in the family relations of schizophrenics. *Psychiatry, 71,* 205-220.

Wynne, L. C., & Singer, M. T. (1963). Thought disorders and the family relations of schizophrenics: A research strategy. *Archives of General Psychiatry, 9,* 191-198.

Zeitlin, S. J. (1980). An alchemy of mind: The family courtship story. *Western Folklore, 39,* 17-33.

Zeitlin, S. J., Kotkin, A. J., & Baker, H. C. (1982). *A celebration of American family folklore.* New York: Pantheon.

Zetterberg, H. L. (1963). *On theories of verification in sociology* (2nd ed.). Totawa, NJ: Bedminster.

Zimmerman, C. C. (1947). *Family and civilization.* New York: Harper & Row.

Zimmerman, C. C., & Broderick, C. B. (1954). Nature and role of informal family groups. *Marriage and Family Living, 16,* 107-110.

Zimmerman, C. C., & Broderick, C. B. (1956). The family self-protective system. In C. C. Zimmerman & L. F. Cervantes (Eds.), *Marriage and the family* (pp. 101-117). Chicago: Regnery.

Zimmerman, C. C., & Cervantes, L. F. (1960). *Successful American families.* New York: Pageant.

Index

About the Author

Carlfred B. Broderick is Professor of Sociology and Director of the Ph.D. program in marriage and family therapy at the University of Southern California. A graduate of Harvard University (A.B. in social relations) and Cornell University (Ph.D. in child development and family relations) with postdoctoral clinical training at the University of Minnesota, he is one of those relatively rare specimens who have standing in both the academic world of family scholarship and the applied world of family therapy. He has served as editor of the *Journal of Marriage and the Family,* as president of the National Council on Family Relations, as chair of the Family Section of the American Sociological Association, and as president of the Southern California Association for Marriage and Family Therapy.

He anticipates that this, his 13th book, will appear at about the same time that his 13th grandchild appears.